WITCH-DOCTORS

CHARLES BEADLE

1st WORLD
LIBRARY
Literary Society

Witch-Doctors

Charles Beadle

© 1st World Library, 2008
PO Box 2211
Fairfield, IA 52556
www.1stworldlibrary.com
First Edition

LCCN: 2007935367

Softcover ISBN: 978-1-4218-9320-4
Hardcover ISBN: 978-1-4218-9420-1
eBook ISBN: 978-1-4218-9220-7

Purchase *"Witch-Doctors"*
as a traditional bound book at:
www.1stWorldLibrary.com/purchase.asp?ISBN=978-1-4218-9320-4

1st World Library is a literary, educational organization
dedicated to:

- Creating a free internet library of downloadable ebooks

- Hosting writing competitions and offering book publishing
  scholarships.

Interested in more 1st World Library books? contact:
literacy@1stworldlibrary.com
Check us out at: www.1stworldlibrary.com

1ˢᵗ World Library Literary Society

Giving Back to the World

"If you want to work on the core problem, it's early school literacy."

- James Barksdale, former CEO of Netscape

"No skill is more crucial to the future of a child, or to a democratic and prosperous society, than literacy."

- Los Angeles Times

"Literacy... means far more than learning how to read and write... The aim is to transmit... knowledge and promote social participation."

- UNESCO

"Literacy is not a luxury, it is a right and a responsibility. If our world is to meet the challenges of the twenty-first century we must harness the energy and creativity of all our citizens."

- President Bill Clinton

"Parents should be encouraged to read to their children, and teachers should be equipped with all available techniques for teaching literacy, so the varying needs and capacities of individual kids can be taken into account."

- Hugh Mackay

CHARACTERS

LUCILLE CHARLTRAIN—A Photograph
(Mrs. Gerald Birnier)

USAKUMA—An Idol
(The Incarnation of the Unmentionable One)

GERALD BIRNIER—A Professor

ZU PFEIFFER—German Kommandant
(Hermann von Schnitzler und)

ZALU ZAKO—Heir apparent
(son of Kawa Kendi)

BAKUMA—in love with Zalu Zako
(daughter of Bakala)

MYALU—a chief in love with Bakuma
(son of MBusa)

BAKAHENZIE—Chief Witch-Doctor
(son of Maliko)

MARUFA—another Witch-Doctor
(son of MTungo)

KAWA KENDI—King-God and Rainmaker
(son of MFunya MPopo)

MFUNYA MPOPO—Predecessor of Kawa Kendi
(son of MKoffo)

KINGATA MATA—Keeper of the Sacred Fires (son of Kabolo)

SAKAMATA—deposed Witch-Doctor and spy

YABOLO—another Witch-Doctor

MUNGONGO—Birnier's servant

SCHULTZ—German sergeant

LUDWIG—German sergeant

SCHNEIDER—German sergeant

CHAPTER 1

In a bayou in the south-eastern corner of the Victoria Nyanza was the station of Ingonya, a brown scab on the face of the green earth. The round mud huts of the askaris were like two columns of khaki troops marching rigidly on each side of the parade ground. To the north, upon a slight rise of ground, were the white men's quarters; the non-commissioned officers had four bungalows to the south of the orderly room and Court House; and beyond a green plot flanked by a store house and an ordnance building, was a bigger bungalow, florid in the amplitude and colour of the red pillared verandah, the residence of the Kommandant, Herr Ober-Lieutenant Hermann von Schnitzler und zu Pfeiffer.

On the northern side, overlooking the swamp and the distant lake, was a flagpole, before which paced an ebon sentry in a uniform of white knickers, tunic and lancer cap, red faced. The glow of sunrise stained the green of the moon with crimson. A trumpet blared. From the rear of the Residence marched with stiff-legged precision a squad of askaris and the stocky figure of a non-commissioned officer in a white helmet. Simultaneously appeared on the verandah of the large bungalow the tall form of a white man in pink silk pyjamas. The sergeant barked. The squad presented arms. A coloured ball slid up the flagpole. The first rays of the sun splintered the bloodied waters beyond into silver spikes and caressed a fluttering black, white and red flag.

Then the squad ported arms, relieved the sentry, and retired, their black legs gleaming blue points as they rose and fell. The pink figure disappeared. Sergeant Schultz strutted back to his bungalow, in the verandah of which squatted a native girl clad in gay trade cloths. He emerged lighting a cigar, and sjambok in hand, returned to the orderly room. Another trumpet blared. From beyond the askaris' camp came a line of natives, young and old, their scrawny necks linked together by a light iron chain which clanked musically. Filing on to the parade ground they were divided into gangs by Sergeant Schneider to labour under guard at the interminable work of the camp.

The air above the swamp began to sizzle in the heat. The same slender figure clad in immaculate white reappeared upon the south verandah of the florid bungalow. Herr Ober-Lieutenant stood staring about the small square with a peevish glint in the fair eyes. A big negro in spotless white hurried around the house bearing a brass tray set with a cup, a liqueur glass and a decanter. Herr Lieutenant sprawled his legs on either arm of a Bombay chair. As he delicately mixed cognac with his coffee, his jewelled fingers sparkled in a shaft of sunlight which set afire the sapphires mounted in an ivory bracelet.

At a yard from the table stood the servant as rigid as the flagpole. With a lazy insolence which marked his movements, the lieutenant sipped the cafe-cognac and smoked a cheroot, as if he were seated on the terrace of the Cafe de la Paix. The brutality of the round skull, emphasized by the cropped blonde hair, seemed at variance with the boyish rotundity of the face and the small, but dominant, nose. Two separate moustaches bristled so fiercely that they suggested sentries on guard over the feminine softness of the lips.

Charles Beadle

When he had finished zu Pfeiffer arose languidly, lighted a fresh cigar, adjusted his helmet with care, took a gold-mounted sjambok from his servant, and strode across the square. The lines of his torso were so perfect that they suggested artificial aid.

The orderly room was square and whitewashed; grass matting was upon the floor, and high screened doors opened on to the north verandah. Zu Pfeiffer sprawled in a swing chair before the office desk placed at an oblique angle to the wall, encumbered with books and papers. After tapping reflectively on a book cover with a polished nail zu Pfeiffer's hand sharply struck the bell. Instantly a corporal appeared at the farther door and stood as if petrified, black hand to black temple. Zu Pfeiffer snapped instructions in Kiswahili without removing his cigar. The man grunted, shot his hand away at right angles with as much energy as if he were trying to knock down an elephant, and vanished.

"Sergeant!"

"Ja, Excellence."

At the other door like another Jack-in-the-box appeared Sergeant Schultz in exactly the same attitude. At a nod the sergeant melted into the semblance of human movement: he drew aside a chair, selected a certain document from a pile of them, and handed it to the lieutenant. Zu Pfeiffer pushed a box of cigars across the table, lolled back with one foot on the table, and began to peruse lazily. The sergeant retired respectfully with the cigar to the outer office. A fly buzzed hopefully at the mosquito wire. The tap of a typewriter sounded like some other insect. On the hot air came the faint barks of a drill-sergeant on the parade ground. From behind the building rose fitfully the murmur of voices from a herd of natives squatted in the sun awaiting the opening of the Court

House. Leaves rustled largely under the Lieutenant's fingers...

At length he pitched the report on to the table, carefully placed the butt of his cigar in an ash-tray, lighted another, and disposed of the match with equal care.

"Sergeant."

"Ja, Excellence!"

Zu Pfeiffer indicated a chair by a thrust of the chin. The sergeant sat. Tapping the report with the highly polished and very long finger-nail of the left hand, the lieutenant demanded:

"Who is the man who gave you this report?"

"Ali Ben Hassan, an Arab trader, Excellence."

"Trustworthy?"

"Ja, Excellence. He has done much work for us."

"Where?"

"On the Tanganika district, sub-division B II, Excellence. He brought papers of first-class recommendation from the Kommandant."

"Ben Hassan speaks of one Sakamata, nicht wahr?"

"Ja, Excellence."

"Of what tribe is he?"

"Wongolo."

"A witch-doctor?"

"Ja, Excellence."

"He is here? Let him come in."

The sergeant rose, saluted and departed. Gutturals sounded lazily. The sergeant reappeared and behind him shuffled a native. Clad only in a dirty loin-cloth, his brown skin was wrinkled in scaly folds upon his chest and belly; his face was like an ancient tortoise; the small lack-lustre eyes were bloodshot and furtive; the limbs were almost fleshless. He squatted upon the ground and with lowered lids appeared to be absorbed in the contemplation of a white man's table leg. Zu Pfeiffer regarded the man as one would a stray dog and nodded to the sergeant, who sat down.

"Does he speak Kiswahili?"

"Nein, Excellence. Only his monkey speech."

"Why do you suppose that he is trustworthy?"

"Because, Excellence, his interests are with ours. There is no competition. The Schweinhuende Englaender have no interest there—yet. They are too busy with the Uganda railroad."

"Ja, ja. Again what is the tribal system there, King-God or— "The lieutenant permitted a slight smile—"or Dis-established Church?"

"King-God, Excellence," replied Sergeant Schultz gravely.

"This fellow then is an apostate priest, nicht wahr?"

The sergeant noticed the movement of one of the sentry moustaches. A twitch of the lips recognized his superior's pleasantry.

"Ja, Excellence."

Zu Pfeiffer stuck the cigar into the corner of his mouth and regarded idly the dumb figure on the floor against the wall.

"We must have the Wongolo country, c'est entendu. Now what's your opinion of the method, sergeant?"

"With due deference, Excellence," responded Sergeant Schultz, "I propose that we advance and bring them to subjection in the usual manner."

Zu Pfeiffer fingered a ring and stared out into the yellow glare.

"Nein," he said at length, meditatively, removed the cigar from his lips and delicately knocked off the ash. "Circumstances alter cases. That method is too expensive. Son Altesse cannot afford the blood of the Fatherland in return for such ignoble carcasses. We—the price paid in the Herrero campaign was insupportable."

"Pardon, Excellence, but Treitschke said—"

"I know, sergeant. But Treitschke did not live in Central Africa."

"True, Excellence."

"Die Schweinhuende Englaender have had more experience than we have. Even a fool learns wisdom by experience—sometimes."

"True, Excellence."

Again fell a silence save for the buzz of the persistent fly.

"Also psychological research is more valuable than artillery —sometimes—in spite of Napoleon and Treitschke." Zu Pfeiffer glanced at the sergeant who, beneath the mask of his features, appeared shocked. "Blasphemy, nicht wahr, sergeant?"

"If your Excellence thinks—"

"But remember if Napoleon invented the science of artillery, we invented psychology."

"True, Excellence."

Zu Pfeiffer smiled complacently and stroked his moustaches.

"Now for this animal here. Who and what was he?"

"One of the principal witch-doctors, Excellence, wealthy and powerful. He attempted to overthrow the Chief Witch-doctor, one Bakahenzie, and was discredited."

"How discredited?"

"He attempted some form of magic, Excellence, which failed. Details are not given."

"Who gave the dossier?"

"Ali ben Hassan, Excellence."

"From whom did he get his information?"

"Name given as one Yabolo, another witch-doctor and relative."

"This Saka—Saka"—zu Pfeiffer glanced at the document— "Sakamata. Is he in communication with this Yabolo?"

"Ja, Excellence."

Zu Pfeiffer smoked reflectively.

"When did the last agent come in?"

"But yesterday, Excellence."

"And no report of any other white men in the country? No British missionaries or traders?"

"Nein, Excellence."

"Where is Saunders?"

"On Lake Kivu."

"No report?"

"Not since the last three months ago, Excellence."

"Umph!—Now, pay attention." Schultz leaned forward dutifully. Zu Pfeiffer unrolled a map on the wall beside him. "Here's Ingonya. The Wongolo country is twenty days' march from here, but across the lake it's twenty hours with the launch, and five days from there." The delicate finger-nail indicated a spot on the opposite side of the lake. "From here—what's the place? Ach—Timballa. To hell with the British boundary! We must not give them time to get the news. Always rush the seat of government. Surprise them and they're done."

"But, Excellence, Treitschke says regarding retreat—"

"There will be no retreat. At MFunya MPopo's is the idol, the fetish. We destroy it and they're done!" He brought down his fist with a crash on the table. "Faith unites a people; in unity is strength. Break the faith and you've broken the people."

"But, Excellence!" exclaimed the Lutheran sergeant, aghast.

Zu Pfeiffer's blue eyes hardened.

"Understand, you fool, these are savages. *You* have an abstract deity—which you cannot break in the concrete— obviously: they have a concrete god which we can and shall smash."

"Excellence, you are right," said the sergeant humbly.

Zu Pfeiffer flicked cigar ash from his sleeve and lolled back.

"Those are your orders. Commandeer the necessary canoes and notify Ludwig to have the men in readiness for the full moon. Work out the details and give them to me to-morrow."

"Ja, Excellence." Schultz stood to attention. "But, Excellence, this creature—"

Zu Pfeiffer glanced casually at Sakamata.

"Oh, that? Take it away!"

Schultz saluted smartly and wheeled about.

"Njoo!" he commanded sharply.

Sakamata rose up quietly and disappeared through the door without glancing to the right or the left.

"The Court awaits your Excellency," reminded the sergeant.

As zu Pfeiffer nodded languidly, a booted foot clopped on the verandah.

"Wa da?" queried Sergeant Schultz, startled at the intrusion of a stranger.

"Oh, only I," responded a soft voice in English.

Through the screen door a tall figure in a Tirai hat was silhouetted in sepia against the yellow glare. A brown hand pushed open the door.

"Mon nom est Birnier, Gerald Birnier—er—Does any one speak English?"

Zu Pfeiffer, in the act of rising, sank back into the chair, placing his left leg in a favourite position and selecting a cigar simultaneously.

"Yes," said he, almost without accent. "What do you want?"

"I wish to see the—the Herr Kommandant."

Zu Pfeiffer struck a match without looking up.

"I am he."

One hand upon the open door, Birnier stroked his shaven chin perplexedly with the other. He glanced from the sergeant, standing rigidly by the table, to the lieutenant engaged in stoking his cigar to a nicety.

"Well, it's usual to invite a white man to sit down, isn't it?" suggested Birnier, with a note of irritation.

Zu Pfeiffer looked across the table.

"Nein. This is the Orderly Room; not a general office."

"Oh, I see. I beg your pardon!" There was a note of laughter in the voice. "Will you kindly instruct me where I am to apply?"

Zu Pfeiffer continued to regard the stranger from head to foot, smoking slowly.

"Please to come in," he said at length, gesturing with his cigar, "and sit down."

"Thanks so much!"

The trace of irony seemed to escape zu Pfeiffer. He gave a guttural order to the sergeant, who saluted and disappeared. The stranger placed his Tirai hat on the table, revealing rumpled brown hair flecked with grey, a high white forehead, and long features; the slight stoop of the shoulders and general carriage rather suggested a professional type than a hunter or trader. He regarded the slim figure staring insolently at him with a hardening look of disapproval.

"What is it you wish?"

"Well, principally I require an elephant licence and the usual permit to trade."

"Where are you going?"

"To the Kivu country."

Zu Pfeiffer regarded his cigar tip interestedly.

"You are going to the Wongolo country," he stated.

Birnier's mouth tightened.

"Quite possibly."

"You have been to the Wongolo country already?"

"Yes, I have been there, but what has that to do with it?"

"We know all about you," stated zu Pfeiffer coldly, twiddling his cigar between slender fingers. He glanced at a gold repeater. "Pardon, but I must request you to return later. The Court is already awaiting me." Birnier frowned slightly. "If you will be so good as to return at, let us say, five o'clock, I will be pleased to listen to your application."

Birnier rose, taking his hat.

"Certainly," he said curtly. "Good morning!"

Zu Pfeiffer watched him depart; then he struck the bell sharply. Sergeant Schultz appeared, a line of nervous expectancy upon his sallow face.

"Why have you not reported that man's arrival?" demanded zu Pfeiffer harshly.

"Excellence," returned Schultz, saluting, "he has but arrived within the hour in a launch, loaned to him by the Englaender."

"Ach! An English spy!"

"I do not know, Excellence."

"We ought to know. Why have you not a report of the man's movements? He admits that he has been in the Wongolo country."

"Excellence, it is already done." Schultz hurriedly searched a card index cabinet and handed a document to the lieutenant. "There is Saunders' report, Excellence; more than six months old."

Zu Pfeiffer glanced at the page indicated and began to read while the sergeant stood stiffly at attention.

"You may go, sergeant," announced zu Pfeiffer without looking up. Schultz saluted and departed. Zu Pfeiffer finished the report leisurely, put down the paper, and stared meditatively.

No, he decided, as he rose, all the English are spies.

CHAPTER 2

Like a topaz set in a jade ring was the city of the Snake, the place of Kings, a village of some eight hundred huts huddled upon a slight rise above a sea of banana fronds, some two hundred miles to the west of Ingonya.

On the summit was a large conical hut like an enormous candle snuffer, the dwelling place of Usakuma, the spirit of the Snake, whose name was forbidden to all save the Priest-God and Rain Maker, King MFunya MPopo, who was so holy that after succeeding to the sacred office he was doomed to live within the compound, even as were the Kings of Eutopia, Sheba and China, a celibate for the remainder of his life: for, as the incarnation of the Idol, Usakuma, and therefore the controller of the Heavens and the Earth, his body must be kept from all danger of witchcraft lest the rains cease and the blue skies fall.

From the compound, looking towards the north-west where the snow-capped Gamballagalla rose violet against the horizon, another brown cone peeped above the green fronds, the late residence, and now the tomb of King MKoffo, predecessor of MFunya MPopo. For where a King-God dies there is he buried, he and his wives after him; the site becomes holy ground, a place of pilgrimage and sanctuary.

In each of the small huts to the rear of the temple of MFunya MPopo, but outside the sacred enclosure, lived his wives who, although forbidden to their husband, were permitted a royal promiscuity. Just within the precincts was a small replica of the temple where dwelt a young chief, also bound to celibacy, whose duties were to keep the royal fire burning as long as the king should reign. No one was allowed to converse with the king, save on matters of state, except this man; through him was spoken the royal will—what there was left of it—to the council which sat in a long rectangular building opposite to the temple entrance and open to the village, a body of witch-doctors and chiefs.

Solely the kingly office existed as a beneficent agent, a matter of self-preservation on the part of the tribe. The King-God's functions were divine; to make magic for the victory of his warriors and principally to make rain, on which, of course, the alimentary needs of his subjects depended—an incarnation of a god who was in reality the scapegoat of the god's omissions.

The office was hereditary. Perhaps no one else would willingly accept such an onerous post. The making of magic was performed before the god with the assistance of the chief witch-doctor, an exceedingly lucrative post won upon merit, occupied by one Bakahenzie, a tall muscular man in the prime of life, whose bearing was that of the native autocrat, fierce and remorseless. The King's personal wishes could be safely granted as long as he did not endanger the existence of the people by a desire to break any of the meshes of the tabus designed to ensure the safety of his sacred body, and therefore that of the tribe, on the assumption that if the incarnation were injured the god would be injured, and so would his creations be affected: any infringement of these laws entailed the penalty of death, a code which revealed the native logic in the confusion of cause and effect, the concrete and the abstract.

In the door of a hut on the outskirts of the village squatted a wizened man with a tuft of grey beard upon his chin. He was clad in a loin-cloth fairly clean, and about his neck was suspended by a twisted fibre an amulet wrapped in banana leaves containing the gall and toenail of an enemy slain by a virgin warrior, a specific against black magic whose powerful properties were proven by the undisputed influence and wealth of the owner.

A tall lithe savage, bearing upon his arms and ankles the ivory bracelets of the royal house and the elephant hair chaplet of the warrior, advanced leisurely towards him from the banana plantation. Marufa continued to gaze in rumination at the opposite hut. But as they had not met since the rising of the sun, he did not fail to make the orthodox greeting at the exact moment that the chief's shadow passed in front of him, which Zalu Zako returned punctiliously, thereby averting an evil omen. As soon as the young man had passed beyond the next hut appeared in the grove a girl, modelled like a bronze wood nymph. She wore the tiny girdle of the unmarried and walked furtively, carrying in her hand a parcel wrapped in banana leaves. In the shadow of a compound fence she halted, one slender brown arm set back in apprehension as her eyes followed the lithe figure of Zalu Zako.

Motionless sat Marufa staring in mystic contemplation. Bakuma glanced swiftly about her. Apparently satisfied that no one was observing her save a lean dog and two gollywog children, she continued on as if to pass the old man, her eyes still ranging like a fawn's. But when she was beside Marufa she subsided on her haunches beside him, clutching the bundle as she whispered:

"Greetings, O wise one!"

"Greeting, daughter," returned Marufa without lessening the fixity of his gaze.

"I would talk with thee."

"Aye."

Again she glanced around furtively.

"I would talk in thine ear, O my father."

"The knots of my hair are tied."

"I thank thee. There's a fluttering bird in my breast."

"And a snake around thy heart, O my daughter."

"Aie-e!"

"The grandson of the snake hath tied thy girdle."

"Ehh!"

The girl clasped her breast in surprised terror.

"How dost thou know?"

"All things are known to the son of MTungo," declared Marufa solemnly, still regarding the opposite wall. "Thou desirest a love charm... at hast thou?"

Tremulously Bakuma put down the green package on the ground, darting terrified glances to right and left. Slowly the skinny hand of the wizard gently tore open the leaves; very impressively the eyes slanted down to appraise the stock of blue and white beads.

"The spirit of Tarum hath a big belly," he announced tonelessly.

"O wise one, intercede for me," pleaded Bakuma, "for more have I none, I, Bakuma, daughter of Bakala, a girl of the hut thatch."

"The true love charm, infallible and powerful, is difficult to obtain, O Bakuma. The young huntress aims at big game."

"Ehh! But I have no more, great one!"

"The hair of a rutting leopardess, the liver of a forest rat, the tongue of a Baroto bird—these must I have to mix with thy blood to be drunk by thy man when the moon is full."

"Ehh! Ehh!"

"Such is the magic that no young man can resist."

"Ehh-h!"

"But these things are difficult to obtain."

"Aie! Aie!" wailed Bakuma, clasping her hands in despair.

"Difficult to obtain."

"Aie-e!"

"On the night of the half-moon will I take upon me the leopard form."

"Ehh!"

"I will talk with the spirits."

"Ehh! Ehh!"

"But they must be propitiated with the blood of a fat goat."

"Aie! Aie! But I have no fat goat."

"If there be no fat goat then will the spirits be wroth with me."

"Aie-e-e!"

Bakuma sat staring in dismal perplexity.

"No fat goat have I, a girl of the hut thatch! Aie! Aie!"

Marufa fumbled within the loin-cloth and thrust a tiny package along the ground.

"See and know the power of my magic." Bakuma greedily snatched up the amulet. "Begone!" he whispered, jerking the parcel of beads behind him. "MYalu approaches."

"Ehh!"

Bakuma rose and fled with the grace of a startled antelope as appeared a tall, strongly built man, having a low-browed face, across which was a deep scar. Behind MYalu came two young slaves bearing a small elephant tusk. Opposite to Marufa the slaves stopped. Their master, careful that his shadow fell well away from the figure of the magician—for the shadow is one of the souls, so woe unto him who shall leave his soul in the hands of an enemy!—squatted gravely.

"Greeting, son of MTungo!"

"Greeting, son of MBusa!" returned Marufa.

Gravely they spat into each other's palm, the sign of amity as they who exchange bonds of good behaviour inasmuch, as is well known, magic can be worked upon that which has been a part of the body as upon the body itself. Then solemnly they rubbed the spittle upon their respective chests.

"The spirit of the snake nourisheth not the life of the banana."

"Nay, for nigh unto two moons hath there been no blood of the snake," returned the old man perfunctorily, as he lifted his eyes from a swift appraisement of the tusk to his favourite mud wall.

"Nay, the crops sprout not. Maybe the Dweller in the Place of the Snake hath been visited by one from the forest."

"Aye, but old blood runs not as swiftly as young blood."

"Nay," replied MYalu, in answer to the reference to himself, "but the girdle is not yet tied by another."

"When the first twig of the nest is laid," remarked Marufa, indolently eyeing the tusk, "it is difficult to entice the hen to another tree."

"Here is a goodly twig with which to tempt spirits of the forest," and significantly, "Maybe there are others."

"A mighty potion shall be prepared for thee, O son of MBusa," declared Marufa, moving slightly to conceal the package of beads. "A mighty potion, infallible; made from the hair of a rutting leopardess, the liver of the forest rat and the tongue of the Baroto bird; these must she take that she shall speak thee softly, together with a portion of that which remains from the ceremony of the lobolo. Infallible is it; never known to fail."

"Ehh!"

Marufa stared interestedly at a wandering hen. MYalu watched him covertly. Like bronzes sat the two young slaves. From the distance came a faint chanting and the beat of a drum...

"The tusk is here, Marufa," remarked MYalu casually.

"My eyes see it," observed Marufa, without altering his observation of the hen.

"Where then is the potion?"

Marufa glanced at the tusk, appraised it again, and fumbling within his loin-cloth, thrust another tiny package along the ground. MYalu greedily picked up the amulet and stared in awe, turning it over and about.

"The tusk," murmured Marufa.

MYalu gestured to his slaves. They rose and placed the tusk beside the old man, shuffled backwards and squatted again. After lifting one end to test the weight, Marufa examined the grain. Then sliding it behind him as if he wished to sit upon it, remarked:

"The potion must be eaten at the full moon."

"Ehh!"

MYalu glanced up from an absorbed examination of the amulet.

"And within the quarter shall the fruit be ripe for the plucking." The whites of MYalu's eyes gleamed. "Unless," continued the old man uninterestedly, "there be stronger magic made against thee."

"Ehh!"

The two hands holding the amulet came down.

"If," explained Marufa, "another hath tied the grasses of her father's roof, will there be required a stronger spirit to overcome such magic."

"But thou hast told me," expostulated MYalu, regarding the tusk regretfully, "that this is a mighty magic, powerful and infallible, never known to fail."

"Thus is it," asserted the old man imperturbably, "for all save a stronger magic."

MYalu's eyes wandered from the tusk to Marufa and back. He scowled.

"Why didst thou not tell me?" he demanded sourly, dropping the amulet on the ground.

"It is for thee to tell the wizard all that thou knowest. How else may he reckon with thine enemies?"

"Enemy!" exclaimed MYalu. He stared questioningly at Marufa. "Enemy! Dost thou know whom I seek?"

"Do not all the hens remark the strutting of the cock?"

inquired Marufa unconcernedly, tapping his snuff box.

"Ehh!"

MYalu observed the taking of snuff as if he had never seen the operation before.

"Ehh!" he remarked again succinctly.

Marufa replaced the cork of twisted leaves, let fall the snuff box made of rhinoceros horn suspended from his neck by a copper wire, and contemplated a skinny goat scratching itself violently. MYalu stirred as if to rise, but subsided, cogitated and said slowly:

"In the house of MYalu are four more tusks."

"Four more tusks," repeated Marufa dreamily.

"Bigger than this one," said MYalu suggestively.

"Bigger than this one."

"Knowest thou by whom the girdle is tied?"

"By the grandson of the Snake."

"Ehh!"

MYalu squatted motionless. The old man appeared to doze. Women bearing gourds of water upon their heads passed in single file, their loins swaying rhythmically. The shadows dwindled. From close at hand began the rapid beat of a drum. A stir began through the village as each man herded his women and slaves to his own hut.

"O Marufa," said MYalu, speaking with a slight snarl, "hast thou such a powerful medicine that can surely trap the soul of Zalu Zako when perchance it wanders (in sleep)?"

"All things are possible to the son of MTungo," mumbled the old man.

Two chiefs appeared walking through the grove at a middle distance. MYalu glanced round apprehensively.

"Two tusks will I give thee," he whispered, "if thou wilt do this thing."

"Three tusks. No less, for the matter is dangerous."

"Two, two."

"Nay."

The old man stirred to rise.

"Three be it," gasped MYalu. "But I must see the magic done."

They rose together.

"Bring me of his toe-nails one paring, of his hair one, and his spittle and a footprint. Then shalt thou come with me to the sacred grove where the magic shall be done."

"Ehh!"

"But the three tusks must be given to Yanoka, my first wife."

MYalu hesitated.

"Aye, thus shall it be done," he assented reluctantly.

"It is agreed?" inquired Marufa.

"May my cord be lost!" swore MYalu, and gesturing to the slaves, hurried away.

A slight grin flecked the old man's eyes as he turned into the hut.

"Already hath he drunken of her blood," he mumbled. "Ya, Inkombana! take the tusk!"

When Marufa emerged, a head-dress of the tail feathers of the green parrot, professional uniform and potent specific against evil spirits, fluffed gently as he slowly stalked towards the council house. From the other side of a hut walked MYalu as if he had come from a different direction. In the open gate of the royal enclosure sat a muscular young man upon his haunches, tending the royal fire, which fed hungrily upon small faggots. Beyond him across the yellow glare upon the cleared ground beneath a thatched awning, stood an idol of wood, whose lopsided mouth snarled beneath a bridgeless nose; narrow slits for eyes squinted; baby arms stuck down beside triangular breasts above a melon belly having a protuberant navel like a small cucumber—the incarnation of the Snake-god, Usakuma.

Without the palisade of the sacred ground was a taller one, barring the doings of the council of witch-doctors and chiefs from the lay public, who were confined to their own huts under the penalty of a hideous death, or an enormous fine, as the witch-doctors should decide.

To the rear of the idol, cross-legged against the wall of the entrance to the conical hut, were the musicians beating a monotonous rhythm upon big and small drums and twanging a primitive lyre of five strings. Just as Marufa and MYalu took their respective places without among the wizards and the chiefs, a young goat skipped into the open and stared inquisitively at the Keeper of the Fires. As the man waved the animal back from the sacred ground, the goat lowered its head and threatened to charge, suddenly recollected its mate lying in the shade a few feet away, and began to bleat absent-mindedly.

Gravely and silently sat the assembly: continuously throbbed the drums. The sun beat diagonally. As a lizard darted like a flash of a prism from the grass palisade, the band ceased. A man emerged from behind the idol. Although the grey woolly tufts upon his chin, the sacred snake skin around his waist above the cat skin loin-cloth, the jingle of the ivory bangles on arms and ankles, and his stature, imparted an air of barbaric royalty, King MFunya MPopo advanced with the manner of a pariah dog ordered to his master's side.

As the King approached, the Keeper of the Fires hastily threw on a handful of faggots and bowed his head. In the centre of the opening of the enclosure the King squatted down with his back to the fire which streamed blue smoke. Not a limb or a muscle moved among the group of wizards and chiefs in the council house. Attracted by the movement, the goat stopped bleating and stared at the King; then, putting down its head, charged him.

With a horrified click, the Keeper of the Fires sprang. But he was not swift enough to prevent the impact of the animal's horns with the royal arm thrust out in self-defence. Three young chiefs came running; one caught up the goat and carried it away bleating bellicosely; the others knelt, and while one carefully collected a gout of blood upon the King's forearm in a piece of banana leaf, his companion wiped the wound. When they were satisfied that the bleeding had ceased, the pieces were meticulously wrapped in another leaf and borne away by the Keeper of the Fires to be deposited in the temple: for as every man knows, the royal blood must not be spilt upon the ground lest the site be accursed for ever and like the tooth of the dragon of Colchis, arise from the spot ghostly warriors to annihilate the tribe.

Neither upon the face of any of the elders nor upon the features of MFunya MPopo, the King, had a muscle moved. Yet the incident was regarded as an evil omen... Then suddenly did Baka-henzie, the chief witch-doctor, plumed with a tall scarlet feather in addition to the green ones and a necklace of finger bones upon his bronze chest, who sat in the centre with Kawa Kendi, the King's son upon his right, and Zalu Zako, the grandson, upon his left, begin to chant in a high wailing voice to the rapid rhythm of the drums:

"Is there not a shadow come over the land?
The frown of the One-not-to-be-mentioned?
I, Bakahenzie, have seen it! have seen it!"

And from the group within the council house, immobile, came the bass chorus of assent:

"Ough! Ough!"

"Is there not a dry curse come over the land?
Is it not the hot breath of the soul of the Snake?
I, Bakahenzie, have seen it! have seen it!"
"Ough! Ough!"

"Where is the false spirit that hath sinned in the act?
He that hath sinned in the shade of the name?
I, Bakahenzie, have seen him! have seen him!"
"Ough! Ough!"

"Does not the keen sting of him scorch up the land?
Hath not the young bread of our bellies been slain?
I, Bakahenzie, have seen it! have seen it!"
"Ough! Ough!"

The throb of the drums grew faster. Bakahenzie leaped from the crowd. Immediately in front of the King he began to dance and to scream:

"Is the Burden too great for the Guard of the Name?
Aie! Aie!
Hath the Bearer, too, fumbled the weight of the World?
Aie! Aie!
Is His spirit bewitched by the soul of a girl?
Aie! Aie!
Hath His magical power been slain by the sin?
Aie! Aie!
Hath a prophet made words in the act of a goat?
Aie! Aie!
Does a saviour in hairs thirst the blood of a King?
Aie! Aie!
Shall we hearken, O Chiefs, to the wish of the One?
Aie! Aie!
Or be shrivelled and die in the drought of His wrath?
Aie! Aie!"

Kawa Kendi, a man in early middle age, powerful and lithe-limbed, sat as motionless as the King, his father, staring, as did all, with the fixed stare of the anagogic.

Abruptly the drums ceased. Again came a hot silence as Bakahenzie paused in front of MFunya MPopo. Then with a piercing yell, the witch-doctor spun on his toes. The drums broke into an hysterical rhythm. Bakahenzie leaped high in the air; whirled around and around screaming hoarsely; leaped and spun continually.

The chiefs and doctors began to grunt; continued in crescendo until the whole body throbbed and grunted to the rhythm of the drums. Yet immobile sat MFunya MPopo.

Suddenly Bakahenzie changed the erratic course of his wild dance. He whirled and screamed in front of the King and fell headlong, as if in a fit, with eyes injected and foam upon the black tufts of beard. Bakahenzie clutched his belly and began to howl like a hyena at the moon. The drums stopped. Howl and writhe did Bakahenzie as if a thousand fiends were tearing out his entrails.

He lay rigid. The air seemed to quiver. The lines of every man's limbs, except the King's, were drawn in tension. Then from the prostrate body of the witch-doctor, whose legs and arms were twisted as in agony, whose dribbling mouth was closed like a vise, came a ventriloquous falsetto:

"Aie-e! Aie-e! I am the spirit of Kintu!
Aie-e! Aie-e! I am he who first was!
Aie-e! Aie-e! I am the banana from whom I was made!
Aie-e! Aie-e! The Keeper of the Name hath betrayed me!
Aie-e! Aie-e! The Bride of me is defiled!
Aie-e! Aie-e! Let him arise who is pure!
Aie-e! Aie-e! Let him arise who is bidden!
Aie-e! Aie-e! Let the fires be put out!
Aie-e! Aie-e! Let a new fire arise from the ashes!
Aie-e! Aie-e! I have spoken, I, the Father of men!
Aie-e! Aie-e! I, Tarum, the soul of your ancestors!"

From the assembly came the belly grunt of acceptance. In silence rose Kawa Kendi, the heir-apparent. His face was as expressionless as his father's. He stepped around the body of Bakahenzie and across the open space followed by a young man, Kingata Mata. Ten feet away from the enclosure, Kingata Mata sank upon his haunches. Before MFunya

MPopo squatted his son. They spat each in the other's hand and swallowed the spittle. Then the head of Kawa Kendi bent to the lips of MFunya MPopo to receive the sacred Name.

In unison with Kawa Kendi rose Kingata Mata, who to him handed a cord of twisted bark. Bending behind the King, who remained motionless with the closed eyes of one already dead, Kingata Mata swiftly adjusted the cord and handed it back to the son, Kawa Kendi...

When the muscular young Keeper of the Fires had poured solemnly a gourd of water upon the royal fire of MFunya MPopo, he knelt submissively and was strangled beside his master...

From the assembly went up a great shout:

"The fire is put out!"

And from the village, listening in awe to the mighty doings, came like an echo:

"The fire is put out! Aie! Aie-e!"

Then shouted the elders and wizards:

"Let there be a new fire!"

Again came the wailing repetition from the village:

"Let there be a new fire!"

As in the Place of Fires was kindled a new fire by Kingata Mata with two sacred sticks, one of which is male and the other female, the assembled chiefs and magicians groaned in allegiance to the new King-God of the unmentionable spirit of the Snake, Usakuma, the Idol.

CHAPTER 3

At five-thirty zu Pfeiffer was stretched in the long Bombay chair in the coolest portion of the screened verandah. On the table beside him was a tall glass, a decanter of cognac and a box of cigars; and suspended from the roof swung a canvas bag of water with a syphon attachment. A gape fly, which somehow had gotten through the screen, hit the lieutenant's forehead, fell on to the book and whirred up against the wire.

"Ach, Gott verdammt!" exclaimed zu Pfeiffer irritably and shouted: "Ho, Bakunja—la." Instantly appeared the tall negro in white. "You son of a god! Look at that!"

Bakunjala looked, leaped, and caught the fly in his hand.

"Ow!" he exclaimed as the hornet stung him.

"Ach, you woman of shame, catch it instantly!"

Without hesitation Bakunjala made another grab, and clutching the fly tightly, made to open the screen door.

"Halt!" commanded the lieutenant.

Bakunjala obeyed.

Charles Beadle

Zu Pfeiffer regarded the man standing with the wasp sting buried in his palm with a slight smile of amusement.

"It hurts?" he inquired amiably.

"Indio, Bwana!" asserted Bakunjala.

"Good! Now stop there."

Motionless remained the negro. Zu Pfeiffer leisurely selected a fresh cigar, lighted it, stoked it, and inhaling smoke stroked his left moustache.

"It still hurts?"

"Indio, Bwana!" said Bakunjala with a high note in his voice.

"Splendid!" assured the lieutenant: and after a full minute added: "Now you may go. And remember if you are frightened of a fly's pain again I will give you twenty lashes."

"Indio, Bwana," answered Bakunjala humbly and departed swiftly with the hornet in his clenched fist. Zu Pfeiffer smiled, again stared reflectively at the violet shadows creeping lazily across the square, sipped some brandy and picking up his book, began to read...

"Excellence!"

Zu Pfeiffer frowned and looked round. Outside the screen stood Sergeant Schultz at the salute. Zu Pfeiffer nodded.

"Well?"

"Excellence," said the sergeant at attention, "the Englishman is here."

"Ach, tell him to go—" The lieutenant drew out his gold chronometer. "It is my bath time. I cannot see him."

"Ja, Excellence."

"Wait." Zu Pfeiffer withdrew his legs and rose. "Ach, tell the fool to come over here and wait till I have had my bath."

"Excellence!" agreed the sergeant and saluting, marched away. Zu Pfeiffer entered the bungalow. Across the square came Birnier with the sergeant who ushered him into the screened portion of the verandah.

"His Excellence gom bresently," said the sergeant and left him.

Birnier put his Tirai hat on the table, and seeing no other, sat in the Bombay chair; looked about him; idly examined the brand on the box of cigars and smiled. "Makes himself mighty comfortable," he remarked to himself. "Pity he appears such a boor." He glanced at the book on the armchair. *Allgemeine Geschichte der Philosophie* von Prof. Dr. Paul Deussen. "And a philosopher, eh!" Having little German he turned away and lighted his pipe. After a while he began to fidget, wondering how long he was to be kept waiting. "Damn the fellow!" he muttered and picked up one of the books on the table, *Les Ba-Rongas*, par A. Junod, opened it at random and began to read.

The shadows of one bungalow reached the verandah on the opposite side of the square. And still he read on, the dead pipe in his hand. Just as the twilight was snuffed out like a candle, a sharp step heralded the arrival of the lieutenant. Birnier rose, the book in his hand.

"Good evening, sir!"

"Good evening," responded zu Pfeiffer, who was in an undress uniform of white. "What is it that you require?"

"Well," said Birnier, "first of all I must apologise for using your chair and reading your book. Most interesting, by the way."

"That is nothing," said zu Pfeiffer as Bakunjala came in with a lamp and a chair. "Please to be seated."

"Thank you."

Birnier took the small chair and the lieutenant the Bombay.

"I—er I—am sorry that I disturbed you this morning," began Birnier diffidently. "But I did not know—"

"That is nothing. It was the fault of the sentry. He should not have allowed you to pass."

"Regarding my application for the licence, Herr Lieutenant?"

"I regret," said zu Pfeiffer coldly, using a cigar cutter, "that I am unable to grant you the licence you ask."

"You cannot grant me a trading or shooting licence?"

"I regret, no."

Birnier stared.

"May I inquire why I am refused?"

"You may. We do not wish undesirables in the country."

"Undesirables!" Birnier's lips tightened. "I am afraid that I do not understand you." The lieutenant was engaged in carefully stoking his cigar. "Will you kindly afford me a reason for—for such an insulting remark?"

Zu Pfeiffer blew smoke luxuriously. Birnier stared for a moment, stuck his pipe in his mouth and bit the stem; removed it and snapped:

"You can have no adequate reason for such action... If you intend to continue this ridiculous farce I shall be compelled to make a comp-laint through Washington."

"Washington?" Zu Pfeiffer removed one leg from the chair-rest and the cigar from his mouth. "You are an American?"

"I am."

"So? We understood that you were an English agent. You have papers?"

"Certainly. If you wish—"

"We do not demand. No. My agent was wrong. He shall be punished." Then in an amiable voice: "I, too, have been a long time in America. Please to have a cigar, Mr. Birnier."

Birnier hesitated, puzzled.

"Thank you," he said diffidently, selected one, bit off the end and spat it into the corner. Zu Pfeiffer shuddered delicately; but as Birnier lighted his cigar he studied his face in the glow of the match; noted the breadth of the jaw, the width between the eyes and the slightly hard line at the corner of the mouth.

"And forgive me!" Zu Pfeiffer shouted to Bakunjala. "I presume that you have been in Africa a long time," he continued.

"Some ten years."

"You do find the Wongolo country interesting?"

"Oh, yes."

"You were there long?"

"No, I had been two years in the Congo and passed through on my way to Uganda to refit."

"Ach. You permit me? You are mining?"

"No." Birnier smiled thinly. "I have a professorial job in the American Museum of Natural History, Anthropological department."

"Professor! Ach!" Zu Pfeiffer looked at him interestedly.

"Yes. That is why I was so absorbed in *Les Ba-Rongas* which I found here. You are interested in anthropology?"

"Ach, yes, I love to study the animals. I have a library—a small one, here. You must see it."

"Thank you."

"You were studying the animals' ways and how d'you call it?—das Volkskuendliches—in Wongolo?"

"Yes. I do nothing else."

"So?" Bakunjala arrived with fresh glasses and vermouth. "Which do you prefer, French or Italian, Herr Professor?"

"French, please."

"You will dine with me, please?"

"That is very kind of you, Lieutenant." Birnier gazed quizzically, rather amused at the complete change of manner. Quite charming when he likes, he reflected.

"From what part do you come, Herr Professor?" inquired zu Pfeiffer as he set down his glass.

"Oh, I'm a Southerner. Louisiana. My name is French, you know."

"Ach so? Che les aimes, les Francais. Les femmes sont adorables!"

"Oui, je les trouve comme ca!" agreed Birnier, smiling. "Ma femme est francaise."

"So?... I, too, Professor, I am in love with a Francaise. She is wonderful! superbe! Ach, ent zueckend!" The lieutenant gazed into the warm darkness. "Always I see her—in the darkness, the—chaleur—parmis les animaux." In the glow of the lamp, the blue eyes were soft, the feminine lips curved in a tender smile as he murmured:

> "Die Jahre kommen und gehen,
> Geschlechter steigen ins Grab,
> Doch nimmer vergeht die Liebe,
> Die ich im Herzen hab!
> Nur einmal noch moecht ich dich sehen,
> Und sinken vor dir aufs Knie
> Und sterbend zu dir sprechen:
> 'Madam, ich liebe Sie!' "

"Thank you," said Birnier quietly. "I, too, would say that."

"Ach, sprechen Sie Deutsch?" demanded zu Pfeiffer quickly.

"No, unfortunately I don't speak it, but I understand a little; and particularly Heine."

"Ach, Gott!"

The note was of satisfaction. A gong sounded. Zu Pfeiffer turned sharply: "Come, Herr Professor, let us go to dinner. You would wish to wash?"

The bungalow, unusually lofty, was divided into three compartments. The ceiling, made of stout white calico, to shelter from snakes and the continual dust from the wood borers, was suspended from the rafters like the roof of a marquee tent. The centre room was furnished with cane lounge chairs like a smoking-room and decorated with skins, native musical instruments, spears and shields; drums served as small tables with elephant's toe-nails for ash trays.

In the bedroom was a brass bedstead and mosquito net. Behind was a bathroom having a corrugated cistern upon the cross beams which gave force for a shower. The towels and appointments were specklessly clean. When Birnier appeared he found zu Pfeiffer sprawled in the lounge. On a red lacquer tray upon a great war drum, covered with the striped skin of a zebra, was a crystal liqueur set and a large silver box of Egyptian cigarettes.

"Ach, Professor," said he, "it is good to speak to a white man again" (by which he meant an equal). "Please be seated, I beg you. A little liqueur is good for the aperitif and a cigarette; for there is no time for another cigar."

As Birnier sat he remarked the blonde head of the lieutenant in his meticulous uniform touched with gold and caught a glimpse of the jewelled bracelet of ivory and the Chinese finger-nail.

Another summons of the gong brought zu Pfeiffer to his feet. As he led his guest out through the side verandah along a screened porch to the mess room, built away from the main building to keep away the plague of flies, a native girl whose close-wrapped white robes revealed a lithe figure, flitted through a doorway. The table was set in immaculate linen, aglitter with glass and decorated with a profusion of wild orchids. Behind the chairs stood two negroes in spotless white, immobile. On each plate were hors d'oeuvres of anchovy and cheese upon a patterned piece of toast. Salted almonds, sweets, and olives were in green china; wine glasses of three kinds. Broiled fish followed the soup.

"So, Professor," remarked the lieutenant, "you will go back some day to Wongolo?"

"Yes, I—unless I discover some tribe who have a more interesting system of—er—theology."

"They are a powerful tribe, nicht wahr?"

"Oh yes, very. Their system ensures unity which provides for concerted action. Here I believe it is different."

"Yes, yes; they are poor here. Each village was at war with the other—before we came. Their superstitions are not—how would you say it?"

"Systematised?"

"Yes. They have neither any supreme chief nor god. There you see," he added, smiling, "that autocracy is the only form of government. Democracy—pah!... I apologise, Professor!"

"Please don't," replied Birnier, "although of course I cannot agree with you."

"But the Wongolo, they have a god and king?"

"Yes, the King-Priest system. One of the most interesting I have ever encountered or read of."

"You did see the King-God, MFunya MPopo?"

"Oh no. He is forbidden to be seen by a foreigner—a similar law to that of the Medes; only by the witch-doctors—and by the people once a year at a harvest festival. That is why I intend to go back. It is impossible to procure reliable statistics of their customs, practices and real beliefs without —without winning their confidence. That is my mission."

"I do not longer wonder, Herr Professor, that you were most justly annoyed. Ach, yes. But please do not worry about your ridiculous licence. It is not necessary in my jurisdiction, I assure you. You may come and go as you please, shoot what you wish. I will always be so glad to help so distinguished a professor."

"I thank you very much."

"It is nothing. And perhaps when you are there, you will be so kind as to write to me? To tell me things that are not known—so that I may, too, continue to study the animals— again what is it? das Volkskuendliches?"

"Folk-lore, isn't it?"

"Yes. Please to have some more wine, Herr Professor. Please, I insist. It is the real Mumm. That is a promise? I thank you. And if—Were there any others—whites—when you were there?"

"Only one."

"Where was he, I wonder?"

"On the southern boundary."

"Near lake Kivu?"

"Yes."

"Saunders," muttered zu Pfeiffer.

"I beg your pardon?"

"It was nothing, but I do not like to have—aliens in my province. They are—missionaries and traders—spies."

"Indeed."

"Yes, it is always so. Herr Professor, I ask you a favour. Will you be so kind as to write to me if some other white comes into the Wongolo country?"

"I shall be delighted," said Birnier... "Do you intend to come there some day, Herr Lieutenant?"

"Ach, no, it is not—not our territory; although I should very much like to see it and to shoot. There is much elephant there?"

"Oh yes, quantities."

"Please to try some of this curried egg, Herr Professor. It is excellent, I assure you. I thank you... And rubber, is there much rubber there?"

"Yes, I believe so."

"Now I wonder if you noticed whether it was tree or vine?"

"I really couldn't say." Birnier smiled thinly. "I am not interested in such things."

Zu Pfeiffer glanced at him keenly and changed the subject. When they had finished the best boned chicken that Birnier had ever tasted in Africa, zu Pfeiffer rose.

"Let us go to my study, Herr Professor, if you so permit, for some coffee and a little good port—and I will have the pleasure to show you my little library."

"I should be delighted," assented Birnier willingly.

Around the white walls of the cool room which was zu Pfeiffer's study, ran low bookshelves made of native wood, containing some hundreds of volumes which had been carried five hundred miles on the heads of porters. Grass mats and leopard skins were upon the floor. In the centre, upon a heavy table, was a green shaded lamp set in a silver-mounted elephant's foot. Upon the bookcases were various odd curios, and a coffee service in copper; and from opposite sides, marbles of Bismarck and Voltaire stared into each other's eyes. On the south wall was a large oil of Kaiser Wilhelm II; and in the centre of the other wall a photograph of a woman set in an ivory frame made from a section of a tusk.

Zu Pfeiffer strove to be more agreeable than ever. They talked mythology and folklore. With the port, zu Pfeiffer rose, an erect martial figure above the glow of the lamp.

"Herr Professor!" he remarked. "I beg you."

Slightly bewildered, Birnier rose, too, glass in hand. Wheeling with military precision zu Pfeiffer raised his glass to the great portrait on the wall.

"Ihre Hochheit!"

Politely Birnier followed suit, his democratic ideas slightly astonished at the veneration of the kingly office; almost, he reflected, as curious as the native superstition of the King-God. Then zu Pfeiffer turned to the left and lifting his glass to the portrait in the ivory frame, drank silently.

"I was wondering, Professor," remarked he, as he resumed his seat without explanation, "from what college—you call it?—you come?"

"Harvard," said Birnier, rather amused and noticing that as a true connoisseur, zu Pfeiffer refrained from smoking while drinking his port.

"I have met many of the Harvard men—at Washington."

"Ah, you know Washington?"

"Yes, I was there nearly two years."

Zu Pfeiffer drained his port, selected a cigar, lighted it and gazed abstractedly towards the ivory frame. The lips softened and he smiled gently.

"Do you know many people there?"

"Oh, a few."

"Ach... I wonder... You must know that I met her there, my divine Lucille!"

"Lucille! How strange! That is my wife's name too."

"Really?" Zu Pfeiffer still peered dreamily at the corner. He gathered up his legs and rose like an eager boy. "Permit me, Herr Professor, she is so—so—" He bent over the portrait and struck a match. Politely Birnier stooped to look. He saw a portrait of a French woman in an evening gown, a woman of charm with the vivacious eyes and tempting mouth of the coquette.

"My God!"

Birnier bent closer and stared intently. Across the corner of the photograph were written in ink in familiar characters the words: 'a toi, Lucille.'

"Lucille!" he gasped. "Lu—Good God!" He stood up abruptly. "I—What in God's name—who is this woman?"

The match fell to the floor. He was vaguely conscious of the tall white figure stiffening as a dog does.

"That lady is my fiancee."

"Fiancee! She—Good God, you're mad! She is my wife!"

"Wife!... Gott verdampf, der Teufel solls holen! Das ist der Schweinhuend!"

The gutturals exploded from zu Pfeiffer. The sleeve of his white jacket quivered, the arm came up to the gold braided chest and jerked out a silver whistle. He hesitated, glaring at the astonished figure of Birnier. Suddenly zu Pfeiffer sat down by the table. His blue eyes were as hard as malachite.

"Sit down!" he commanded harshly.
Birnier did not appear to notice him. He struck a match and bent over the photograph again.

"Good God!" he muttered. "I—I—don't understand—O God!"

"Sit down!" shouted zu Pfeiffer. Birnier merely blinked at him.

"Would you mind explaining?" demanded Birnier.

"Explain!... Is your wife Mademoiselle Lucille Charltrain?"

"Why, of course. That is her professional name. But how on earth has this mistake happened? I—I—that is her writing—but it can't be. I mean it's impossible..." Birnier put his hand to his head. "I—God, it can't be! I or you must be mad! Which is—"

A prolonged whistle startled him. He saw the whistle at zu Pfeiffer's lips, but the act conveyed no meaning. He turned away, struck another match and peered again at the photograph.

"Lucille! Lucille!" he whispered. "What on earth—"

A powerful clutch closed upon his arm. He was whirled backwards into a chair. For a moment he was too dazed to grasp what had happened. He saw zu Pfeiffer's face. The sentries over his moustaches quivered like a row of fixed bayonets. The eyes seemed needle points. Then the fact of the assault penetrated beyond the unprecedented incident of finding his wife's photograph in another man's room. The ugly line about the mouth hardened. He rose slowly.

"Am I to understand that you have laid your hands upon your guest?" he began, stuttering over the choice of words. "I am—I am—"

The scuffle of many feet interrupted him. Into the room rushed Sergeant Schultz and several soldiers. Zu Pfeiffer stood up and pointed.

"Sergeant, arrest that man!" he barked.

"Ja, Excellence!"

The sergeant saluted and barked at the askaris. Birnier gazed stupidly at the uniforms around him as if unable to comprehend. He looked at zu Pfeiffer who stood erect, his face lost in shadow above the lamp, and back at the soldiers.

"Is this a joke, Lieutenant—or are you mad?" he demanded angrily.

"Sergeant, put that man in the guard-room," zu Pfeiffer commanded.

Zu Pfeiffer sat down with his back to Birnier and facing the photograph. Birnier's face twitched; he raised his arm. The sergeant barked and the line of bayonets lowered menacingly.

"You gom with me, Herr American," ordered the sergeant.

Birnier controlled himself.

"One moment, sergeant, please! Herr Lieutenant, on what charge do you arrest me?" The perfect lines of the white-clad back did not quiver. "Very good! I give you warning, Herr Lieutenant, that you have committed an assault upon an

American citizen."

"Gom! Gom!" insisted the sergeant impatiently.

Birnier raised his head and walked as indicated by the sergeant. As the footsteps plodded across the square zu Pfeiffer turned to the table, examining his left hand.

"Ach!" he growled gutturally, "the dirty pig has broken my nail!"

CHAPTER 4

Over the city of the Snake the sun sank red dry, leaving the Place of Kings hot in the electric air of magic and world happenings. The people were still confined to their huts, trembling in the knowledge that for three days love must be eschewed, no water drawn nor any food cooked with fire; nor might any man, woman or child leave the precincts of the compound.

All the night Bakuma crouched in her hut listening in awe to the swish of the ghosts through the air, to the moans, groans and howls of the wizards doing battle with them. Tightly did she hold the amulet as she strove to conceal curiosity regarding the welfare of Zalu Zako; for did her mother suspect the presence of this evil spirit would she cause Bakuma to take a decoction of the castor-oil plant in order that the demon might be expelled; and the more to aid her conquer this unlawful impulse to peep without did she most persistently recite to herself the fate of the daughter of MTasa, the foolish Tangulbala whose body had been discovered impaled upon a tree by the angry spirits of the dead, because she had rashly ventured forth the third day after the death of the grandfather of Zalu Zako. Bakuma dared not mention the name of one who had died, for, as everybody knows, such an impious person runs the risk of summoning the ghosts to their presence.

The "putting out of the fire" had changed Bakuma's prospects, had made Zalu Zako heir-apparent, implying half a hundred responsibilities, the chief of which was that now he was compelled to choose his official first wife, she who would be the mother of the "divine" Son of the Snake: an alteration that excited Bakuma to frantic clutching at the amulet. Would the charm work or would it not? How to insure that it would be efficacious? Marufa's greedy demands worried her. She feared even if she obtained the goat that he might require something else as well. Anybody knows how greedy doctors are and how wealthy. He would be sure to increase the fee, knowing the value of the prize. Bakuma only possessed one really valuable article, and that was a charm against sterility; but this was the last thing that she wished to part with as the only possible occurrence that could ever divorce her from the position of chief wife, once she had won Zalu Zako, would be failure to provide the male heir. She was impatient, too, at the delay caused by the three days' tabu. Time was important. Soon she would be under the ban of the unclean which entailed the curtailment of her liberty again, and she dreaded that possibly the charm might grow stale. The greatest need for speed was MYalu's suit. As her father was dead she belonged to his brother. Already MYalu had offered four tusks of ivory and three oxen for her. Her uncle was lazy, mean, and greedy. Fortunately he thought that by waiting he could get double that amount. Yet MYalu might decide to pay the price demanded. Once Zalu Zako had selected her as his bride, her uncle dared not accept any other man's offer, no matter how wealthy he might be; besides, the old man would not wish to refuse a relationship with the heir to the king-godhood.

Again her cousin was sick. The diagnosis of Yabolo, the wizard, was that her soul had wandered in sleep down to the river and had been swallowed by a fish. Yabolo had caught the fish and lured the soul into a tree, but now he demanded such a big price to restore the errant soul to the girl that her father, Bakuma's uncle, would not pay it, so she would surely die; then they would all have to be exorcised, which inferred a further loss of relative freedom for another four days. Indeed with all these actual and possible delays it seemed to Bakuma that some one had made much magic against her. Unless she knew who he or she was, how could she employ the same means to annul the terrible effects? And more, how could she obtain the wherewithal to pay the fees of the best doctors? Life was very complicated to the daughter of Bakala.

Up on the hill of MFunya MPopo had the magicians been busy all the afternoon after the "putting out of the fire." Zalu Zako and the chiefs also were barred from the sacred enclosure; for being mere laymen they could not hope to withstand the evil spirits of the dead. Even Bakahenzie and the inner circle of the cult were compelled to employ the most potent methods of protection to preserve them from being bewitched or slain outright.

After Bakahenzie, Marufa, Yabolo and two other master magicians had released the souls of the dead King by making incisions in the body with a sacred spear to the thrumming of the drums, the mighty groaning of the other wizards, and the persistent wailing of the dead man's wives, the corpse was borne by twelve doomed slaves to the temple and there interred with the gouts of blood shed by the prophetic goat, the nail parings and hair clippings of his lifetime, and his personal effects.

Upon the hill of MFunya MPopo, soon to be a temple and sanctuary, sat Kawa Kendi beside the New Fire tended by Kingata Mata, facing Zalu Zako, MYalu and the lay chiefs, while upon his own hill slaves were tearing down his old hut, erecting a temporary palisade around the quarters of his wives who were forever forbidden to him, and beginning the building of the new temple.

As the violet shadows were creeping from one hut to another did Bakahenzie and his satellites return from the ghoulish offices of the dead. Zalu Zako, the chiefs and magicians arose to the wild beating of the drums and the wailing chant of the hereditary troubadour with the five stringed lyre. With Kingata Mata carrying a brand of the newly lighted sacred fire, was Kawa Kendi led in procession through the deserted village to his sacred home.

Under the hard stars set in a dry sapphire, the fire cast yellow flickers upon the carven features of Kawa Kendi. In the still heat the distant wailing of the women from the opposite hill drifted into the continuous throb of the drums, the plaintive wail of the singer, and the hysterical groaning of the magicians, yelling ferociously ever and again to intimidate the baulked spirits around the magic circle.

Then was a white goat, previously selected from the flock of Kawa Kendi, slain by Zalu Zako, disembowelled by Bakahenzie, and the entrails rubbed upon the brow, the chest and the right arm of the slayer of man, a ceremony of purification designed to protect the royal executioner by appeasing the justly angry spirits of the dead; to Marufa were given other parts of the slain beast to smear likewise upon Zalu Zako, the son; and Yabolo ran screaming with portions to the quarters of the women of Kawa Kendi: for must every blood relative be so enchanted lest the vengeful ghost seek substitute victims.

As a pallid moon rose, as if fearfully, above the deep ultramarine of the banana fronds, was a magic potion brewed from certain herbs in enchanted water, with which the King, Zalu Zako, his son, and the King's wives were laved. Amid a tempest of screams and drums rose Kawa Kendi purified, to be driven by Bakahenzie and the wizards back to the hill of his father, leaving the assembled lay chiefs squatting humbly and in dread of the spirits abroad in the night. While the procession leaped and twirled, screamed and groaned to the frantic thrum of the drums through the blue darkness, the magicians ran and pranced through and around the village, seeking any blasphemer who dared to look upon sacred things; banging on hut doors and shaking thatches, the more to terrify the shrinking inhabitants.

Without the gate of the old enclosure all remained, except Bakahenzie and the four wizards who encircled Kawa Kendi and Kingata Mata and hustled them across the clearing. With his back to the dim form of the idol stood Kawa Kendi as behind it grouped the master magicians. From the base Bakahenzie took two large gourds and gave them into the keeping of Kingata Mata.

Came an abrupt cessation of the drums and cries. The wailing of the women behind the temple died. The tense air pulsed with electricity. A cock crowed feebly in the village. Then at a rippling splash of the drums and the sudden screaming of the wizards, they began to push the idol. The base had already been loosened in the earth by the slaves. The idol began to totter. Louder screeched the magicians; faster fled the drums. Slowly the idol leaned and subsided on to the shoulders of Kawa Kendi. Grasping the mass firmly upon his bent back, he bore the burden out of the enclosure and down the hill.

Behind his unsteady steps pranced and yelled the doctors with more prodigious a noise than ever before as they scourged the King's legs and arms with cords of fibre. Through the listening village panted the King. As he gasped slowly up the hill the thrashing was redoubled. But into the new enclosure the King staggered, let slide the heavy mass into a hole prepared for the sacred feet and, gleaming blue points of sweat in the faint moon, let out a hoarse yell, proving to the assembly of magicians and chiefs that he was powerful enough to bear the burden of the world and moreover that none could wrest his office from him.

No time was given for the incarnation of a god to recoup from his labours. The motive principle of the accusation and for the death of the king was the drought. That only concerned the soul of the tribe in the person of Bakahenzie. For him and his brothers of the inner cult, while certain pretensions of power over the supernatural were for the "good of the people," the truths of magic and divine functions were inviolable. The person of Kawa Kendi, heretofore merely one in whom was a potentiality, became after the purification and "coronation" the very incarnation of the god. Kawa Kendi had crossed from the comparative safe haven of the potential into divine activity.

Also there were, as ever, political reasons for the hastening of the offices of the god. Should the new King-God fail, as his father had done, to accomplish the duties of the rain-maker, then, as no precedent had ever been known for the failure of two kings in succession, an enemy might accuse Bakahenzie of having committed some sacrilege which had displeased the Unmentionable One. Politics and religion are often inseparable. Therefore, as soon as Zalu Zako had witnessed the ascent of his father into the dangerous zone of the gods, was he bidden as the victim apparent, to produce the sacred rain-making paraphernalia. From the Keeper of the Fire, Kingata Mata, Zalu Zako received one of the large gourds, which he deposited at the feet of his father squatting before the sacred fire, and retired to his allotted place among the other lay chiefs. Only Bakahenzie and the four of the inner cult were permitted within the enclosure.

Fumbling within the pot Kawa Kendi produced a bundle of twigs tied with banana fibre, which he unbound and cast into the fire. The herbs smouldered and sent up a pungent smoke forming a heavy cloud like some strange blue tree sheltering the form of the idol against the green sky. Save for the faint wailing of the distant women there was silence, in which an owl screeched harshly, a good omen. Little flames flickered. The smoke grew denser, obliterating the figure of the King. The drums began to mutter, Bakahenzie cried out in a loud voice:

"O great God, the Unmentionable One! let thy powers be made manifest!"

The Keeper of the Fires came forward upon his hands and thrust the other sacred gourd in front of the King, a deep one containing water, and a wand made from a sacred tree which had upon the end a crook. To the groaning of the magicians, the King took from the one gourd two stones of quartz and granite, the male and the female, and spat upon each one, thus placing part of his royal body upon them; then did he put them on the ground, and pouring water, chanted:

"Go forth, male spirit, with my ghost in thy hands!
Go forth, female soul, with my ghost in thy breast!
Make love together in the shade of great Tarum,
Of him whom fear of me hath frozen the breath!"
"Ough! Ough!"

grunted the priests and magicians.

"Go forth, male spirit, with my ghost in thy hand!
Go forth, female soul, with my ghost in thy breast!
Love one another that the crops of our land
May marry as well and be as fruitful as thee!"
"Ough! Ough!"

"Go forth, male spirit, with my ghost in thy hand!
Go forth, female soul, with my ghost in thy breast!
Rise high up to heaven and mount on the black back
Of the bird of the wet wind: poke your hands in his eyes!"
"Ough! Ough!"

Save for the distant wailing, there was the silence of those waiting for a miracle. In the sky, at the back of the idol, was the paling of dawn. Suddenly, as if exasperated by the non-obedience of the elements, Kawa Kendi sprang to his feet, with the magic wand in his right hand, turned and stared apparently into the face of the idol. For a full two minutes he stood as if carven, while the doctors and the chiefs moaned dismally. Around him like a pall still hovered the smoke of the magic fire. From the village a cock's challenge was answered from point to point. Then shooting out his right hand, Kawa Kendi made gestures as if hooking something invisible and began to scream furiously:

"Thus do I, the One-not-to-be-mentioned,
Drag forth from the belly of heaven
The disobedient One, the lazy One!
The insolent One who sinneth in sleep!
The black-snouted One whose udders are choked!
The womanly One whose nipples are dry!
The sluttish One who refuseth her milk!
The gorbellied One whose voice is a wind!
Come forth, lest I give thee sorrow and pain!
And make thee to weep the bitterest tears!
Come forth, lest I tear out thy black bosom!
Tear out thy guts for a feast unto Tarum!
Come forth, lest I throw off the yoke of the burden
Of the Earth and the Sky upon thy sweating black belly!"

In a slight puff of wind, the smoke, lace-edged with the dawn light, swayed, seeming to twine about the figure of the King as he stood with the wand outheld, as if firmly hooked in the guts of the recalcitrant elements.

Against the rose of the dawn appeared a dark line which increased as the magicians and chiefs moaned and groaned in sympathy with the furious efforts of the rainmaker, who threatened and pulled with the magic crook, so that everybody could see that he was indeed dragging the reluctant clouds from over the end of the earth. As the dark mass swelled the more he wrestled and screamed abuse at the dilatory spirit of the rain.

And behold, within half an hour, great black spirits sailed across the scarlet sunrise and wept exceeding bitterly; while from the village went up a great shout of praise to the triumphant King still prancing and cursing to such good effect up on the hill.

CHAPTER 5

The same vast balloons of sepia rolled over the lake, vomited a host of liquid ramrods and, after short intervals of brilliant glare, were succeeded by others. The gutters of the station were turned into burbling brooks and the grass plot into a morass.

Behind the screen on the south verandah sat zu Pfeiffer in his pink silk pyjamas, a scowl upon his brow. He sipped his cafe cognac distastefully and inhaled a cigarette so fiercely that the heat burned his tongue. He had not slept. Yet the broken nail on the left little finger had been cut and polished. Half the night he had sat before the photograph in the ivory frame, pondering upon, and rehearsing, the past; muttering aloud to Lucille, sometimes words of love and sometimes savage curses; wondering what she was doing and where she was; gritting his teeth at visions which aroused insane jealousy; calculating what the consequences of his action would be were he to obey the impulse that had leaped into his mind in the first flush of passion. If he were to release the prisoner the fellow would probably expect an explanation and an apology which was, of course, out of the question. No, he must carry out the thing thoroughly without leaving any chance for the man to make trouble at the coast, or through the Embassy at Washington; at all costs not through Washington. For him, Birnier merely existed as a person whose feelings mattered nothing.

With the greening of the moon zu Pfeiffer had retired. As he had lain sleeplessly watching the pallor of the dawn he had savagely corroborated the decision. Now the roar of the deluge appeared to him in the form of an abettor to his plan. He watched the grey wall of rain with satisfaction, stroking the left sentry moustache as if to tame the fierce bristles of an outraged dignity. When he had emerged from the bath, the pink of his face appeared to have spread to the whites of his eyes, a fact which Bakunjala had noted with sullen dread.

Between the storms the sun glared yellow upon the smoking earth. Across the square squelched zu Pfeiffer to the orderly room. He grunted at Sergeant Schultz's greeting and sprawled in the chair. When Schultz proffered him some official documents he waved them aside irritably.

"Bring the prisoner to the Court, sergeant. I will try him immediately."

"Excellence!" said the sergeant, saluting. "What charge am I to enter against him, Excellence?"

"Arms and liquor running," responded zu Pfeiffer quickly. "I hold papers which prove the case completely; moreover you will see that Ali ben Hassan and others are prepared to testify. But—the charge will be margined as political: not criminal. Understand, sergeant?"

"Perfectly, Excellence. Ali ben Hassan and the others have to testify before your Excellence now?"

"There will be no need."

"Very good, Excellence."

"And, sergeant, what is the personnel of the launch and the prisoner's party?"

"The launch returned immediately to Jinja, Excellence, as soon as the prisoner had landed."

"Ach, good."

"The prisoner has a considerable battery, equipment and provisions; a headman and personal servants. He intended to obtain porters here, Excellence."

Zu Pfeiffer meditated, tapping the desk with a gold pencil.

"What is the headman?"

"Bambeeba, Excellence."

"Good. And the servants?"

"One is a Wongolo youth, the others are mixed Walegga and Kavirondo."

"Arrest them all and see that none gets away."

"Excellence!"

Schultz saluted and departed. Zu Pfeiffer frowned at the glare which was suddenly extinguished by falling water. He lighted a cigar and waited. Presently the sergeant returned in a waterproof cape, dripping, and announced that the prisoner was ready. Zu Pfeiffer gathered up his long legs and marched stiffly into the Court House adjoining.

Upon a slight dais was a large desk and a cane armchair beneath the Imperial Eagles and a portrait of the Kaiser

Wilhelm II. Pale, stubble bearded, and tense eyed with anger, sat Birnier upon a form against the wall; beside him stood Sergeant Schneider, for it is not usual etiquette to put a white prisoner in charge of a black guard. The grizzled sergeant stood stuffy to attention, which zu Pfeiffer acknowledged. Although he did not meet Birnier's gaze, he scowled as if he had expected him to salute the majesty of the judge as well.

But as zu Pfeiffer mounted the step to the chair of justice he looked up at the portrait of the Kaiser, stopped, and hesitated; then he wheeled abruptly, and barked:

"Sergeant, bring the prisoner to the orderly room!"

In the orderly room Birnier was placed between Sergeant Schultz at his table and Sergeant Schneider by the door. Birnier watched zu Pfeiffer intently, but zu Pfeiffer regarded him icily as if he were a piece of furniture. Without a word Birnier reached out and lifted a chair. Sergeant Schneider started forward, evidently fearing that the prisoner was about to attack his officer. Birnier said acidly: "I merely wish to sit down."

Zu Pfeiffer scowled again, but he made no objection. He took up some papers at random and began to peruse them. Said Birnier sharply:

"When you have finished with this farce I shall be obliged if you will kindly explain your insane actions!"

The tap-tap of a typewriter sounded from another room. A fly buzzed. Zu Pfeiffer's eyelids did not blink. The sergeants stared woodenly to the front. Birnier looked from one to the other, bit his lips, and then exclaimed in exasperation: "What in hell do you mean by this damned nonsense?"

The tap-tap continued; the fly buzzed irritatedly. Birnier clenched his fist. But he sat still. Another storm so darkened the room that zu Pfeiffer could scarcely have seen the print, but apparently he read on. The deluge roared, passed, and the glare came as suddenly. Zu Pfeiffer lifted his head and said in German:

"Sergeant, record the opening of the Court."

"Excellence!" assented Sergeant Schultz and poised his pen ready to write.

"The prisoner, a Swiss subject—"

"I am American, as I have told you," said Birnier in leashed anger.

"A pseudo trader and hunter, named Carl Bornstadt," continued zu Pfeiffer imperturbably, "is charged under sub-section 79 of section 8 with supplying guns and liquor to the native subjects of his Imperial Majesty."

"Good God!" began Birnier. But as he realised zu Pfeiffer's purpose and his own position, he closed his lips tightly.

Methodically the sergeant finished the entries and waited. Zu Pfeiffer stroked his favourite moustache and considered. He glanced at Birnier, but without a vestige of expression and continued:

"Make a special note, sergeant, that we have reason to suspect that the prisoner is in the political service of"—a slight smile flicked the lieutenant's face—"in the service of the Portuguese, and so under sub-section 109 of section 8, I am referring the case to Dar-es-salaam for investigation; witnesses, documentary and personal, to accompany the

Charles Beadle

prisoner. Owing to unusual pressure of service we are unable to afford the prisoner, although apparently of European descent, a white guard; therefore, Sergeant Ludwig will detail a corporal and six men for the duty."

He paused. The sergeant's pen scratched on. Zu Pfeiffer lighted a cigar and added impersonally:

"The prisoner and escort will leave to-morrow morning. Sergeant Schneider, remove the prisoner!"

Birnier's face was a little paler, the eyes were slightly more bloodshot; but he did not attempt to speak. Zu Pfeiffer rose. The sergeants stood to attention and saluted. As he left the room towards the Court House, he smiled with slight satisfaction as the gruff voice of Sergeant Schneider barked: "Prisoner, shun! Right turn! Quick marrch!"

But zu Pfeiffer did not remain long in the Court House. After fidgeting about with papers on the table and reprimanding Sergeant Schultz because he had not arranged the next native case to his satisfaction, he rose abruptly and marched swiftly across the square in the brilliant glare without his helmet and into his study. There he straddled a chair and leaned on the back sucking a dead cigar absent-mindedly. As he stared at the portrait in the ivory frame, the blue eyes grew soft and the delicate lips quivered like a child about to weep. He sighed heavily and then rapping out an oath, rose violently, overturning the chair, poured out a half-glass of neat cognac, and drank it at a gulp. As he neared the Court House the sentry, turning at the end of his short beat, was so startled at the proximity of the Kommandant, or incompletely disciplined, that he became flurried. Zu Pfeiffer clicked his heels together and haughtily watched the fumbled efforts to salute. The bolt caught in the man's tunic. Gold flashed in the sun as the sjambok descended. Zu Pfeiffer walked on unconcernedly, leaving a grey weal on the terrified native's face. To Sergeant Schultz, rigid in the doorway, he snapped an order to have fifty lashes given to the "clumsy dog."

Sentences were harsher than usual that morning. All the native world about him knew that a demon had taken possession of the Eater-of-men; he was usually inhabited by an evil spirit, but this time the demon of Bakra who, as everybody knows, tears the vitals with hot claws, making the victim to have fits, to foam at the mouth, to be quite mad, had entered the white man. Bakunjala, coming to the Court House with vermouth and biscuits at eleven o'clock, distinctly saw the devil glaring through zu Pfeiffer's eyes, and was so scared that he let fall the tray, which was the reason that he also was doomed to have twenty-five lashes that evening. Even the stolid Sergeant Schultz remarked that the Herr Lieutenant had gotten a touch of the sun; but the grizzled Schneider, who came from Luthuania, opined that the Herr Kommandant had left his table knife edge uppermost.

When zu Pfeiffer went across to tiffin the hot sun had dried up the gutters and the plot of grass. He did not return to the Court House, much to the gratitude of many innocent and guilty. After drinking more wine than usual he lay down for the siesta and fell asleep. But at five he awoke with a mouth like a burnt cooking pot and the temper of the said devil. He yelled for Bakunjala, who came, so trembling with fright that he stuttered. Zu Pfeiffer threw a glass which missed him and broke a mirror.

"Another seven years' ill luck!" shouted zu Pfeiffer, sitting on the bed in his shirt. He glared at Bakunjala standing in the door, too terror-stricken to flee, convinced that he would be blamed for breaking the glass. "You—you superstitious nigger!" yelled zu Pfeiffer, and added more calmly in

Kiswahili: "Fetch me a brandy-soda! Upesi, you son of a baboon!"

"Bwana!" exclaimed Bakunjala and fled gladly.

Zu Pfeiffer sat and scowled at the scattered pieces of mirror until Bakunjala arrived with the drink. An hour later he emerged in his immaculate undress uniform and sat on the north verandah, drank vermouth and smoked cigars, staring out across the flat swamp where the pewter of the lake was flecked with silver and blood of the sinking sun. From beyond the fort came the yaps of the drill-sergeant busy in the cool of the afternoon. At the bark of the relieving guard, zu Pfeiffer rose and walked around the house to watch, with tetchy eyes, the saluting of the flag.

As he stalked off to dinner in the messroom eyes glimmered in the darkness about him. Bakunjala, after receiving punishment, was indisposed, in fact incapable of attending to his duties in the spritely manner required. Another servant, who had taken his place, was nervous of the probable conesquences, and had a keen eye for the appearance of the devil so realistically described by Bakunjala. But the demon apparently slept, for zu Pfeiffer took the dishes placed before him with an unaccustomed meekness, pushed them away absent-mindedly, and rising, retired to his study. Even when the deputy brought the wrong bottle he reprimanded him mildly without taking his eyes off the photograph in the ivory frame.

Yet, with the port, he did not omit to rise, and heels together, raise his glass to the "Ihre Hochheit." Then sprawling in the chair he began to drink and to smoke steadily.

As the notes of the last post stuttered out in the clammy stillness he summoned the "boy" and bade him fetch

Sergeant Schultz. At the sound of the sergeant's steps on the verandah zu Pfeiffer stiffened up and patted his lips as if desiring to erase the lines that were graven thereon; and with one foot pushed the chair from the direct angle to the photograph.

"Take a cigar," said zu Pfeiffer, when the man had entered. The words were rather an order than an invitation. Sergeant Schultz obeyed. Zu Pfeiffer smoked reflectively, still regarding the photograph out of the corner of his eyes as if unable to resist the fascination.

"How long have you been in this benighted country, sergeant?"

"Nine years, Excellence."

"You wish to retire on the pension at the year's term?"

"I have not seen my wife and children for three years, Excellence."

"You shall have special leave as soon as the Wongolo affair is over."

"I thank you, Excellence."

"And I will recommend you for the special colonial service medal and pension."

"I thank you, Excellence."

"Take a drink, sergeant."

"I thank you, Excellence."

The sergeant obeyed with some semblance of initiative and he remarked that the lieutenant drank half a tumbler of neat brandy at a gulp. As if to drag himself away from the contemplation of the photograph zu Pfeiffer stood up and sat on the arm of the chair with his face in shadow above the lamp-shade. Gazing keenly at the sergeant, he said sharply:

"You are quite aware of the regulations regarding official secrets, sergeant?"

"Ach, yes, Excellence!"

As the sergeant paused to answer with the glass in his hand there was just a suspicion of astonishment in the tone.

"Good. Don't forget it!" A note of menace was in zu Pfeiffer's voice. He added more mildly, "Political reasons may cause stringent measures sometimes."

"Yes, Excellence."

Zu Pfeiffer smoked, coldly regarding the sergeant.

"Who is Sergeant Schneider detailing for the prisoner's escort to-morrow?"

"Corporal Inyira, Excellence."

"A long service man?"

"Ja, Excellence."

"Good. Go and fetch him here."

Not a shadow of surprise showed on Sergeant Schultz's face as he departed. Zu Pfeiffer smoked hard and drank another brandy thirstily with a slight unsteadiness as he lifted the glass to his mouth. The sergeant returned and stood at attention just within the door.

"The man is here, Excellence." Zu Pfeiffer nodded.

"Forward, quick marrch," commanded the sergeant in a muffled bark. "Halttt!"

"Very good, sergeant, you may wait."

Schultz saluted and retired without. The tall powerfully built native in uniform stood as if he had a bayonet beneath his chin. There was a slight nervousness about the blues of the eyes as he squinted in the attempt to look straight ahead and to watch the Kommandant at the same time. One nostril was slit, in the lobes of the ears were three can keys, and the temples were tattooed with tribal scars.

"Corporal Inyira!" said zu Pfeiffer sharply. The black body twitched at the voice. "You are to leave to-morrow for Dar-es-salaam and you will take as a prisoner a white man who has been taking your tribe as slaves and selling them to the Abyssinians. The Bwana Mkubwa protects you from these evil white men and Arabs. You know that?" sharply.

"Bwana!"

"Very good. You know what would happen to you if you were sold as a slave? You have had many brothers who have been sold to the Abyssinians?"

"Bwana! Many, Bwana!"

"Very good. Now listen! This white man is very bad. He leaves with you to-morrow morning for Dar-es-salaam, but—he is never to arrive there. I give him to you. You may do what you like with him, but never let me see him again. You have my protection. Understand?"

"Bwana!"

The rubber lips pouted in the emphatic utterance.

"These are your secret orders. But you are not to tell them to any man, woman, or child here; you may tell your men when you are gone. If you disobey I will cut out your tongue and give you three hundred lashes. Understand?"

"Bwana!"

"This man is the enemy of the Bwana Mkubwa. His enemies are your enemies. His goods are yours. Begone!"

The black hand came up jerkily to the black forehead, shot away out and down; the polished calves moved like the eccentrics of an engine, and Corporal Inyira melted into the shadows.

"Sergeant Schultz!"

To smart heel taps on the verandah entered the sergeant.

"You will see that Corporal Inyira and the escort leave before daybreak; moreover, that he talks with no one before he leaves."

"Excellence."

"Take a drink, sergeant."

With legs as stiff as his sjambok, Sergeant Schultz obeyed

the order; lifted the glass and drank.

"You may go! Good night, sergeant."

"Excellence, good night!"

As zu Pfeiffer shifted from the chair-arm to the seat his movements were slightly erratic. He sat forward, staring at the photograph, as he drank more brandy. Outside, the paean of the frogs pulsed steadily. From a distance came the throb of a native drum. A cricket shrilled intermittently.

"Bwana!"

The ghostly figure of Bakunjala whispered from the doorway. Zu Pfeiffer started nervously.

"Zingala," began Bakunjala timorously.

"Gott verdamf—Emshi!" snapped zu Pfeiffer, his ring flashing in an irritable gesture.

Bakunjala melted. Came a mutter of voices and a subdued giggle.

Zu Pfeiffer sat and drank and stared. Above the insectile anthem of the night, rose a gurgling voice in a drinking song... Later the crash of a breaking glass was accompanied by an oath. The glimmer of three pairs of eyes through the window screen vanished and reappeared... Once more rose the voice singing:

"Scheiden tut weh,
Scheiden, ja scheiden, scheiden tut weh!"

Just as the cricket began anew, after having politely ceased to hear the lieutenant's song, trickled out upon the clammy air the sound of weeping.

CHAPTER 6

In the violet shadow of his square hut inside the compound, squatted Zalu Zako. The lips and nose were nearer to the Aryan delicacy than the negroid bluntness; for the Wongolo, like the Wahima, are a mixed Bantu-Somali race. In colour his skin had the red of bronze rather than the blue of the negro, and the planes of his moulded chest were as light as the worn ivory bracelets upon his polished limbs. Broad in the shoulders he had almost the slender hips of a young girl and his carriage was as balanced as a dancer's.

From a group of small round huts behind his square hut, where dwelt his two wives, concubines and slaves, came the clutter of voices. A distant drum throbbed gently on the hot air. Away in the cool green of the banana plantation rose the crooning chant of the unmarried girls and slaves bringing water from the river.

Apparently Zalu Zako was absorbed in the movements of a diminutive chicken scratching in the soil. The omen of the goat was occupying his mind: that and the death of his grandfather, MFunya MPopo. There was no sense of grief, for he was not a woman. Now, at the beginning of his warrior's career, he had not any desire for divine honours and celibacy. No man had. Yet Zalu Zako no more dreamed of questioning the necessity than of spitting in the face of an enemy. Always had the first born male of his family been doomed to the kingly office. There was never a second born male, for it was not meet that a god should have paternal brothers. The wives of his youth and his concubines could have as many children as they could bear; but according to the law, did he select the chief wife from whom should spring the one regal son only when he had become heir apparent; for then was he not already half divine, being so near the sacred enclosure up on the hill?

The choice of that chief wife was free as there were no royal families in the sense of divine descent save the direct male line of the King-God. But the mind of Zalu Zako dwelt more upon his personal career. The life of a warrior was frequently short and that of a god even briefer. MFunya MPopo had reigned but twenty moons; MKoffo, so said the elders, had reigned for full two hundred moons; but then he had been a mighty magician.

With a harsh squawk a brilliant scarlet and blue bird with an enormous yellow bill perched on the palisade of the compound. Immediately the young man forgot his musing and rose, calling for his spear. A stocky man, coal black, with a fuzzy tuft of a beard, came out of the hut. From the slave Zalu Zako took a broad-bladed spear with a short haft. Watching to see that the bird was still sitting on the fence as he passed out of the compound, he set off rapidly through the village and into the banana plantations in search of a wart hog which had been rooting up one of his fields of sweet potatoes. Just as he came within sight of them a black field rat sprang out of the grass in his path, glanced round at him, and disappeared. The young man's steps slackened, for he knew that the black rat had spoiled the luck which the banana eater had portended. Scarcely troubling to glance around the field, he diverged across at an angle making for a break in the jungle where he knew was the trail of the boar.

But he grunted contemptuously as he examined the last spoor, which was at least half a day old. Of course the hog would not be there.

He bethought himself of another field where sometimes came buck. But there was no game. The black rat again! Yet if one waited long enough a good omen might appear. As he squatted beneath a banana plant to take snuff came a squawk and the banana eater—for it appeared to be the same one— alighted on a frond near to him. Zalu Zako waited. Leisurely and cautiously he arose. The bird peered at him. Zalu Zako passed and left the banana eater still sitting there. He felt the weight of his spear tentatively, for a double omen of luck must mean big game: possibly an eland or a leopard.

He circled right round the outskirts of the plantation. But he saw no signs. As he began to make the big circle again the shadows were lengthening appreciably. Passing by the ford of the small river, which was swollen from the rains, he heard a group of young girls chattering on the river bank as they filled their gourds. He paused to test which way the wind was blowing in order to avoid going down wind where the sound of their voices would scare away any game.

But as he turned to move on he caught a glimpse of a figure mounting the incline. The motion was as lithe as a young giraffe; the legs were as straight as spears and as supple as a kiboko; the moulded hips swayed rhythmically like a banana frond in the breeze; the fluted arch of her back swelled proudly upwards to the resilient shoulders; and an arm as slender as a lizard's tail steadied the gourd upon a small black head set upon a neck like a sapling. The dappled shadows of a tree played hide and seek upon the tiny hills that were her firm young breasts, upon the smoothness of her torso of light bronze. As he gazed her face came into view in speaking to a comrade just beneath. An errant shaft of sunlight glinted the pearl of teeth, glowed the tiny nose and blued the whites of eyes which were as soft as any antelope.

Zalu Zako clicked the syllable that means astonishment.

"Wait there, O Bayakala," she called, "for I have to do the making of mighty magic with the spirits of the wood."

"Eh, eh!" responded one of those left by the water edge, "a girl of the hut thatch hath nought to do with spirits of the wood for their bellies are as big as a pregnant woman!"

The young girl laughed and her notes seemed to Zalu Zako like the dripping of water upon a river rock.

"Thou knowest less than the Baroto bird who as everybody knows is the spirit of one!"

"'Tis more than thou wilt ever be!" retorted the rival beneath.

"Ehh! Ehh!" exclaimed the girl at the sneer, "thy girdle is rotted long since with juice!"

"And thine," shouted the insulted one, who was old for a spinster, "wilt rot with the dryness!"

"Tscch! It is dry for the lord whom I will conquer with magic such as thou hast never dreamed on, O Bayakala!"

"And who is he for whom thou makest magic, O daughter of the hut thatch?" demanded Zalu Zako, stepping from the shelter of the tree.

"Ehh!" ejaculated Bakuma. "I—we do but tickle the fronds (jest), O Chief!"

The only sign of her nervousness was the slight swaying of the gourd of water upon her head as she turned up her eyes to the young chief who regarded her slowly. She edged away. He moved a pace in front of her. She clutched at the amulet around her neck as she turned her eyes and said:

"The cooking fires are low, O Chief, and need be tended."

"Thy breasts are like unto small anthills," he said, "and thy belly is as smooth as yonder river rock."

"Thy tongue is sweeter than the honey of the kinglan tree."

"Thy voice is softer than the muted lyre and thy nose is formed of two petals of an orchid."

"Thy praise is more refreshing than the morning dew to a thirsty flower."

"And by thy figure am I made more drunken than by the wine of the Soka palm."

For a full minute they stood, a study in light bronze against the dappled green foliage. The shrill chatter of the other girls approaching startled Bakuma into action. She swayed to one side.

"The spirits of the cooking pot cry aloud for me, O Chief."

"Who is thy father, little one?" he demanded.

"I am Bakuma, the daughter of Bakala, O Chief."

"There has been a veil before my eyes that I have not seen thee before."

"The mountains see not the tiny brooks amid the mighty forests," murmured Bakuma and sped up the path.

Zalu Zako stood motionless watching her form melt into the green, and as he turned towards the river he met Bayakala and the other women who shrank aside from the path to allow the Son of the Snake to pass in silence. Yet at the ford he paused. He had forgotten the omen of the banana eater and the purpose for which he had come.

As Bakuma sped along in a gliding lope the amulet swayed rhythmically to the whispered praises of the power of Marufa, mixed with ardent prayers to the spirits to provide the fat goat with which to propitiate the spirit of the woods; for had not the love charm already manifested its wondrous power? As she hastened through the banana plantation she could not resist diverging a little in the direction of the magician's hut. As she passed, she saw him seated on the threshold of the compound gathering inspiration from his favourite wall. But Marufa observed her demeanour, and being something of a student of men, he deducted that the charm had already begun to work.

Marufa, as all successful men, had a strain of luck. Before the shadows had crept a hand's breadth came MYalu, indignant and exasperated. The three tusks had been paid and the footprint obtained; but he had discovered that it was no easy matter to procure the other ingredients which he suspected the wizard had known well and intended as a means to extract more ivory. After the ceremonious greetings he protested that the task given was almost impossible to execute. Marufa remained imperturbably interested in his wall.

"But as thou knowest," insisted MYalu, "the hair and the toe-nail and the spittle of the Son of the Snake are more than difficult to obtain. Does a man so carelessly render himself unto his enemies, and he the Son of the Snake? None save one of his household could purloin a single hair. Even this morning was his hair shaved and the remnants, as thou knowest well, deposited in the temple with him who was his father."

"The hair, the toe-nail, and the spittle," mumbled the old man, "must I have for such mighty magic."

"Ehh!" snorted MYalu, "with a man of the clay, but with one who is half divine, the Son of the Snake! Ehh!"

"The bow is useless without the arrows," mumbled the old man.

"Tsch. 'Tis a mighty hunter that hath not the arrows for his bow," sneered MYalu.

"Verily," retorted Marufa disinterestedly, "and still more a mighty man who cannot do his own hunting!"

"No warrior hath been purified more frequently than I," boasted MYalu, referring to the ceremony incumbent upon those who have taken life to appease the ghosts of the slain.

"The spirits obey not the crowing of a cockerel," reminded Marufa.

"Tsch!" For a while both sat silent, MYalu gloomily watching a hen.

"Aie! Aie!" he lamented at last, "what is there that I may do, for indeed she hath caught my soul in a trap. Aie! Aie!"

"If the hunter cannot make arrows, he may buy them,"

remarked Marufa, who had been patiently waiting for this state of mind.

"Eh! The bowstring hath been costly but the arrows! Aie! Aie! What would'st thou?"

"The rich man payeth in his kind. Four tusks of fine grain."

"Eh! Eh!"

"Maybe there are others whose hands are not withered."

"Others than the Son of the Snake?" demanded MYalu quickly.

"Who knows? There are more fools than chickens," muttered the old man.

MYalu stared disconsolately at the distant bananas. Perhaps, he reflected, it would be cheaper to pay the price the girl's uncle demanded, yet—MYalu had bought other wives whose unimpassioned charms had quickly staled. His soul, as he put it, had indeed been tempted into a trap by Bakuma; for he wished only that she should desire him as he desired her. Yet was he angry. Love seemed to be a costly business. Marufa tapped out snuff and sniffed delicately with the air of a connoisseur devoting himself to the pleasure of the moment. Replacing the cork of twisted leaves he stirred as if to rise.

"Canst thou procure then the nail and the hairs that are asked by the spirits?" inquired MYalu sulkily.

"All things are possible to the son of MTungo," asserted Marufa. "Four tusks, and these things are found; but of fine grain, for the others were old and coarse."

"Ehh! How wilt thou procure these things?" demanded MYalu sceptically.

"The ways of the wise are not the ways of fools."

"The tusks are thine," said MYalu reluctantly, "if thou wilt tell me how thou wilt procure them."

"Thy words are like unto the vomit of a dog," muttered the old man.

"But how? My heart is not bound in clay."

"Tch!" clicked Marufa contemptuously. "Every fool must needs see the spoor of the god which he cannot read. I have spoken." MYalu regarded the old wizard incredulously. "Tch! Send the four tusks as we have agreed and so shall it be. Begone!"

Slowly MYalu rose, made his greeting, and departed more impressed than ever that the old man was a mighty magician.

During the hour when the soul is small and dwells timidly around the feet Marufa dozed in the cool of his hut; but later when it spread boldly out was he squatted once more in his favourite seat at the entrance to the compound, taking snuff and contemplating. The shadows grew from violet to blue; the small hens pecked for worms with avidity and the goats scratched with vigour in the cool. Patiently Marufa sat. At length that for which he had waited with a sound though primitive knowledge of psychology, came to pass. Bakuma appeared, apprehensive, but with yet an abandon which sang her happiness. Beside Marufa she sat so as to avoid the shadow of one foot protruding beyond that of the fence.

"O great and mighty magician," she began eagerly, after the

formal greetings. "Indeed all that thou hast said hath come to pass. Thy charm is infallible."

"Ugh!" grunted Marufa unconcernedly.

"All that my heart desireth hath already begun to be. I thank thee."

"Ugh!"

"O mighty son of MTungo, what must I now do?"

"Thou knowest," mumbled Marufa, fumbling for the snuff case.

"Aie! Aie! but I have no fat goat!" cried Bakuma, who had hoped fatuously that the wizard would have forgotten. "I, a girl of the hut thatch, how should I have a goat?" Marufa tapped snuff as if no romance were in the making. Bakuma's bright eyes, sharpened by the proximity of the promise of her love, watched the old man keenly. "Listen, O great and mighty son of MTungo, to whom all things are known, who canst accomplish all that thou desireth, Bayakala, my cousin, hath a goat, but it is old and skinny. Perhaps—"

"In the nostrils of the spirits," asserted Marufa instantly, "all odours are the same except that of the fat goat whom they love."

"Aie! then am I undone, for no fat goat have I!" wailed Bakuma. "Know I not one who hath a goat who would smile on me, a girl of the hut thatch."

"Ugh!"

Bakuma regarded him imploringly, but Marufa's gaze was

fixed upon the wall as if his mind were turned to matters of more importance.

"O mighty wizard, what must I do?" implored Bakuma desperately.

"Ugh!"

After a prolonged contemplation, said Marufa: "If thou canst get no goat, then is there another path by which thou mayest accomplish thy end."

"Eh!"

"But it is very difficult."

"By my cord, will I do all that thou canst bid me to do!" swore Bakuma in anxious haste.

"Ugh! This path is more certain of success for the will of the spirits are oftentimes chary of their favours."

"O mighty one!" breathed Bakuma, as he paused tantalisingly.

"But the matter is exceedingly difficult—and dangerous."

"If the flower hath no sun hath it ever lived?"

"As even thou shouldst know," mumbled Marufa, more casually than ever, "he who possesses a part of the soul may do magic thereon."

"Aye! Aye!"

"Bring me then of the nail parings one, of his hairs one, and of his spittle. Then may I do magic thereon which he cannot resist."

"O mighty magician!" gasped Bakuma, appalled at the difficulty and the danger of the task.

"That path is sure. There is no other."

"Eh!... But if they of thy craft should know then am I doomed!"

"There is no other."

Torn between her love and the dread of the penalty incurred by the sacrilege of the theft of the parts of one who might any day be King-God, Bakuma stared distraught.

"Were not my words white? Hath not the love charm thou hast already had done even as I did say?"

"O mighty one!"

"But that is only as the goat to the leopard. The trap must be dug—or the scent of the bait will be blown."

"Ehh!" gasped Bakuma, in desperation, "by my twin soul which dwells beneath the banana plant, will I do it!"

CHAPTER 7

Gerald Birnier had flattered himself that he was a philosopher with a sense of humour, fairly well developed by ten years' wandering about Central Africa, but deep emotions submerge such cherished qualities.

The presence of the photograph was explicable by several surmises: zu Pfeiffer might have met Lucille at Washington, Paris, or Berlin: she might have given him the photograph or he might have bought it, or even stolen it. But—the signature "a toi, Lucille"! There lay the sting which maddened Birnier and strangled reason, the fact at which his mind yawed futilely.

So great had been the shock that the arrest had seemed but a secondary matter in accord with the insanity of zu Pfeiffer's statement that he was engaged to Lucille. The affair had been so sudden that for some time he could progress no farther in an attempt to think than a gasp, pawing mentally at an intangible substance which eluded him like a child's small hand trying to grasp a toy balloon. Sense of reality appeared to have been dissolved. He had followed the sergeant across the square meekly without realising what was happening, and when he had been placed in a whitewashed room at the back of the native guard house which served as a jail, he sat down upon a chair, too bewildered to comprehend where he was. That "a toi, Lucille" rang like the clanging in a belfry, drowning the sound of other thoughts.

By the light of a hurricane lamp he regarded the soldiers bringing in an old camp bed with indifference. When they had gone he began to pace up and down the small room frantically trying to gain control. To the first prompting of a logical reason for the whole affair he did not dare to listen. The disrupting cause was the complete inability to explain the familiar signature. To his Anglo-Saxonised mind, bred in the strict code of the south, tutoyer was only permissible to dogs, inferiors, most intimate relations and lovers. He was far too unbalanced to see the humour as he solemnly announced that certainly zu Pfeiffer was not a dog, nor in the social code an inferior; he was not a relation; therefore... His mind baulked and raced into incoherence.

A point of view which added false premises, as well as his attitude to those two little words, was the consciousness that many would consider that he had not treated his wife as a husband should do. This possibility had never occurred to him before, so that it came with disproportionate emphasis.

As a young man he had been too absorbed in his profession to be a lady's man; and of love he had reckoned little until he had met the Lucille Charltrain with whom half the world was in love. And she doubtless, like many a spoiled beauty, was a little piqued that the professor did not join the throng of her courtiers. In Birnier's mind there had ever been associated with love the fear that the woman would demand too much, that no woman could understand that a man's profession must of necessity come before all things. Lucille was the first woman whom he had met who really seemed to understand this point of view, as she, too, was devoted to her art. This had grown to be the biggest bond and attraction between them. Most men wished to make of love a nuisance, as

Lucille once put it. So the good-looking professor had won the beauty. They were married on the mutual understanding that each should pursue their respective professions. Shortly afterwards Birnier was offered a special mission to go to Africa for the purpose of studying the customs and superstitions of the natives. Lucille had consented, forbidden, relented, and laughed.

So Lucille sang from musical height to height and her husband sped from depth to depth in the seas of human fatuity. Whenever he took a furlough he went, of course, straight to her, wheresoever she was, in Berlin, New York, or Paris. To Birnier the situation was ideal. He had never dreamed of any other woman. Indeed the tracts of his mind were so filled with statistics of anthropology and Lucille that there was little or no room for any one else. The delight and satisfaction in Birnier's mind were so sincere that he never had dreamed of questioning whether Lucille's point of view had remained the same. But now?

That "a toi" stung and baited him into the unprecedented realisation that after all women had been known to change their opinions. Perhaps pride had prevented her from ever openly demanding other ways. Lucille was young and beautiful, courted and flattered on every hand. Perhaps he had been wrong to leave her for years at a stretch. Of her loyalty he had had no doubt, but for the first time in his marital life the professor's profound knowledge of human nature was shot like a spot-light on to his own affairs. Yet his erudition did not in the least relieve him from the laws of emotional reaction.

Perhaps in an emotional moment... That knowledge of the frailties of genus homo was too deep for comfort in such actuation.

"A toi, Lucille! A toi, Lucille!" rang and echoed as he paced that room, striving for control... And—and—why else should zu Pfeiffer have gone crazy?—why had he exclaimed: "Das ist der Schweinhuend"? The husband, of course, whom he wanted out of the way, and he had immediately seized the opportunity to secure that end, seemingly indifferent to consequences— symptomatic of the state of "being in love."

Around and about, about and around a field of weeds which had sprung from that seed "a toi," had paced the professor all night. When the green was creeping through the high barred window, Sergeant Schneider had brought to him some coffee and biscuits. Birnier had drunk the coffee thirstily, and as the sergeant had no English nor French, had tried in broken German to extract some information. But the sergeant had merely grunted and retired. At seven he had returned again and escorted Birnier to the Court House. He returned from the mock trial a little more in touch with reality, and more impressed with the malignity of zu Pfeiffer. Yet the gratuitous insults, the laboured farce of the registering of an alleged Swiss trader, Birnier saw through, and was relieved, for it argued that zu Pfeiffer's intention was to make Lucille a widow. No other reason could account for the homicidal intentions displayed.

At the glow of dawn next day he was aroused by the big corporal who ordered him out. The tone of the man's voice naturally stimulated a violent reaction. But Birnier realised that his sole chance lay in controlling himself to accept stoically whatever treatment was offered; for he saw instantly that any protest or indignation would be interpreted as insubordination and possibly be made an excuse to shoot him down.

Outside in the grey light he saw under the guard of six native soldiers, the five others of his party. Mungongo, his personal "boy," cried out at the sight of him, asking what was the meaning of these strange happenings. Before Birnier could reply, the big corporal struck the man savagely with a kiboko, bidding him to be silent. In spite of his resolution, the reaction made Birnier turn angrily upon the soldier, who deliberately repeated the order, and struck the white man across the face. As Birnier raised his fist the man lowered his bayonet and grinned, adding, apparently for the benefit of his men, that now the white would learn what it was to be a slave.

Furiously Birnier looked around for Sergeant Schneider: but no white man was in sight... He turned to Mungongo and said quickly: "Take no heed. Do as they bid thee for the moment."

"Be silent!" shouted the corporal, but as he raised his kiboko, Birnier looked him quietly straight in the eyes. The black hand was lowered; the man turned away, ordering the party in general to march.

Dishevelled and without any camp equipment, Birnier began to march as the blood of the sky paled to orange. At the bottom of the great parade ground he turned in time to see the relieving guard falling in behind the Court House. For one moment he hesitated whether to put all to the test by refusing to go; but a significant gesture with the ever ready rifle of the corporal signified that he would not be given a chance. Humiliated, he obeyed. But just beyond the last hut, waiting by the path, was a group of women loaded with the soldiers' gear; and beside them were some carriers bearing his green tent and apparently all his equipment. The sight cheered him a little. He attempted to find immediate consolation in the idea that the savagery of the corporal might possibly abate when they were away from the neighbourhood of the inciting agent, whom he was sure was zu Pfeiffer.

Leading the caravan was a soldier; next to him came Birnier and behind him was another soldier, after whom walked Mungongo and the four other prisoners, with a soldier between each; and then the corporal, strutting portentously important within easy shooting distance of the white man. The carriers and women brought up the rear.

The path led for some miles through the dreary swamp following the course of the small bayou, crossing and recrossing small streams swollen with the rains, through which the white man was forced to wade to his hips. For the first mile Birnier was so angry and humiliated that he dared not catch the troubled eyes of Mungongo. But by force of will he attained a reasonable plane of philosophic resignation, temporary at least, and smiled at the boy, who grinned back like a tickled child. At any rate, soliloquised Birnier, he had at least one man upon whom he could rely.

At the head of the bayou they reached higher ground and the path zigzagged through dense jungle thick with fan palms. The longer Birnier pondered upon the situation the nearer he came towards the conclusion that he had better make his escape as soon as possible, or he would never have the chance. Rather by the uneasy glances of Mungongo, who dared not speak, did he guess that they had left the regular trail to the coast. What their destination was he could not imagine. Probably, he thought grimly, to make an end of the whole party and return to the camp. Yet why trouble to travel so far? And another good reason to hasten an escape was that, although for the moment he was in good health, a few days of exposure would subject him to fever and consequent weakness.

Now and again the theme "a toi" would return like the refrain of a song to which he found himself keeping step; but the words sometimes became meaningless; for in the merciful way that nature has, the impulse of self-preservation so occupied his mind that he had scarcely leisure to worry over marital troubles.

At the end of about two hours, when the heat of the sun was beginning to be felt severely, the corporal called a halt in the shade of a great baobab. Birnier sat down with his back against the bole. Alongside him squatted the corporal deliberately and called to the women for a gourd of juwala. There is a certain acid odour which native beer has that is particularly irritating to a dry palate. The corporal drank deep, sighed with satisfaction and set the gourd beside him almost touching the feet of the white. Involuntarily Birnier swallowed. The corporal saw and grinned. Birnier understood and turned his back to the man. Immediately the corporal arose and lowering his bayonet until it pricked the sleeve of Birnier's coat, ordered him to get up. In the knowledge that he would be instantly shot by the others if he attempted to resist, he had perforce to obey.

Outside the shade of the great tree, in the full glare of the sun, was the white man compelled to sit while the black corporal, with the rifle ready across his knee, drank deep and handed the gourd to his fellows. Again Birnier turned his back to him. But he began to realise faintly what treatment he would receive before the end came and an intimate knowledge of native ingenuity made him feel physically sick.

Half an hour later they were on the march again. The path became rugged and difficult, passing through thorny ground, following burbling watercourses of rough stones. To make the going more trying Birnier wore light moccasins intended for camp use instead of his high field boots. Once when a long thorn penetrated the flank of his shoe he stopped to extract it. The corporal shouted at him; the soldier behind called him unmentionable names in the dialect and pushed him with his foot. The insult and the heat of the sun maddened him. He leaped to his feet. The corporal raised his gun promptly and jeered. For a moment Birnier stood trembling with passion; then he closed his eyes as if to shut out sight and sound and limped forward, fighting with himself.

With natives had Birnier always been able to negotiate, to live, and to quarrel when necessary, on terms of amity; but this black "swine," as he termed him in his wrath, prinked out in a masquerade of a white man's clothes... He jammed his heel down savagely upon the thorn to divert the southern passion. After all it was not the man's fault but zu Pfeiffer's. Put a white man in a uniform and he becomes a beast; put a nigger in a uniform and he becomes a devil, Birnier forced himself to reflect.

The sun grew incandescent. The heat and the flies quickened his thirst. He plodded on, stumbling over the stones, sagging heavily in sandy patches. They had left the comparative shelter of the jungle and were crossing a flat plain approaching, he judged, to a river bed. The carriers, he noted, had lagged behind. Soon they must halt. Even the fiend of a corporal would not fatigue himself too much for the sake of tormenting a white man.

Then a new idea was added to the plagues. He had tasted nothing save the coffee, canned beef, and native bread which had been given him for dinner on the previous evening. The corporal had manifested his conception of humour by refusing him beer and water on the march; was he going to torment him by starvation as well as by thirst? And if torture were reserved for him by that grinning black brute, then he knew what would be the end that awaited him.

Within an hour they came to a river about forty yards broad, a swollen rushing torrent. There was no village as he had expected. The corporal halted. Birnier slid down the bank and thrust his muzzle into the flood. There was torture in the restraint not to drink too much. He clambered up the slope to find the corporal grinning at him. He turned his back and lay down. There was no shade; only short scrub and grass. Small sand flies buzzed and stung. He heard the gurgle of the corporal's military water-bottle. But this time the sting was extracted; his belly was moist.

Birnier stretched out, shielding from the glare the little that he could with his hands. Faint echoes of "a toi" strolled across his field of consciousness. He observed the apparently stoical indifference of Mungongo squatted a few feet from him, a soldier sprawling between them; but he cursed because investigations had taught him that that "stoical" should usually be read as "bovinity," as he had termed it; and he smiled dismally at the ancient story that so well illustrated the point, of the peasant who expressed his occupation through the long winter hours as "sometimes we sits and thinks but mostly we just sits."

Mungongo "just sits," he repeated, and envied him. Yet in that heat and hunger, waiting for his savage captor to wreak some new fancy upon him, so saturated with philosophic interest in life was Birnier, that he wandered off into a meditation upon the mechanical fatuity of human conduct; illustrating his reflections by his own actions when stirred by emotion. "The loaded gun may be as wise as Solomon was reputed to be," he remarked beneath his hands, "but all the same when some one pulls the trigger the damn thing goes off," and sat up to confront the muzzle of the corporal's rifle, who was ordering him to get up. Birnier rose. But to the savage's amazement, he smiled.

The corporal backed away.

"Ah, my friend," remarked Birnier blandly in English. "You've lost, for I have found that which was lost!"

The corporal scowled and bade him to follow. Birnier obeyed but he felt that he was obliging the man. The carriers had arrived and the green tent was pitched, invitingly cool against the grey flood of the river. He followed the corporal gladly, but at ten feet from his tent, beside a thorn bush four feet tall which spread in a fan shape, he was bidden to sit. For the moment, newly arrived from his philosophic dreams, he did not comprehend.

"But that is my tent!" he said in Kiswahili.

"Sit down!" commanded the corporal, grinning. "The white seller of slaves sits in the place of the slave, but his owner dwells in the place of the blessed."

"O God!" remarked Birnier as he bumped his head against black reality.

CHAPTER 8

Bakuma sat in the shade of the reed fence preparing the evening meal of boiled bananas. From her slender neck swung the precious amulet at which, as if to reassure herself of its safety, she clutched occasionally. Her half-sister, who had not yet passed through the initiation at maturity, sprawled upon her belly in the dwindling rays of the sun, scratching her woolly head. Beyond her were two slaves tending a fire beneath two large calabashes, preparatory to the brewing of banana beer, which had of course to be done by the chief widow, Bakuma's half-sister's mother.

The mind of Bakuma was occupied by percepts of the charms of Zalu Zako; particularly as memorised on that afternoon by the river when the effect of the love charm had begun to work. These memories, as sweet as they would have been to any maid, were shot with gay colours by the words of the wizard; for he had assured her that with the toe-nail and hair to work magic upon, Zalu Zako would be bewitched by her charms for all time. And she had obtained them! She could have gotten the goat, not a skinny goat as described under the inhibiting influence of a wild hope that the wizard would relent. Her cousin, smarting under the reproaches of her husband, had such a goat, fat as goats in Wongolo go, and she was eager to exchange it or anything for an infallible charm against sterility. Bakuma feared to part with the charm, yet the matter was pressing; immediately she was the wife of Zalu Zako she would be in a position to purchase all the charms in the village.

But difficult to obtain as they were, for as everybody knows no man leaves portions of himself around that may fall into the hands of an enemy to work magic upon, least of all a rich man, "half divine," she had obtained some nail parings and one hair. With that charm against sterility, the only thing of value Bakuma possessed, had she bribed a concubine of Zalu Zako's household to steal the ingredients required from the hut thatch where they had been hidden after the official shaving and paring following the ceremony of his father, pending their removal to the sacred precincts of the temple.

Above her passion for Zalu Zako was her natural feminine appreciation of a good match. The Son of the Snake was far better from a woman's point of view than union with a successful wizard. In the event of the death of the King-God, Kawa Kendi, the wives of his son and successor, although denied to him, were accorded special privileges; and upon his demise these royal wives retained their home upon the hill which had become his tomb. Moreover, as Bakuma knew well, now that Zalu Zako was heir-apparent, he must choose the principal wife who would for her life remain paramount in the household, avoiding the dread of every ageing woman that her husband would take unto him another wife younger and more supple.

The one mosquito in paradise was the fear that as soon as her uncle, her father's brother to whom she belonged by inheritance, learned the august personage who desired her, he would raise the price to a prohibitive figure; for he was mean as well as stupid and lazy, wherefore he had few goods, and although Zalu Zako was a rich man she knew that any man save a fool loves to drive a good bargain if only to prove his astuteness. Therefore was another imperative necessity to procure every means of magic and charm to fan the flame of her lover's desires.

Yet always flashed a bright-hued lizard in the sun of her joy when she imagined herself installed as the chief wife in the household of Zalu Zako, an unassailable position as long as she had one male child; the practical mistress of his first two wives as well as the retinue of slaves.

Bazila, the younger wife, Bakuma knew well; the favourite and haughty, covered with the most expensive amulets against every ill and black magic, she was overfond of sneering at young girls of the hut thatch whose charms had not yet netted a victim.

"Ehh!" gasped Bakuma and flashed her teeth as she rolled the warm leaves around the sticky mess, "then will the scent of my body be more bitter than the flower of the fish-faced cactus!"

And so through the night did Bakuma nibble at anticipatory joys as she lay upon her reed mat on the slightly raised dais of the floor which was her bed, watching the smoke of the fire in the middle of the hut lose itself in the shadows of the roof, and listening in the hope of hearing some voice of the spirits whom Marufa was to invoke on her behalf. Save for the occasional bleating of a goat and once the harsh scream of the Baroto bird, which made her heart contract, for it is a bad omen, the night was still. However, at the hour of the monkey Bakuma arose to replenish the fire. As the western star was melting in the warm green she left the compound. On the outskirts of the village the tall figure of MYalu appeared from the shadows of the plantation.

"Greeting, daughter of Bakala," said he, his eyes greedily

devouring her.

"Greeting, O Chief!" returned Bakuma, as she politely stepped to one side to avoid standing on the vague shadow of the chief.

"The fawn seeks the pastures early," remarked MYalu.

"Before the breath of the sun the grass is sweeter," retorted Bakuma, edging away.

"Aye," remarked MYalu, with a hungry glint in his eyes, "thou art eager to slake thy thirst? But in the valley will no buck walk this day!"

"Ehh!" gasped Bakuma, recollecting instantly the omen of the Baroto bird heard that night. "What meanest thou?"

"Maybe the soul of him hath wandered and been caught in a trap or maybe—" He paused to watch her closely—"maybe an enemy hath made magic upon the parts of him."

"Ehh!" Bakuma started nervously.

MYalu smiled and touched her upon the shoulder.

"Thy flesh is cooler than the dew."

"Nay, nay, O Chief, thou hast not tied my girdle," she protested, as she backed away from him, her eyes wide like a terrified deer's.

"Nay, but will I untie it soon," he retorted.

But as he stepped towards her she turned and fled. As MYalu watched her running as swiftly as a pookoo into the plantation he grinned and called out: "Even now is the cooling draught steaming in the breath of the Unmentionable One! But the goblet shall hold a sweeter draught for me!"

"Aie! Aie-e!" wailed Bakuma, her heart beating furiously, "what devil hath bewitched me! O, that father of many goats hath betrayed me! Aie! Aie-e! O, the cry of the Baroto bird! Aie! Aie-e!"

And when Bakuma, distraught with terror by the menace that she had only procured the nail paring and hair to give her lover into the hands of the false magician who, of course, had been bought by MYalu, arrived at the "pastures" by the river, as MYalu had foretold, no buck walked there.

The sun spilled blue shadows on the village from the sacred hill where another scene was being enacted, and it was not as imagined by the amorous MYalu.

In the council house, which was within the outer fence and before the sacred enclosure, was in progress a meeting of the doctors. In the door of the enclosure squatted Kawa Kendi, with Kingata Mata in attendance tending the royal fires. Before him, in front of their fellows, were seated Bakahenzie and Marufa in full dress of green feathers and the scarlet plume. The left side of the idol, which was so set that the shadow never fell upon the entrance to the compound, was gilded by the sun; the mouth grinned in one corner, one eye was closed in shadow, seemingly like a prodigious wink.

To the thrumming of the sacred band Bakahenzie was rocking himself to and fro mumbling incantations. Kawa Kendi squatted immobile, but the others swayed and grunted softly in rhythm. Then on a sudden did Bakahenzie lift up his head and cry in a great voice. The drums ceased and the body of witch-doctors remained motionless, expectant.

Bakahenzie dropped his head and began to chant:

"Behold! I have heard the voice of the trees
Crying softly by night!
Lo! the soul of the plant is in labour!
As a woman with child!
Behold! is she not to break forth?
For she crieth for aid.
Unless she be heard the infant will slip!
The fruit will not be!
The plants will not break!
The milk will be sour!
The beer will be green!
Women will not bear!
Our spears will be blunt!
Our magic will wane!
And He will be wroth!"

"Eh! Ah!... Eh! Ah!... Eh! Ah!... Eh! Ah!... Eh! Ah!..."
grunted the chorus of the doctors. Then chanted Marufa:

"Lo! I have slept and been that which I must!
Preying swiftly by night!
Behold! I have bloodied my fangs in the throat
Of a mighty bull eland!
Blood succoured the earth and upsprang a plant!
Which panted for blood!
The sap of the plant is the soul of the tree!
Take heed to the thirst
Of Him who first was!
Who lusts for a maid!
Full breasted, soft thighed!
Supple, bow arched!
Clean blooded and strong!
Whose name is forbid!
Whose name is a sin!"

"Who hath stolen the name?" screamed Bakahenzie, leaping to his feet. "Who is she that hath stolen the name?"

"Eh! Ahh!... Eh! Ahh!... Eh! Ahh!... Eh! Ahh!... Eh! Ahh!..."

As the drums throbbed swifter Bakahenzie began to shuffle in a stooping posture as if he were snuffing a trail. To the continuous grunting he continued this dance for fully a quarter of an hour. Then stopping abruptly in front of the king he screamed:

> "Let her be bidden
> To come to the feast!
> Let her be oiled!
> Let her be shaved!
> Let her come dancing!
> Let her be joyful!
> Let her be decked!
> Let her be glad!
> Lips of the groom
> Thirst for her mouth!
> Let her be drunken
> To bear his sweet weight!
> That the crops will be full!
> That the cattle grow fat
> Wives will throw men!
> Spears will slice foes!"

He sank suddenly upon his haunches. The drums ceased. A slave appeared bearing a pure white kid. Kingata Mata took the animal and held it before Kawa Kendi, who muttered a long incantation over it and cut the throat with a spear head. Then to Marufa was the bleeding carcass carried and while still alive he slit open the belly, smeared the liquid over his chest and right arm, and tore out the guts. The corpse was removed. Marufa, working only with the enchanted arm, turned the entrails over and about, peering closely.

There was silence. The shadows grew in depth. From the village came an occasional bleat and the voice of a distant girl chanting.

After a prolonged and studious search, Marufa caught up and wrapt round his neck an intestine. As he rose, the group of witch-doctors broke out into a mighty groaning. Marufa speeded across the small clearing and kneeled before Kawa Kendi. Through the bloody necklet he whispered two syllables: "kuma."

The groaning ceased as suddenly as it had commenced. Kawa Kendi cried out in a loud voice:

"The bride is found!"

Instantly the drums began a furious beat. A mighty shout rose from all assembled and they fell to the chest and belly grunting: "Eh! Ahh!... Eh! Ahh!..." as Bakahenzie and Marufa began to dance the dance of thanksgiving.

Ba*kuma* had been doomed to be the victim for the Feast of the Harvest Festival, to be sacrificed in the orgy as the Bride of the Spirit of the Banana, because Marufa had discovered by divination that two syllables of her name were those of the secret name which only the King-God knew, of the Unmentionable One, the Usa*kuma*.

CHAPTER 9

Before the green tent strutted a sentry as pompously as if he were on duty before the Kommandant's bungalow. Inside, sprawling in a camp chair, was the corporal, in blue striped pyjamas, smoking a cigarette. Upon the floor crouched one of his women with a safety razor stuck in her woolly thatch, opening a can of beef. On the camp table were a bottle of brandy which had had its neck knocked off, a shaving mirror and an open tin of cigarettes. Squatting on the bed was another woman in field boots, cleaning up a can of salmon with one finger. The rest of the tent was a litter of broken cases, bottles, cans and papers.

Ten yards away under the thorn shrub, lay Birnier, and near to him were Mungongo and the others. Mungongo's regard shuttled between this scene in the tent and the white man with a mingled expression of terror and amazement: terror at the temerity of the corporal in treating a white in such a manner and incredulous bewilderment that the white did not immediately strike them all dead. But the others, more sophisticated to the white man's ways, were solely occupied in envying the corporal's debauch.

The mauve shadows turned to blue as they lengthened. The clouds of small flies thinned and their ranks began to be refilled by the mosquitoes. Birnier lay with his back to the tent with a fly switch of grass, but he watched the doings of the corporal covertly. The corporal and his women had been drinking a good deal of the brandy and now he was supplying generous quantities to his men. Once he had come out to jeer. Birnier had taken no notice, nor even of the kick implanted by one of his own field boots on the foot of the woman. Already there was a bloodshot glint in the corporal's yellow eyes and a pronounced uncertainty in his movements. Whether the man had had any particular instructions regarding the manner of his death Birnier did not know until he became loquacious and took to shouting insults at his white prisoner. The great white chief had given the white man to him as a slave, he yelled, and now he was going to take him home with him. This idea seemed to tickle him vastly and also his women, who giggled and applauded as the corporal began to describe what obscene acts they would make their white dog perform every day, what they would give him to eat, how he should be made to dance.

They grew noisier and the women began to sing lewd songs. The soldiers too revealed signs of their frequent potations. Soon the whole crowd would go mad, Birnier knew, and sooner or later collapse, which would give him a chance to escape, unless they chained him, or, what was far more probable, they decided to bait him to death during an orgy. What they would probably do to him was unthinkable. Somehow he must find a way out by self-destruction. Even should he escape, he would be unarmed and without food, and there was every possibility that they would trail and overtake him in the morning. He was lame and footsore; also he was weak from want of food. Once, when despoiling his chop boxes, the corporal had contemptuously thrown him a half eaten tin of sardines and a cigarette. He let the cigarette lie. Nourishment he must have; and so after an inward struggle he had eaten it, having to claw out the fish like a monkey, while the big black and his women sprawled and laughed.

The soldiers, except the one on sentry who still paced a trifle erratically, were grouped on their haunches around the fire in front of the tent on the threshold of which the corporal presided with as much pomposity as if he were the great Mogul, all drinking and smoking and eating. Now and again the women would screech insults over their heads at the white; and once the corporal threw an empty bottle at him, evoking a gale of applause. The women began the belly dance, crooning while the men accompanied with the rhythmic grunt, which ever leads to hysterical exaltation.

The sun was dipping. They might come for him at any moment. He watched the sentry and contemplated making a rush, taking a venture on the man's bad aim and unsteady hand. They would not follow him far in the dark for dread of the spirits that walk by night. The only alternative to suicide was the river, in flood and full of crocodiles, a slender chance. He determined to try it. He considered making the attempt then. But the darker the better; they would more easily miss. At any risk he must never let them get their hands upon him. He drew himself together, flexing his limbs for a leap and a rush, anxiously observing the chanting crowd around the fire in the sunset glow.

The leashes of discipline were fraying. The sentry still plodded up and down, but with a rolling eye for his comp-anions. The working of his mind was revealed when he walked round tying knots in the long grass which, as every Munyamwezi knows, is a sure method to prevent a prisoner's escape; then he halted in front of Birnier, grinned, and pointed to the fire; evidently he knew or had heard that an orgy was coming. The man stood and watched him. Fearful that the fellow was about to drag him over or suggest that the victim be seized, if only in order to release him from his irksome duty, Birnier snatched up the cigarette lying in the grass and asked for a light to distract the man's attention. The sentry shook his head and pointed to the fire. Hastily Birnier searched his pockets for a match; recollected that he had used the last, and took out a small tin box of wax vestas wrapped in oiled silk which he kept as a reserve in a special pouch of his belt. In the very act of striking the match Birnier ejaculated: "God!"

"Nini?" demanded the sentry.

"I burned myself," returned Birnier.

"Nothing to what you will soon!" retorted the nigger, grinning, made an obscene suggestion and swaggered across to the fire.

Birnier cursed his own stupidity as he thought swiftly. If Mungongo and the others ran at the same time the numbers would confuse the soldiers the more. He spoke across to Mungongo in the Wongolo dialect, hoping that the Munya-mwezi would not understand.

"Let thy heart be like unto the bullet of my big gun, and obey me! When I throw up in the air this cigarette, thou shalt run and plunge into the river, but not into the depth; lie hidden in the reeds of the bank until thou shalt hear a frog croak thrice and then once. Come out and go to the frog, and be not afraid, for thou shalt see me in the spirit form. Dost understand?"

"Truly, my master!"

"Tell the washenzie that they also obey or shall my spirit eat them up as it shall these children of dung!"

"Truly, master!"

Birnier glanced at the horizon. The shadows had melted into the violet twilight, which in equatorial Africa is almost as short as the snuffing of a candle. The stars were popping out. Dusky forms were circling round the yellow of the fire which threw pale flickers on the figure of Corporal Inyira, revealing the beginning of the hysterical gleam in the yellows of his eyes as, reverting to habit, he squatted on his haunches in the chair. They might make a rush for the victims at any moment. The sentry, excitement overcoming discipline, was, rifle still in hand, dancing round the outskirts of the throng.

Birnier threw the cigarette towards Mungongo. As he dived round the thorn bush he heard the rustle of movement and the "boy's" gasped exclamation to the others. The bank of the river was not fifteen yards away. On the brink Birnier crouched and listened. He heard a splash a little to the right, which was Mungongo or one of the others literally obeying his instructions.

The mosquitoes buzzed and stung in clouds. A cricket shrilled persistently above the chorus of the frogs and the throb of the hand-drum and the chanting. The sentry had not yet discovered the flight; he was probably drunker than Birnier had guessed. By raising himself on his hands he could see the gleam of the fire and the inverted V of the tent through the scrub. He hesitated whether to begin operations immediately or wait until after they had discovered the flight and were further intoxicated. Yet the excitement of the loss of the prisoner might sober them a little, Birnier reflected. No, it did not matter even if they were completely sober. The spirits of the night would be perhaps more real to them then than when they were drugged by alcohol. Yet he would wait. They might come as far as the river with lanterns and should he be compelled to take to the water he would have to take the risk of crocodiles seizing him. Almost had he begun to curse the askaris for being so slow, when a rifle cracked and a bullet hummed over his head.

He scrambled hastily down the bank, thinking for a moment that he had been spotted. But it must have been a random shot. The chanting ceased. A hoarse shout from the sentry was echoed by uproar from the others.

Birnier crawled up the bank cautiously and peered. He could not see well, for one eye was nearly closed by mosquito bites, but he could make out vague forms passing and repassing across the glow of the fire. Lights glimmered. Amid shouts and yells, figures began to advance towards the river. Whether the water was deep or shallow he could not know; only could he make out in the sheen of the stars a dark patch of reed or bushes for some yards. He slid down the slope as noiselessly as possible, although the pursuers were making noise enough to scare all the spirits in Africa. He sank to his chest, standing on stones. He waded out a little, buried his head and shoulders behind a half-submerged bush, and remained still.

For some time he could only hear the shouts and yells. He kept the water up to his chin and continuously splashed his face in the endeavour to slacken the efforts of the mosquitoes. The cries approached. He saw men outlined against the stars and then some gleams of lanterns. Some-thing stirred ponderously near to him. It might be a crocodile, but he dared not move. The figures seemed to stay on the top of the bank for hours. He remained rigid, expecting a swirl of water and teeth.

Suddenly a spurt of flame shot out above him and was followed by a fusillade of shots in the direction of up river. Had they spotted Mungongo or were they merely letting drive at a bush or the spirits in general? The latter was most probable. The water swirled near to him. All his will power was required not to leap frantically for the bank. Yet a crocodile would be far more merciful than those black devils. Again a swirl and something passed close to him at high speed. Probably an otter scared by the firing; at any rate it was not a crocodile. The lights and figures on the bank disappeared.

Shots rang out again, and were followed by a wild outburst of yelling. Birnier began to wade for the bank, continually splashing water at the mosquitoes which were so thick that they reminded him of the bayou Lafourche in far-off Louisiana. Crouching, he waited on the edge of the bank to listen. The corporal might have had enough sense to post men in the grass. Yet he might be too fuddled to think of that, and no native would willingly stay there in the dark, unless under white discipline. Voices still muttered, but they sounded as if from the camp. Had they given him up for the night, relying on the chance that if he had not been taken by a crocodile they could trail him in the morning? Probably.

Birnier squatted in the water, ready to plunge back, until he was sure they were in camp. Then as cautiously he crawled up the bank. Through the scrub with his uninjured eye he could make out the figures around the yellow of the fire which had gone down considerably. Now what would they do? He could hear the mumble of the corporal's voice. Would they be sufficiently sobered to be ready for the chase in the morning? Birnier did not think so with that case of brandy there; the corporal would not, at all events. There was a scream of pain and the chatter of women's voices.

Was the corporal punishing the sentry for having let the prisoners escape, or were they beginning to fight among themselves? The latter was improbable, as non-commissioned officers are usually chosen from petty chiefs and the men under them, as far as possible, from their own village. Had they captured Mungongo or one of the others? Birnier listened again. Another scream was stoppered to a groan.

"Devils!" muttered Birnier. Lying flat to watch the grass and shrub tops against the stars, he gave the frog croaks arranged, at intervals of ten seconds. About five minutes later he saw some grass tops quiver unnaturally. He croaked again. Came a whisper:

"Is it thee, Infunyana?" (a name given in reference to Birnier's gold fillings).

"Aye." A dark form glided towards him. "Where are the other men?"

"I know not. I told them as thou hadst told me to do. When thou didst give the sign, I fled and plunged into the river."

"Thou wast not frightened of the crocodiles?"

"Nay; for I have a mighty charm against all river beasts, enchanted by Bakahenzie, the greatest of magicians."

"Ehh!" commented Birnier, contorting his swollen lips in the dark, "would that I had such an one! Thinkest thou that the men did as they were bidden?"

"Who knows what is in the heart of a goat?" returned Mungongo contemptuously, for they were of another tribe.

"Ah, listen!"

The mutter of the hand-drum grew swifter as a high tenor chanted to the accompaniment of the abdominal grunting and the laryngeal shrilling:

"We have come from afar from the Place of the waters!
From the place where dwells the mighty Eater-of-Men!
Hard was the road as the hills of Kilimanjaro!
Hot was the sun as the wrath of Inyira the bold!
The son of Banyala!
Ough!...Ough!
E-e-e-e-e-e-e-e-e-h!

But strong are we still as the trunk of an elephant!
For have we not walked in the shade of a great chief!
Blacker and fiercer than the male rhinoceros!
Swifter and more terrible than the mother of whelps?
The son of Banyala!
Ough!... Ough!
E-e-e-e-e-e-e-e-h!

What hath he given us to tickle our spears?
A dainty white dog whose meat is so tender!
Fattened and groomed by the Eater-of-Men!
A gift from the great Chief to his ally and friend.
The son of Banyala!
Ough!... Ough!
E-e-e-e-e-e-e-e-h!

We will tickle his white flesh with the tongue of our
spears!
Our women shall pluck out his hair and his manhood!
He shall dance to our liking in the midst of the fire!
His girl screams for mercy shall lave hungry ears of—!
The son of Banyala!
Ough!... Ough!
E-e-e-e-e-e-e-e-h!

Great was the gift of the great Eater-of-Men!
A white slave so sleek to dance the dance of the ants!
Eh! We'll slit up his nostrils and pull out his hairs!

A white slave and four black ones to wait on one great chief!
The son of Banyala!
Ough!... Ough!
E-e-e-e-e-e-e-e-h!

"Those children of folly have not obeyed," whispered Birnier. "The time is come... Wait here for me, O Mungongo. I go to take my spirit form. When I return be not afraid!"

"Truly," answered Mungongo, as Birnier crawled away and down the bank. By the water's edge he swiftly stripped himself to his moccasins and taking out the wax vestas, damped each precious one and carefully rubbed lines over his face and body, endeavouring to get the most distinctive phosphorescent effect around the eyes. Leaving his clothes he crawled back to Mungongo.

"Ehh!" exclaimed Mungongo in a muffled scream when he saw the glowing apparition. Birnier heard the rustle of grass. As the boy stood up to run he leaped and pulled him down savagely.

"Be quiet, thou fool!" he whispered. "It is I. Be silent!"

"Eh! Eh!" gasped Mungongo, who was trembling violently.

"If thou dost not be quiet will I tie up thy heart," threatened Birnier.

Mungongo continued to quiver, but he remained passive.

"Eh! Eh!" he gasped, "truly thou art a more mighty magician than Bakahenzie."

"Be quiet!"

The drums and the song were still going and the chant had become more obscene.

"Follow me!" whispered Birnier, when Mungongo was more reassured.

They made a detour. As they drew near they could hear muffled screams and groans beneath the howl of the chorus and song. The mighty son of Banyala and his merry men were so engrossed in the orgy that Birnier could have walked right up to the fire before anyone would have seen him. But he would not take any unnecessary risk. Leaving Mungongo outside he crawled under the back flap of the tent. Crouched there he paused. The tent was empty; for all were engaged in the dance. His two shot-guns and two light rifles were stacked in the corner and the big express which the corporal had appropriated, leaned against the tent door behind the chair. He glanced hurriedly around for ammunition, but he could not see any open, and he had left his belt of cartridges with his clothes. Outside the men and women were circling in contrary directions, each with a spear, a knife or a firebrand in hand, around the fire beside which, trussed like bundles of faggots, were the four servants, their feet singeing on the outside hot ashes.

For a second Birnier hesitated. He could not know whether any of the guns was loaded. The fire was of glowing embers which did not throw much light into the tent. Swiftly Birnier rose and glided into his own chair in the deep shadow of the tent flap. Then summoning all his nerve he uttered a yell and began to shout the first song which he could recollect:

"Hurrah! Hurrahhhhhhh! It is the Jubileeeee!
Hurrah! Hurrah! the flag that set you free!"

The native minstrel stopped in the middle of his chant; the

Charles Beadle

whole shuffling, grunting crowd was petrified in as many different poses. Birnier leaped to his feet waving his arms wildly, yelling:

"Thus we sang the chor-uss from Atlanta to the Sea-aa! As we..."

But before he had gotten to "Georgia," only the prostrate forms around the fire had not fled.

CHAPTER 10

On the morning of Birnier's departure there was much movement in Ingonya station. Every sign of preparation for the expedition had been carefully concealed while a stranger was in the vicinity. Trumpets blared importantly. On the great parade ground companies were formed, long lines of rigid, ebon figures, down which strolled zu Pfeiffer inspecting personally kits and rifles. Afterwards they were drawn up before the flag-pole. In an address zu Pfeiffer informed them that they served under a greater Bwana than he, the greatest Bwana in the countries of the white or the black, who was the son of Ngai (an uncertain term meaning "son of God" or the "son of nobody"); that the flag they bore, the brother of the big one upon the pole, was so powerful in magic that none could withstand it, the Totem of the Bwana Mkubwa Kuba. No wives were allowed for black or white, and he himself set them the example; for they were embarking on a war expedition to take a country which they knew was full of ivory, cattle and women.

The row upon row of eyes in black faces bulged, as from the mass came the long grunt of assent and allegiance. The three white sergeants barked at their various companies, which wheeled into column formation and marched past zu Pfeiffer beneath the flag in review order, their alignment and precision a credit to their drill masters. Down below the fort on the mouth of the bayou Sergeant Ludwig superintended the overhauling of the steam-launch, and a native sergeant and a file of men overseered lines of carriers bearing white men's provisions, the bulk of which was zu Pfeiffer's personal supplies. Around the launch was a flotilla of native canoes in charge of a small crowd of nude Kavirondo paddlers, jabbering at the prospect of a war expedition.

Most of the day zu Pfeiffer spent in the orderly room going over documents and giving detailed instructions to the grizzled Sergeant Schneider, who was to take over the station with fifty of the least competent men, pending the arrival of an officer, which again would depend upon the success of the expedition. In zu Pfeiffer's manner was evident the controlled excitement of a boy on the eve of a house match, and indeed for him it was the game for which he was bred and lived, "das Kriegspiel." Perpetually his long fingers caressed the sentry moustaches; an unusual glitter was in his blue eyes.

The personality of Birnier had been apparently wiped from his mind as a spoor in the sand by rain; indeed in addition to the competing excitement of the expedition, the previous night's alcoholic and sentimental debauch had served to exhaust the emotions stimulated by jealousy. To him had appeared an obstruction in his emotional life in the shape of the husband of the woman whom he adored; therefore, according to his nature and training, he had endeavoured to remove that obstacle as swiftly and as efficiently as possible. Superlative confidence in himself, reflected in his pride of family and nationality, the apotheosis of which was the Kaiser, enabled him to devote all his energies to the business in hand, never doubting that his interpretation of native psychology would ensure the extinction of his adversary.

Beyond the mere joy of the game of war was present the

fundamental impulse to win the approval of the All Highest by gaining another place in the sun as well as the half-suppressed conviction that such a distinction would naturally further his suit in love. In the orbit of these two poles revolved the life actions of zu Pfeiffer.

That evening zu Pfeiffer dined as leisurely and as sumptuously as usual; drank his port and smoked his cigar while his servants packed the last of his kitchen battery. Then at the first green of the moon he gave the order to march.

The three companies of askaris fell in, marched down to the bayou and embarked without fuss or confusion, each group under a non-commissioned officer to the appointed canoe.

The launch laboured busily out of the bayou past misty reed-girt islands into the indolent waters of the great lake, dragging after her the fleet of forty odd canoes. A cigar under the awning of the tiny poop suggested a great firefly in the blue shadows, where lounged zu Pfeiffer with his favourite brandy and seltzer at his elbow.

Resembling an enormous water-fowl leading a strange black brood, the launch towed the flotilla through the night. A war chant pulsed like a fevered heart as the moon upon her back lazily chased the stars into the dawn upon her way to her home in the Mountains of the Moon, to be in turn extinguished by a furious sun. And all that day, while incandescent heat tried to boil illimitable waters, the strange fowl waddled on with her noxious brood. Huddled in the cramped canoes the soldiers slept and snuffed and sang, to which zu Pfeiffer contentedly listened beneath the awning. Three times grey walls of falling water enveloped them, sending frantic black hands to bailing. Once more the moon made the skies to laugh. When the sun had played his part of a flaming Nemesis, a fringe grew upon the horizon like the stubble upon a white man's chin.

Zu Pfeiffer had calculated to arrive at the village of Timballa just within the river at sundown. The headman came down to the strand to meet them. Immediately he was seized, and the soldiers, as joyous and as mischievous as children released from school, surrounded the village.

Sitting in full uniform upon the poop of the launch, together with the two sergeants, zu Pfeiffer held a shauri and demanded sufficient paddlers to man his forty canoes. The headman, to whom all white men were alike, thought they were British and hastened to proffer his services, promising that the Bwana should have the men within two days. Zu Pfeiffer curtly ordered him to procure them before the sun was overhead on the next day; and to insure that he was obeyed, detained him as hostage and forbade any man to pass his line of pickets around the village. The old man protested that they had not sufficient men in the village, but zu Pfeiffer's spies had afforded him practically correct information. He gave the headman the right to send a number of messengers, each accompanied by a soldier, to the neighbouring villages and promised him fifty lashes and to rase his village, if the paddlers were not forthcoming.

Solely because he wished to give his men time to recover from their stiffness did he not insist upon starting that night upon the river trip. As a good commander he considered his men from every point of view of efficiency. They loved him. He was a warrior chief as they understood such to be; carefully he fostered their warrior pride; never were they ordered to work at menial offices, to fetch or to carry; only to drill and to fight; his punishments were ferocious, but he gave them liberty in pillage and rape. Eh! but the Eater-of-Men was a mighty chief! and of his name they boasted to every man.

With foresight he had demanded twice as many men as he needed, knowing that the panic-stricken chief would round up the halt, the blind, and the sick. By an hour after the stipulated time they were assembled in the village, a motley crew. Those of the most powerful physique he selected to man the soldiers' canoes, and the next in competency he allotted to the baggage canoes.

They started immediately. They made about two and a half miles an hour, for although the river was swollen it was sluggish and slow streamed, tortuous. Each canoe load of soldiers was made responsible for the paddlers and the speed was set by zu Pfeiffer in a large canoe with Sakamata as guide. Never had those paddlers driven canoes so speedily and persistently. At sundown they halted in a convenient bend where there was no village near; pickets were set on the bank and no other man allowed to land, no lights and no talking. They were ordered to rest.

At the first glint of the moon they started again. The canoes were hauled by the aid of the soldiers over the slight rapids which divided the river into pools in the dry season. Throughout the night the misty forest and swamp slipped by to the perpetual rhythm of the paddles. About the hour of the monkey a hippopotamus charged the flotilla and upset two boats. Zu Pfeiffer forbade any shooting, nor would he permit the expedition a moment's delay to pick up the occupants. Just as they heard the distant crowing of cocks from the village for which they were bound, four paddlers collapsed. The soldiers, acting on their own initiative, threw them overboard to swim if they could, and took the paddles themselves. Afterwards they were thrashed for disobedience to orders in having given a possible chance for one of the men to escape to warn the Wongolo. At an hour after sunrise they arrived at the village. The majority of the paddlers were so exhausted that they dropped in the canoes and had to be thrown ashore, where they lay inert, their backs, bloody with the urgent bayonet pricks, caking in the sun.

Beyond this point the river was not navigable, but the village was upon the Wongolo border and within two days or fifteen hours' continuous march of MFunya MPopo's (as zu Pfeiffer knew it). Zu Pfeiffer adopted the same tactics to procure porters. But to the chief, in case he should require his services again, he gave an extravagant present and left bales of cloth for the carriers upon their return. Zu Pfeiffer and Sergeant Ludwig travelled in machilas (hammocks) each with a crew of six; the soldiers carried nothing save their rifles, double cartridge belts, a day's rations; the pick of the carriers bore ammunition and the two Nordenfeldts and two pom-poms slung upon poles, and the chop boxes; the men's blankets and the heavy stuff were to follow more slowly under Sergeant Schultz and fifty men. The country between this village and MFunya MPopo's was mostly forest and very sparsely inhabited, which afforded some shade and concealment, and lessened the risk of a warning being given.

The expedition started at noon. The carriers were kept on the native shuffling lope by the aid of attentions from the askaris. Two unfortunate small villages which lay on the line of march were surrounded and the inhabitants massacred. Twenty porters collapsed; they were bayoneted to prevent any chance of a successful ruse in escaping to give the alarm, and their loads given to relay men brought for that purpose. The column halted at sundown. The men ate their rations, but the carriers were too exhausted to eat; they drank water and lay prostrate. According to Sakamata they were within two hands' breadth of the moon of Kawa Kendi's.

In full uniform of white, girded with sword and revolver, zu

Pfeiffer ate, drank, and smoked cigars until the forest roof was patterned against the cold pallor of the moon. Then, after giving final instructions to Sergeant Ludwig and the various native non-commissioned officers, he ordered the jabbering men to march, with the carriers staggering on at the point of the bayonet.

CHAPTER 11

The doom pronounced by the Council of Witch-Doctors was to Bakuma and all concerned as a Bull of Excommunication in mediaeval Europe. MYalu was the one who exhibited the most emotion. Had he not paid seven tusks of good ivory to have the object of his passion placed under the most terrible tabu? Against Marufa, who had seemingly betrayed him, was his anger directed. But the rage of MYalu was tempered with fear. A man had not merely to kill an enemy: he had also to appease his justly wrathful ghost; and who knew what the disembodied spirit of the most powerful magician in the land, save Bakahenzie, could do! Moreover, no other wizard would give him absolution in the form of the magic of purification. A chief though he be; he dared not slay a magician. He sought Marufa and found him as usual squatting on his threshold contemplating infinity in a mud wall. He saluted Marufa politely, choking back words of bitter recrimination, for if he even offended him, the wizard might cast a spell upon him instantly. Marufa returned the greeting as courteously as ever. When at length MYalu reproachfully reminded him of the seven tusks which he had paid apparently to secure his love's terrible fate, Marufa replied uninterestedly:

"I have done that for which thou hast paid."

"What man buyeth a bride for another?" retorted MYalu.

"When I did make magic upon 'the things' did I place in the power of the spirits the owner. Behold, hath not the owner of 'the things' been accursed?"

"Ehh!" gasped MYalu. "But how may that be? Didst thou not thyself take the paring and the hair?"

"I bade the One who is tabu to bring them that he might be bewitched to her girdle. She thought to deceive me by bringing that which was of herself."

"E—eh!" muttered MYalu, impressed at the awful effect of deceiving a wizard. Marufa continued to stare. MYalu meditated ruefully.

"But the tusks," murmured MYalu at length dismally.

"It is not I who have two tongues," responded Marufa indifferently.

And with that MYalu had to rest content. Marufa indeed had no interest at all in the passions of Zalu Zako, MYalu and Bakuma. Merely the time had come for the witch-doctors to choose the victim for the Harvest Festival: Bakuma was young and good looking, a dainty morsel that should please the taste of the officiating doctors, and her owner and uncle was a man of no importance: so accordingly he had made known the sin of her name through the divination.

In the solitude of his own hut upon the hill Zalu Zako sat and pondered sulkily. His young and fierce temper was stimulated and the seed of rebellion against the domination of the priesthood was quickened by the fate of his new love; although the masonic secrets of the craft were denied to him, he, as son of the royal house, was suspicious of the powers of the Unmentionable One and the priesthood, as many an one had been before him; yet in spite of that the verdict was absolute, for he was too crushed by terror of the conesquences to permit of any hope of annulling it.

The fiat not only doomed Bakuma to a terrible death at the third blooming of the moon, but from that very instant the tabu came into force; for being thus accursed by the possession of two sounds of the sacred name, she was deemed unholy. Her half-sisters and their mother, with whom Bakuma shared the hut, fled to another and were exorcised by the wizard, which, as everybody knows, is an expensive ceremony; gourds and pots, spoons and utensils of all sorts, were left to the sole use of the unclean one and would be burned upon her demise. A magic line was drawn around the hut out of which the soul of the girl as she slept could not escape to bewitch anybody. Neither her name nor anything that had been hers would be ever mentioned again; any word of a household article or any thing or beast which had one syllable of the name "Bakuma" was changed, lest the user be accursed and bewitched.

For the whole day, in this isolation, sat the girl Bakuma, Marufa's useless love charm clutched in her hand, as bewildered as if the earth had suddenly turned inside out under this fact so stupendous and stupefying. She did not weep. She squatted in the door, her eyes staring with the glazed inquiring expression of a dying gazelle, a bronze question to Fate. At the feeding time her mother threw her bananas into the circle. Bakuma looked at them as they flopped near to her as if she did not realize what they were. She made no stir to cook or prepare them. The cool twilight came and passed like a blue breath. Above the insectile chorus of the night beneath the crystal stars came the faint thrumming of a drum from MKoffo's hill. The sound of music and dancing reminded Bakuma of her ambitious dreams. She could neither weep nor wail; she merely emitted a faint gasping sound. But her mind began to work jerkily, yet more fluently. Visions of the form of Zalu Zako were weaved and spun in the darkness: the lithe walk of him, the haughty carriage of the head. Slowly greened the sky until the banana fronds were etched in sepia against the swollen moon. The dismal croak of the Baroto bird shattered the black cocoon of Bakuma's mind.

"Aie-eee! the foul bird of my despair!" she wailed, and at last wept. Then she rose and flitted like some green ghost into the plantation and across to the place of water where her lover had first spoken her sweet, recking naught in her mist of despair of spirits of the night nor of the breaking of the magic circle. The moon spattered the squatted form with blue spangles and turned the falling tears to quivering opals. Bakuma broke into wild lament.

"The black Goat hath cried three times in my hut!
My soul hath wandered and been caught in a trap!
Aieeeeeeeeeee!

A wizard hath stolen a hair from my head!
The beak of Baroto pecketh my gall!
Aieeeeeeeeeee!

A rival hath lain in wait for my love!
She hath slain my bird in the nest of his breast!
Aieeeeeeeeeee!

A porcupine dwells in the place of my heart!
The bird of my soul is fluttering faint!
Aieeeeeeeeeee!

An ember of fire hath entered my mouth!

The milk of my breasts is curdled to-night!
Aieeeeeeeeeee!

The strings of my bosom are tied with fine knots!
My belly is void! My nipples are dead!
Aieeeeeeeeeee!

A monkey hath bitten the back of my tongue!
Hath stolen my breath to make magic by night!
Aieeeeeeeeeee!

The blood in my veins hath turned to sour porridge!
My throat is choked up by the sudd of the Lake!
Aieeeeeeeeeee!

A grey forest rat hath swallowed my heart!
My thighs have been scratched by a poisonous thorn!
Aieeeeeeeeeee!"

As the last quiver of the wail blended with the anthem of the
forest came from a figure squatted above the ford of the
river, his spear a blue flame in the moonlight, an answer:

"My love hath been taken by a greater than I!
Her flesh will be tasted by a hungrier mouth!
Her flesh which is sweeter than honey and wine!
Her flesh which is softer than a newly born kid!
Ough! My spear is bent!

My love hath been taken by a greater than I!
Her breasts will be pillowed by a much broader chest!
Her breasts which do swell like a tender young gourd!
Her breasts which are as firm as the meat of the plum!
Ough! My spear is bent!"

And answered Bakuma's wail:

"Aieeeeeeeeeeeeeeeeeeeeeee!"

"My love hath been taken by a greater than I!
Her chines will be gripped by a far fiercer hand!
Her chines which are smoother than elephants' tusks!
Her chines which are as plump as the breast of a fowl!
Ough! My spear is bent!
Aieeeeeeeeeeeeeeeeeeeeeee!

My love hath been taken by a greater than I!
Her eyes will be touched by longer fingers than mine!
Her eyes which are like unto moons veiled by rain!
Her eyes which are like the starlit river at dawn!
Ough! My spear is bent!
Aieeeeeeeeeeeeeeeeeeeeeee!

My love hath been taken by a greater than I!
Her scent will be drunk by nostrils broader than mine!
Her scent which is pungent and sweet like the smoke!
Her scent which slakes thirst more than driest of beer!
Ough! My spear is bent!
Aieeeeeeeeeeeeeeeeeeeeeee!

My love hath been taken by a greater than I!
Her breath will be sipped by a thirstier throat!
Her breath which is hotter than the flame of a fire!
Her breath which makes more drunken than enemies' blood!
Ough! My spear is bent!
Aieeeeeeeeeeeeeeeeeeeeeee!

My love hath been taken by a greater than I!
Her voice will be heard by ears mightier than mine!
Her voice which is like unto burbling beer!
Her voice which is gentler than the rustle of fronds!
Ough! My spear is bent!
Aieeeeeeeeeeeeeeeeeeeeeee!"

A slight breeze stirred gently the trees. The crickets shrilled their perpetual chorus. A crocodile flopped in the river. Dogs yapped from a village down the river. Again Bakuma lifted up her voice:

"Mightier than elephants was the tread of my man!
Keener than a leopard was the flash of his eye!
Stronger than an oak tree was the strength of his arm!
Swifter than lightning was the stroke of his spear!
Enemies died!

Taller than the wine palm was the height of my man!
Broader than the temple was the span of his chest!
More graceful than antelope was the carriage of him!
More slender than saplings was the build of his legs!
Women lamented!

Sweeter than warm honey was the scent of my man!
Whiter than a spear flash was the gleam of his teeth!
Fiercer than scorpions was the grip of his hand!
Smooth and like stone was—"

A gale of yells and shots destroyed the song of Bakuma like a foot crushing a flower.

Zalu Zako leaped to his feet and stood for a moment listening intently. Across the river some strange beast spat spears of red flames. A little farther down another beast coughed violently like a hippopotamus. The sky seemed falling. Such volumes of sound he had never heard before.

As he raced with the speed of a koodoo through the plantation he saw the glow of fire ahead and heard the moan of some terrible monster near him. He leaped five feet in the air as the world appeared to crack in half beside him. He felt a sting like a brand of fire in his shoulder, but he ran on towards the village from whence fled dim figures on all sides amid shouts and screams and wailing.

Several huts were already blazing. The leviathan coughed and moaned again and once more the earth seemed to crash to pieces near him. Appalled and bewildered, choking with rage, he reached the outer enclosure where his fellow warriors were shouting and yelling that the white gods were attacking. Bakahenzie, gun in hand, was bidding them charge they knew not what. Then out of the clutter of the village broke line upon line of yelling figures clothed in uniform. Screaming the battle-cry, the warriors charged, led by Zalu Zako, Bakahenzie, and Kawa Kendi, who in the excitement had dashed from the enclosure. Howls and yells were drowned in the spiteful crackle and cough. Warriors were mown like weeds under a sickle. Scarce a hundred scrambled inside the enclosure at the rallying call from Bakahenzie.

Again came a short rush of those uniformed figures; again scarlet spears pierced the green moonlight like a hailstorm; small red flames rippled in a line resembling a forest fire as the soldiers charged through and over the palisade. Hand to hand was the fighting, spear and sword against bayonet and rifle around the idol, the askaris outyelling the warriors. The temple was on fire. In the light of the flames they saw a tall figure in white with a glow of fire in his mouth and magic eyes upon his hands, eyes which flashed rays of scarlet and blue as he cut and hacked at the base of the idol...

"Tarum hath come!" screamed some one, and as the cry was taken up, the Unmentionable One tottered and crashed to the ground.

They fled, Zalu Zako, Bakahenzie and those that were left.

CHAPTER 12

The village of Yagonyana, the son of Zahilazaan, was situated some five days' march to the north-west of Kawa Kendi's, in open cattle country near the fringe of the forest. Here were gathered nearly every witch-doctor and warrior of the tribe. Most of the women, children, and slaves had been sent still farther to the west, driving the cattle before them.

Bakahenzie, Zalu Zako, Marufa, and all those warriors who had escaped from the massacre by zu Pfeiffer were distinguished from their brethren by circles of yellow earth around each left eye, and each right breast and arm was smeared with red, which is part of the ceremony of magic purification for those who have slain, lest, as is well known, the ghost of the dead wreak their wrath upon their slayers.

The affairs of the tribe were in a parlous state. The netting of the tabu had been tangled by the death of the King-God, Kawa Kendi, and the unprecedented act of the overthrow of the idol. Kawa Kendi's body, which had not been recovered so that the doctors could release his unhappy soul, might be used to make more magic against the tribe.

For three weeks there had been much discussion among the doctors, the chiefs, and the people. Opinions were at variance; no two men could agree. Lesser wizards, who before had been content with the perquisites of the smaller offices, were now made drunken by the insecurity of Bakahenzie's position. Each of the doctors, seeing a chance to prove his superior merit and win Bakahenzie's post as chief doctor, had busily made magic to destroy the usurper, and each and every one provided a different reason for the failure thereof. Every day came news of the doings of the white god with eyes upon his hands, of shootings and floggings, of the burning of the village including the idol, the temple, and the sacred tombs of MFunya MPopo, of MKoffo, of MZrakombinyana, and other kings before them.

The council of the craft could not even decide whether Zalu Zako was to be King-God or not. Bakahenzie, whose interest lay in supporting the dynasty of the present royal family, maintained that he should be anointed forthwith. But with the downfall of the idol and his own impotence to make successful magic, Bakahenzie's prestige had been badly shaken; no longer dared he issue dicta autocratically. As ever, political ambition tore patriotism to shreds.

Marufa, former close ally of Bakahenzie, but lacking his active principle, continued to mutter incantations most impressively by himself, waiting cautiously to see which side of the river the arrow fell. Bakahenzie became seriously alarmed at the growth of Yabolo's faction and the indifference of Marufa. He knew well that submission would entail the loss of his post as well as his worldly goods; and he was aware that all men knew that his most potent and strenuous magic had failed as utterly as that of the youngest novice in the craft. His only chance to retrieve a portion of his lost reputation was to invent a more plausible excuse for failure than any other doctor had done. He did.

Although he did not know that Bakuma had broken the magic circle of her own volition, he had the shrewd imagination to suggest that she had either fled with the other women during the attack or that, even if she had stayed, the askaris would have taken her from the hut. Therefore did he demand an assembly of the craft and chiefs. One of the reasons, if not the reason, of Bakahenzie's success, as of other witch-doctors before, such as Savonarola, had been a faculty, inspired by, or derived from, hysterical epilepsy, of working himself up at will into a state of convulsion without actual loss of consciousness and the spectacular exhibition of foam, which no other sorcerer had been able to simulate so successfully. Therefore Bakahenzie invoked the great Tarum (apotheosis of ancestors' spirits) who, through the convulsed body, did proclaim that the disaster had been caused by the breaking of the magic circle by one whose name was accursed; and that only could the magic of Bakahenzie be made potent, and the consequent overthrow of the Eyes-in-the-hands be assured, by the sacrifice of the victim to her destiny as the Bride of the Banana.

Marufa, appreciating the shrewdness of this move, immediately abandoned his incantations to reassume his allegiance to the cause of Bakahenzie. The prophecy was hailed by nearly every one as a most timely excuse for the failure of magic in general. The miraculous recall of the Unmentionable One now seemed so easy of accomplishment through the person of Bakuma that many of those who had sided with Yabolo deserted him, foreseeing the renewed ascendancy of Bakahenzie and fearing his wrath.

Yabolo, however, made an attempt to recover the lost adherents by protesting that the Moon of the Harvest Festival had not yet come, and that therefore victory could not be obtained until two more moons had waned. But MYalu saw that by submitting to the new god he might be able to have removed the tabu upon Bakuma—all things were possible to one who had overthrown the Unmentionable One—and thus obtain her by the price of submission; also he might possibly recover his wealth of ivory abandoned after the massacre. Therefore did he with his people go over to the Yabolo faction.

Uproar and confusion ensued. Bakahenzie recovered from his trance with unprecedented rapidity and even did not require to be told what the spirit of Tarum had said through his lips. The tribe was split into fiercer factions than ever. They argued and screamed and cursed. Bakahenzie had lost the hold over them; for as the god, of which he was the sponsor, was dead, his credit had gone too. He dared no longer to remove a troublesome brother or chief by magic. His only hope was to restore the god: so to that end he declared that Zalu Zako must be anointed King-God. Uproar arose once more. But Bakahenzie's purpose had been served; he had diverted their attention from the subject of submission.

From time to time came terrified runners with horrific stories of the burning of villages, of massacre and rapine. Bakahenzie, determined not to yield, secretly dispatched a slave to Eyes-in-the-hands with an arrow which is a sign of war; Yabolo, whose mind ran in the same tracts, sent a banana which is a sign of peace. In the meantime factions grew and multiplied. One chief counselled his followers to take their cattle and women and seek to conquer another tribe to the south-west; another wished to go west. But each and every follower began to bargain with his chief for disproportionate rewards for service. Two chiefs and five hundred men started to the south-west, but they returned because they had met in their path the skeleton of a slain elephant, which is, as everybody knows, a sure sign of disaster.

Bakahenzie sent runners far and wide to discover Bakuma.

Charles Beadle

As she could not be found he concluded that she had been killed or taken as a slave and urged the warriors to fight. Zalu Zako immediately desired the anointing to be delayed in order that he should not be debarred from fighting. Bakahenzie, none too sure of his authority, was compelled to acquiesce. Marufa, observing that the arrow was still in the air, took to his non-committal incantations again. Bakahenzie strove to keep the warriors and chiefs occupied by dissension until the result of his challenge to battle should mature. Yabolo, equally perturbed for his influence, did exactly the same with the banana in view.

Yabolo and MYalu contemplated going in to make submission, but the former wished to negotiate through Sakamata for the best terms, although he tried to persuade MYalu to go; but MYalu was suspicious and would not do so without Yabolo. But at the hour of the monkey one morning came a terrified goatherd crying news that cut the tangled threads of their intrigues as a sword cuts a goat's throat. The white god, Eyes-in-the-hands, was within an arrow's flight of the village of Yagonyana.

Consternation ensued. The village and the temporary camp of grass huts buzzed and hummed. Zalu Zako dashed out, sword and spear in hand, and in the glow of the awakened fires harangued the warriors, urged that they should make a swift detour through the forest and attack the white man as he entered the village. Bakahenzie supported this plan of campaign. MYalu, stung by the recollection of the loss of many tusks to the invader, incontinently abandoned Yabolo and pressed for a frontal attack. Yabolo contended that they send an envoy to make terms, but not very insistently. In spite of the assurance of Sakamata, he was suspicious of the new god's gentle ways. Marufa, the wise, collected those of his household who had remained with him, and quietly made his way to the forest.

But Zalu Zako's martial spirit was overcome by the clamour of those who would flee before worse befell, crying that the white god, Eyes-in-the-hands, would eat them all up with the terrible monsters who coughed flames and death; others screeched that the uniformed devils were spirits of the night and therefore invincible; for always they came in the dark. So they hesitated, shouted and argued. Then came a scout screaming that the enemy was upon them, corroborated by a vicious cough.

A pom-pom shell landed in the midst of the crowded village. Zalu Zako, Bakahenzie and their small following were nearly swept away in the rush of five thousand odd warriors in flight. From the forest they watched with awestruck eyes the burning of the village.

CHAPTER 13

On the morning on which zu Pfeiffer burned the village of Yagonyana, Birnier was encamped upon the southern boundary of Wongolo. By his "coup de superstition" had he recovered all his equipment except several bottles of brandy, some canned goods and two and a half pairs of pyjamas; also the field boots. The noble Inyira, son of Banyala, and his merry men never attempted to recapture their prisoners; no one save the Eater-of-Men in person could have persuaded them to return to that camp even had they had their rifles.

After Birnier had dressed his own foot and the charred feet of his men, had had a good drink and a better meal, he had sought to address the balance of his mind through a medium designed for the cure of melancholy, but efficacious for many other ills, *The Anatomy of Melancholy*. He opened the one big volume which had been his companion throughout his travels at a page marked at haphazard by an ivory paper knife with the American flag upon the flat hilt, an early gift from Lucille, and began to read the remarks of Robert Burton of quaintly glorious memory upon the source of his late adventure.

"Those which are jealous, most part, if they be not otherwise relieved, proceed from suspicion to hatred, from hatred to frenzy, madness, injury, murder and despair... Amestris,

Xerxes's wife, because she found her husband's cloak in Masista's house, cut off Masista's wife's paps and gave them to the dogs, flayed her besides and cut off her ears, lips, tongue, and slit the nose of Artaynta, her daughter."

"Cheerful lady! She ought to have been zu Pfeiffer's wife," commented Birnier and went to sleep.

Birnier arose feeling rational enough to reconsider his position. The recollection of the signature on the photograph now failed to stimulate the emotional reaction as once it had done. The experience through which he had passed had had a beneficial effect in breaking or disconnecting the train of suggestive images. At first in the recess of his mind had lurked the desire to abandon everything, to rush straight to Lucille to demand an explanation. Now the rising sun of reason cast quite different shadows upon the incident. The high light was the fact that should he do so he would be sacrificing his mission for what might prove to be ridiculous. As his mind contemplated the subject the echo of "a toi, Lucille" tended to carry a high note, but this he vented by writing a long letter to Lucille recounting the facts and frankly admitting that he had been sufficiently insane with jealousy to "go up in the air." Once or twice he ceased to write and gazed anxiously into the glare as his imagination suggested the long period of waiting for an answer, wondering whether the echo of that cursed "a toi" might not become unbearably shrill. He became a little more sentimental towards the end of the letter, remarking that perhaps he had been wrong in deserting her for so long and emphasising the rather ridiculous point that he was aware that he was not a young man. However, he let it remain, and at the first opportunity sent off the letter by runner to the nearest station in Uganda, together with an order for certain goods to be sent to a village on the Wongolo border.

Although still inclined to be emotional over the photograph, Birnier did not waste any energy over vindictive thoughts upon zu Pfeiffer, whom he philosophically regarded as irresponsible for his actions, inasmuch as he had been made that way just as any savage. He had gotten out of the toils set for him, so why should he spend time and trouble in seeking revenge which would merely consist in reporting the incident through a British station to Washington, who would open up interminable polite correspondence with the German Embassy, who would again write prodigious letters to the Colonial Minister in Berlin, who would... Ludicrous! No; he would not permit zu Pfeiffer to interfere with his plans. He would continue straight to Wongolo instead of investigating the Kivu country, where zu Pfeiffer might perhaps have another opportunity to cause more trouble. Accordingly he negotiated with the nearest village for carriers and set out, striking due west, thus approaching the Wongolo territory towards the southern boundary.

The people to the south of the Wongolo country was an inferior race, whom the Wongolo periodically raided to replenish their slaves. These Wamongo were split up into several petty chiefdoms, usually at war with one another. They had no defined theology. For they had not progressed beyond the stage of magic as far as any concept of religion, that is of praying for intercession to any power greater than themselves; whereas the mental state of the Wongolo was half-way between magic and religion, mixing and confusing the two as exemplified in the Rain-making ceremony of employing magic and alternately invoking the god and threatening him with dire penalties if he did not behave. There seemed to be no royal family or clan of the Wamongo; chiefs changed constantly as one more powerful for the moment arose; the wizards did not appear to have any political power, acting as general physicians and confining their efforts apparently to simple magic for the growing of corn, the curing of the evil eye and wounds. They were terrified of the Wongolo, much to Mungongo's pride, who never let slip an opportunity of swaggering and bruiting abroad the fame of his master as the greatest of magicians the world had ever seen. Never was he tired of relating to a grunting audience the terrible sight and effect of his master's transposition into a spirit. The yarn lost nothing in the telling.

Progress was slow. Every afternoon, as regular as the sun set, clouds of sepia sailed up from the west to clothe the world in a grey deluge of falling water. Fortunately they were travelling up a watershed so that there were no large rivers to cross. As they approached the Wongolo border rumours began of a white god with eyes upon his hands and live fire in his mouth who, so said the delighted Wamongo, had entirely eaten up the hated Wongolo. They seemed prepared to accept Birnier, when suggesting that he should make magic for them to conquer the Wongolo, as another terrible white god, and were accordingly polite. But Mungongo, vastly indignant, denied the story; according to him, no power on earth could have subdued his race, except perhaps the mighty Moonspirit (the name he had bestowed upon Birnier).

But when Birnier arrived at the first village of the Wongolo the absence of warriors corroborated the wild tales they had heard. The inhabitants of old men, boys and women surrounded the camp to gaze in awestruck curiosity at the white whom they believed to be the brother of the Eyes-in-the-hands. This calumny Mungongo strenuously gainsaid, and anew recounted the marvellous feats of magic of Moonspirit who could, he assured his compatriots, eat up Eyes-in-the-hands as easily as a crocodile would swallow a goat. Yet in spite of their terror they insisted that Birnier must go through the ceremony of purification incumbent upon all strangers in order to exorcise the evil influence of their eyes and souls; also the customary present must be sent to the king and his august permission to enter awaited, although no man knew where he was since the capital had been burned. Mungongo waxed furious. He informed them that Moonspirit was a friend of the Son-of-the-Snake, and moreover had before been in the country; that if they vexed Moonspirit he would enchant the whole village so that no man could move hand or foot. No matter, said they, that was the rule and must be done. They were impressed but obstinate.

From the description of this destroying god, who was the colour of a stripped banana and tall as a palm tree, had fire in his mouth and eyes upon his hands—it was some time before he could recognise the "eyes"—and whose companions were devils strangely clothed, dragging horrific monsters who spat earthquakes, Birnier had no difficulty in recognising zu Pfeiffer, and recollected the significant pumping at dinner regarding the Wongolo country. However he had renounced any idea of revenge, but the discovery of friend zu Pfeiffer as the terrifying god amused him: quickened a desire to overset the gentleman's plans. He smiled with a slight hardening of the line about his mouth as he began to consider what might be done.

As far as he could estimate by recalling the size of the native barracks at Fort Ingonya, he reckoned that zu Pfeiffer could not possibly have more than three hundred men, unless he had been reinforced from the east. Roughly he calculated that the Wongolo ought to be able to put about ten thousand warriors in the field. That number under any sort of leadership, even though they were only armed with spears and swords, should wipe out the three hundred, in spite of the discipline and two or three machine-guns, by sheer weight of numbers. But, from what he had already heard, zu

Pfeiffer had evidently caught them unprepared, wiped out a mass and secured a supernatural effect by destroying the idol. He remembered his talk on das Volkliches and his comment that zu Pfeiffer was unusually well informed upon the psychology of the native mind.

During two days disputing in the native manner news came in of fresh massacres, adding to the general terror. He sent for the headman and with him held a long shauri. The result was that the old fellow conceived the wonderful idea, already suggested by his lesser brethren, of enlisting the services of this white man, reputed to be a most marvellous magician, in their protection.

Then having had his wits sharpened by his own originality and a sheath knife, the headman promptly discovered that the ceremony of exorcism could not be performed because the local wizard had departed with every ounce of magic for the front. Still there were obstinate and fearful persons who wished that Birnier should send a message to the king and wait until he had the permission. Another two days were lost until this objection was overcome by certain presents of "bafta," destined for the king, being handed over to the village.

On the week's march across Wongolo, Mungongo triumphantly held spellbound audiences at every village through which they passed. As they neared the site of the City of the Snake, where they heard zu Pfeiffer was encamped, they encountered deserted villages. When they came upon the smouldering embers of one Birnier consented to turn aside from the regular trail in order to pass to the west of Kawa Kendi's where, so the natives said, were Zalu Zako and Bakahenzie.

Beyond a belt of forest was open rolling country. They came

Charles Beadle

to a village of five huts where dwelt some herdsmen, although most of the cattle had been driven westwards. Mungongo, seeking at Birnier's suggestion for some one who had actually been present at the village when zu Pfeiffer attacked, discovered a young girl who had escaped. He brought the daughter of Bakala into the presence of Moonspirit still pathetically clutching the amulet which Marufa had sold her. But from Bakuma, who had fled to the forest at the first assault and afterwards to this herdsmen's village where the fact of the tabu would not yet have penetrated, Birnier could interpret little of value. Of the whereabouts of Zalu Zako she knew no more than the peasants. She remembered Infunyana, as he had been called on his previous visit to the City of the Snake, and to her it seemed that a god had descended from the blue sky personally to aid her. So utterly incomprehensible and terrifying had the attack appeared that unconsciously the inevitability of her doom was shaken; if such things could happen, she felt rather than thought, then who could say what else was possible? She asked permission to travel with Moonspirit. Birnier, who knew from her dress, or lack of it, that she was unmarried, smiled as he wondered whether she was seeking her lover.

Throughout their journey they had not met a single warrior; but as they neared the place of the king they began to meet groups of them. At the sight of the first headdress Bakuma bolted into the grass, nor did she reappear until after they had gone. Later she came to Birnier and asked permission to hide within his tent when the warriors appeared, and to his question began to explain the fate to which she had been doomed. Naturally this account of the Marriage of the Bride of the Banana at the Harvest Festival was of value as well as of interest to Birnier, from whom it had been concealed when in the country before. He cross-questioned her and made notes; but Bakuma could give him practically no details of what actually happened, a secret well guarded by the craft.

They looked downcast, these warriors, and were doubtful what to do on meeting another white. Many had never before seen a white man and were inclined to bestow upon Moonspirit all the attributes which they had given to Eyes-in-the-hands. Eh! said they, Eyes-in-the-hands is a more powerful god than the Unmentionable One, for has he not eaten him up? Eyes-in-the-hands has imprisoned the thunder and the lightning in a bag which he looses at will. Who could withstand him? Had they better not submit before his wrath had eaten them all up? E-eh! man cannot fight with a god, as any fool knows.

They were returning to their homes to make pilgrimage to the new god, to propitiate him with oxen and with ivory lest worse befall. However they knew where Zalu Zako was hidden, also the wizards whose magic was as a drop of water in a fire. Mungongo did not fail to relate the marvels of Moonspirit which he had seen with his own eyes, he and those with him. The warriors listened without being in the least impressed. That, said they, was merely woman's magic to what Eyes-in-the-hands could do! Aie-e! had not they fallen dead in masses at the cough of one of his monster spirits! Aie-e! had not the look of him burned up the Unmentionable One as a straw in a fire! Therefore was he not greater than the god? Aie-e! was he not burning their villages at will! Aie-e, brothers, they must hasten to appease the wrath of so terrible a god!

Birnier saw that it was useless to attempt to argue with them. Zu Pfeiffer, with his shrewd stroke at the kernel of their faith in the symbol of the idol, had established a kind of godhead; and by his ferocious massacres had thoroughly cowed them. However Birnier secured one man to guide him to where

Zalu Zako, the witch-doctors and those who remained with him, were in hiding.

On the fringe of the dense forest they camped. The warrior guide went to acquaint Zalu Zako of their approach, else otherwise the sight of a white might provoke an attempt at massacre or flight. On the third day the man returned bearing greetings from Zalu Zako personally who remembered well Infunyana, the only white man whom he had ever met.

For two days, on a faint trail, in a steamy heat pulsing with chromatic birds and lizards, they journeyed through the forest, the skirts of the vast Ituri whose deepest recess is the home of the pygmy. One early forenoon they were halted by the warrior in apparently trackless jungle and bidden to camp. Mungongo was indignant, but protest was useless as the man refused to conduct them any farther, saying that Zalu Zako would come to them. So the carriers cut a circle and built a zareba and the messenger was swallowed by the green wall bearing presents of two rifles.

CHAPTER 14

About a mile from Birnier's camp, through forest so dense that even the progress of a native clambering from trunk to trunk and over undergrowth ten feet deep was slow and tortuous, was the temporary village of Zalu Zako; some six or seven hundred huts of branches and creepers straggling over a wide area of ground which had been roughly cleared from undergrowth by a few slaves and women.

The hut of Zalu Zako, as those of most of the bigger chiefs and wizards, was furnished with reeds upon the floor to avoid squatting actually in the green slime, and boasted a palisade run from tree to tree enclosing the huts of his two wives, women and slaves. Every morning the leader of a long line of slaves bringing supplies from the villages in the open, chanting softly the song of the march, entered the village through a mass of creepers which hung like a curtain of humid green. Many hundreds of warriors with their chiefs had deserted their king after the flight from Yagonyana's village.

In the mind of Zalu Zako was doubt and perplexity as in those of his people. All the accepted "laws" and "facts" of his world had been set at naught; it was as if buck lived in the rivers and fish ran roaring through the forests. Fear, curiosity, and resentment filled him. Sometimes it appeared that Eyes-in-the-hands had indeed proved to be a more powerful god than the Unmentionable One, of whom he was, or should have been, high priest and king; that he had eaten him up as they said; so perhaps the better course was to submit to this being invincible. Yet this very anarchy of his beliefs had released once more the passion for Bakuma whom he had renounced, the desire for whom had been inhibited by the sense of the inevitability of the mandate of the witch-doctors. Hereditary custom, which made him feel that it was incumbent upon him—a primitive sense of duty— to be king-god warred with this longing for Bakuma. The fact that he was not yet bound to celibacy quickened the seed of rebellion against the domination of the wizards. If he could escape the godhood then Bakuma was alive again. For to his mind a ban upon the personal ego was far stronger than any ban upon a second person.

Chewing the cud of this sweet grass of hope squatted Zalu Zako one morning in the dignified solitude of his compound on the threshold of his hut. Opposite him sat the brother conspirator of Bakahenzie, Marufa, a brown shadow in comparison to the gleaming of the royal insignia of the ivory bangles. They sat silent, motionless, save for the occasional sparse movement of snuff taking. In the steamy heat a continual mutter and rustle persisted, punctuated by the harsh scream of a green parrot or the squawks of a troop of monkeys. In the faintly spattered sunlight percolating through the bowered roof vivid lizards rivalled in colour the rare finger of an orchid clinging to the great tree beside the hut. Through the humid air came the faint chant of carriers at the end of a journey; swelled louder and ceased. At the mutter of greeting near by Marufa grunted.

"The beaten dog returns to nose in the garbage," he mumbled.

"Maybe he hath news of the doings," commented Zalu Zako after a pause.

"The young dog starts a buck in every tree stump," returned Marufa.

The mumble of voices in the hut of Yabolo near to Zalu Zako's continued. Neither Zalu Zako nor Marufa knew other than that, after his downfall, Sakamata had retired to his native village on the southern boundary where the people, being laymen, had believed the excuse for his absence given by Sakamata that he had retired to the forest for one moon in the guise of his totem, the wart hog, which animal became accordingly tabu to their killing for that period. At length came a young slave from Yabolo who, after saluting, delivered a message from Yabolo requesting that Zalu Zako receive him and his relative, Sakamata, who had weighty news for him.

Presently entered the recusant bearing signs of prosperity in the flowered print about his loins, the ancient cartridge pouch slung around his waist and a huge revolver of the pin-fire model dangling from a neck which appeared more tortoise-like than ever. Before Zalu Zako he squatted and after they had exchanged the usual hostages to hostility, Sakamata inquired most politely after the health of the Son-of-the-Snake, of his cattle and of his fortune, and last of all of his women. Sakamata, aware of the loss of prestige suffered by his old enemy, Bakahenzie, presented Zalu Zako with a duplicate of the pin-fire revolver. Followed an equally extensive greeting to Marufa. Only when these ceremonies had been punctiliously performed did they begin to discuss the news.

At first Sakamata proceeded to repeat the popular saying regarding the doings of Eyes-in-the-hands. Various chiefs

Charles Beadle

had visited the fort of the white man bringing presents in their hands, terrified of what might happen, yet, according to Sakamata, their fears had been dispelled immediately; for the wise new god had received them as brothers and had made offerings to them as was the custom for strangers to do. It was true, he admitted in cross-examination, that whole villages had been put to the sword and burned; but, he demanded, was not that the way of a mighty warrior to those who resisted him?

Moreover, continued Sakamata, to fight him was death. His magic was such that no man could prevail against him. Had any doctor yet succeeded in making successful magic against the Invincible One? His magic was terrible to behold. Spirits which were imprisoned in houses of trees (boxes) spoke and sang according to their tribe.

"Clk!" commented Zalu Zako incredulously.

"These words are as the wind in the trees at night speaking to girls," commented Marufa slowly. "What man hath beheld those things with his own eyes?"

Deliberately Sakamata tapped snuff, inhaled it with relish, meticulously, that not one grain was lost upon his white caterpillar moustache, and said indifferently:

"Even he who sits before you."

"Eh!"

Another point was scored. But both Zalu Zako and Marufa regarded him as one who, having had dealings with the devil and yet had emerged safely, was to be suspected of some ghastly pact. After a calculated pause Sakamata continued nonchalantly:

"There is no magic like unto Eyes-in-the-hands, the Mighty One. A great fort hath he made upon the hill of thy grandfather (MFunya MPopo), O Zalu Zako, girded with a great palisade, around which walk ever the red devils in uniform, each one of whom hath a gun with seven voices. And peering through that palisade, like a terrible black leopard from his lair, are the monster coughing devils. Eh! who are they who can withstand them?"

"Eh!" echoed his audience with lively memories of the "coughing devils."

"And he hath a mighty hut made from the white man's cloth of colour like to the forest full of things to make magic. Seated upon his chair like unto a man plucking bananas, the eyes upon his hands and in his head gleam so fiercely that water is made within a man. He who dares to look sees not only Eyes-in-the-hands, but his two souls, even as thou seest thine own two souls staring at thee with the frightened eyes that are thine!"

"Ehh!"

This time a genuine belly grunt was elicited, and even Marufa moved uneasily.

"Thou hast been bewitched," he added to mask his astonishment. "For a man may see his own soul in any pool, but never two souls!"

"Even is it as I have told thee, O son of MTungo," asserted Sakamata.

Sakamata discovered the use of snuff again to be necessary. He watched covertly the repressed excitement in the eyes of Zalu Zako.

"And what said the great magician unto thee?" Marufa demanded to cover his discomfort.

"He spoke white words as a warrior should," said Sakamata. "He gave words which told me that he was but a small wizard. He made my eyes to see the soul of a greater god than he, who was there and yet was not there; for at the touch of his magic hand with many eyes, behold! there were two more souls of the god which returned even as I looked."

"Ehh! A greater god than he?" demanded Zalu Zako, with a flicker of the white of his eyes.

"Even as I have said, a greater god who is king of all the white man's countries in the sea, who eats up those whom he pleases. Yet, even though he may bewitch with one of his eyes, did he speak softly to Yagombi, the son of Bagazaan, and Zalayan, the son of Kilmanyana, who were with me, bidding us to tell our brethren that if they would not acknowledge the true king that then he would eat us up, even as he ate up the Unmentionable One. But to those who would submit and make due tribute, would he protect in peace from the white men who, fleeing from the wrath of the great god, would soon come to eat up our country like the locusts."

"Eh! ehh! white men as the locusts!"

"Thus he spoke and bade us to go forth and tell our brethren."

This was a wholly new notion and proportionally serious if true. But Marufa, recovering from the first shock, wrapped himself in his professional cloak of omniscient indifference as he recollected that Sakamata was an unfrocked priest of the craft. The group took snuff sternly until Sakamata, having accomplished his mission, deemed it wise to retire to allow the suggestive ideas to germinate. So gravely he arose and departed from the hut of Zalu Zako and went under the patronage of Yabolo to another compound where, to a group of the most disaffected chiefs, including MYalu, he repeated nearly word for word the same harangue.

In the minds of Zalu Zako and Marufa the report of Sakamata had been exceedingly disquieting. Marufa began to wonder whether he had not better make terms with the new god before worse came to the worst in the form of white men like locusts, a menace fraught with dire possibilities which were based upon the rumours which every native had heard of the ways of white men in bulk: to the Wongolo merely vague stories from the north of the conquest of the Sudan by the British. Marufa's ambitions in the craft were almost submerged in the dread that, wizard though he was, he would have small chance of distinction and power among a race of wizards. To Zalu Zako, although the prospect of unlimited white men swooping upon them was terrifying, his semi-conscious mind was rather occupied with Bakuma than with affairs of state which seemed merely to exist to torment lovers. However he, too, was sufficiently impressed to consider seriously the advisability of submitting before it was too late; the motivating principle of the scheme was an idea which suggested that, in some indefinable way, such action might lead to the avoidance of the ban of godhood and thus to the reinstatement of Bakuma in the realm of possibilities.

To Bakahenzie the report was more alarming than to the others, inasmuch as it appeared to portend the irretrievable loss of his power. He saw the effect upon their minds, the inclination to yield to the new conqueror, which, of course, would mean the last of his followers being swept away in the crowd like dry leaves in the wind. But more than the others he suspected the motives of Sakamata, the man whom he had unfrocked. Arguing in terms of his own mental processes he saw correctly enough that Sakamata was surely playing for himself, and guessed equally truly that Sakamata would get, or imagined that he would get, many rewards, political as well as in kind, for his services as jackal to the white man. But he listened and said no word for, or against, him. He was astute enough never to make a move until he had, or thought that he had, all the moves of the game worked out. Marufa was just as wily; he related the news given by Sakamata in a voice which gave no hint by tone or word what any of his opinions might be. Then, as they sat like graven images, supremely indifferent to the doings of Sakamata or aught else, entered the warrior bearing greetings from Birnier to Zalu Zako.

Immediately Zalu Zako, to whose less skilled mind in intrigue this succession of world-shaking events was bewildering, feared that already the plague of white men like locusts had commenced. But when he learned that the white man was alone and was Infunyana, the only white man whom he had ever met, he perceived vaguely some remote prospect of achieving his desires. Almost eagerly, for a native, he commanded the messenger to summon the white man to his presence.

To Bakahenzie the unexpected arrival of another white was an unforeseen potentiality of force which might be utilized to his own benefit; so thought Marufa, which was in effect exactly the same reaction as Zalu Zako's. Therefore Bakahenzie immediately protested upon the ground that no stranger could be allowed to approach the Son-of-the-Snake, or even the village, who had not been purified according to custom. When Zalu Zako demurred he retorted:

"Hath not one white man who was permitted to enter our country without the demon being exorcised wreaked disaster upon us? Wouldst thou then destroy us utterly?"

Zalu Zako was silent. Much as he would have desired to browbeat Bakahenzie, much as his confidence in the powers of the chief witch-doctor had waned in his estimation, yet there remained sufficient to overawe him when the matter was put to a crucial test. Bakahenzie would, so he stated, go himself to see the new white man, thus unselfishly taking upon his person the whole risk of the lasting magic of a stranger unpurified. But Marufa had no intention of allowing Bakahenzie to obtain a monopoly of this possible new ally. Unlike Zalu Zako he was not burdened with awe and had confidence in his own magic to overcome any evil that Bakahenzie might seek to work against him. So when he announced that he would accompany Bakahenzie, that distressed wizard was too conscious of his dwindling prestige to object.

CHAPTER 15

Just after sun-up next morning as Birnier was seated at the door of his tent reading his *Melancholy* and drinking his coffee, a startled "clk" caused him to glance round. He saw Bakuma rise suddenly from the fire and disappear. The next moment materialized out of the miasma of the morning the figures of Bakahenzie and Marufa, followed by a file of warriors.

Portentously Bakahenzie stalked to the fire and squatted down without even a murmur to Mungongo busy with the breakfast. Bakahenzie remembered Infunyana very well, but nevertheless designedly Birnier ignored him in return. So they sat, the two wizards taking snuff with grave concern almost at the feet of the white who continued to smoke and to read.

The sign boded ill, for the insistence upon the punctilious etiquette inferred that Bakahenzie was disposed to be suspicious, if not directly hostile. And indeed the warriors' description of the magic of Moonspirit, vide Mungongo, had made Bakahenzie uneasy.

After a full half-hour Bakahenzie, as if beaten in this solemn game, turned gravely and saluted the white. Birnier looked down from his chair with the affectation of just having noticed that some one was there. After a pause he returned the greeting, a little point which Bakahenzie thoroughly appreciated. Birnier had learned that according to Mungongo and the warrior, Zalu Zako had not yet been anointed king-god; therefore that Bakahenzie evidently intended to keep the young man in the background.

After preliminaries, Birnier inquired after Zalu Zako and informed Bakahenzie that he had journeyed expressly to see him. Bakahenzie ignored the question and began to talk about Eyes-in-the-hands, demanding to know whether Birnier was his brother.

"Nay," said Birnier, "Eyes-in-the-hands is not of the same tribe as Moonspirit," for he sedulously followed up the title which Mungongo had given him. "Eyes-in-the-hands comes from a country twelve moons distant from my country."

Marufa squatting beside him grunted; Bakahenzie took snuff nonchalantly as if he did not believe a word.

"Eyes-in-the-hands is a mighty magician in his own country," said Bakahenzie in the form of an assertion.

"The magic of Eyes-in-the-hands to the magic of Moonspirit," stated Birnier, "is as water to the beer of the banana."

"Eyes-in-the-hands," remarked Bakahenzie indifferently, "hath magic to make the souls of man to be seen by all."

"Those are but the souls of the belly and body, but Moonspirit can enchant so that the spirit of the head of man be seen at night," boasted Birnier, wondering what trick of zu Pfeiffer's had produced the effect.

"Eyes-in-the-hands," insisted Bakahenzie, "hath a spirit in a piece of a tree which cries or laughs, sings or talks to his magic."

"Moonspirit," retorted Birnier (thinking "Gramophone, but I can go one better, my friend"), "hath also a spirit in a piece of tree who will speak words of wisdom unto thee in thine own tongue, who will repeat that which is said unto him in thy tongue or in my tongue, who will speak words of wisdom even unto thee."

Bakahenzie seemed outmatched in the boasting tournament. He tapped snuff woodenly. Marufa scratched his skinny ribs thoughtfully. Then Bakahenzie remarked:

"He that hath not been cleansed may not look upon the Son-of-the-Snake."

"He that hath not been anointed need have no fear of the evil eye."

"Hath not one who was not cleansed entered and cast evil upon the tribe?" demanded Bakahenzie.

"If the fence is not strong the leopard will enter."

"If the leopard be not strong and swift indeed may he not be killed in the hut?" inquired Bakahenzie.

"If a leopard and a wild-cat break in, then wilt thou not kill the leopard first?"

"Even so," retorted Bakahenzie; "then is water stronger than beer, even as the beer does reveal?"

Birnier nearly smiled in recognition of the hit.

"Nay, does not beer make the fool to talk foolishness? Dost thou then cast away the banana? Does not one talk foolishness also who is sick and yet discardeth good medicine, because he feareth to poison his belly?"

"Even so," said Bakahenzie obstinately, "does the sick man exorcise the good medicine lest an enemy hath made magic thereupon?"

"Then," said Birnier, whose only objection to the ceremony was the delay and the messiness, "let the good medicine be purified."

Bakahenzie grunted and covertly took stock of the tent and equipment visible. Upon the pile of cases stacked just inside the tent his eyes rested some time, but he would not make any inquiry. Marufa, too, was occupied in the same manner. Bakahenzie was recalling the previous meeting with Birnier in the village of MFunya MPopo—of that day when Birnier had not made any attempt to impress the native mind with "magic" other than the ordinary "miracles" in the routine of a white man's life.

"When the Son-of-the-Snake," inquired Birnier, who had learned as much of the hagiocracy as Mungongo knew, "hath taken up the Burden, wilt thou then drive Eyes-in-the-hands from the country?"

Bakahenzie slowly withdrew his eyes from the fascinating case as far as Birnier's booted foot.

"Hast thou, white man, the magic twig that makes fire?" he demanded.

"Even so."

Birnier took a box of matches from his pocket and struck one. Bakahenzie and Marufa watched him solemnly. Then a lean bronze hand was outstretched. Birnier gave him the box. Slowly and gravely Bakahenzie, the chief witch-doctor, extracted a match, turned it over and over, smelt it, tasted it, regarded it, and struck it on the top of the box. It was a safety match, so nothing happened. Birnier, without a vestige of a smile, instructed him to strike it only upon the black piece at the side. That impressed Bakahenzie and Marufa. The former tried again as directed and succeeded. Holding the match too near the head he burned the quick of the nail, but not a muscle quivered. He would not even admit that the white man's devil stick had bitten him. But he was still more impressed.

At a sign from Birnier, Mungongo brought from the tent a nickel-plated revolver and cartridges, which he placed at the feet of Bakahenzie without comment. Apparently Bakahenzie did not notice the action or the gift. He held out the matches to return to the white man. Birnier requested him to keep them. He wrapped up the box in his loin-cloth and fell to further contemplation of the cases. He was cogitating. The value of this white had suddenly increased. Evidently he could make small magic. Perhaps he could make as much big magic as Eyes-in-the-hands. Who knew? But then if that was so he could make greater magic than he, Bakahenzie, could. Bakahenzie saw that if Moonspirit were such a great magician he would be difficult or impossible to control. Naturally Bakahenzie could only understand his own motives in others. His problem now was to discover some means by which he could control Moonspirit, make of him a familiar to work to his own ends. Why was he so insistent upon seeing Zalu Zako? Bakahenzie became more and more suspicious. He saw another reason why the white man must be kept away from Zalu Zako. To refuse to purify him would give a valid excuse that he may not look upon the Son-of-the-Snake. But he did not wish to displease him; also Marufa could perform the purification.

Again Birnier repeated the question regarding the overthrow of Eyes-in-the-hands. Bakahenzie took snuff, regarded the revolver lying at his feet idly, and deigned to reply.

"When that which must be hath come to pass, then shall the children of the Snake eat up their enemies as a lizard eats flies."

"And what is that which must come to pass?"

Bakahenzie sat silent awhile, slightly shocked at the directness of the question; then as if to humour the white man, he replied:

"When the Bridegroom hath taken the Bride."

The ceremony of purification could not take place until the following day, because such things may not be hurried; and moreover, various potent charms had to be sent for to the native village. Meanwhile Bakahenzie squatted by the fire, contemplating the nickel-plated revolver and affairs of policy, and opposite him sat the meditative Marufa.

From the hour of the monkey, Bakahenzie, unconscious of the small face and anxious eyes watching the camp from the tangle of green, was busy muttering spells over a calabash containing a magic concoction composed of the entrails of a white goat, certain herbs and the eyes of a black wild-cat. When the roof of the forest was a patterned ceiling against an incandescent glow, Birnier stripped to the waist, and submitted himself to the hands of the wizard who, after scattering the feathers of a scarlet parrot into the calabash, smeared the left breast, the forehead and the right arm of the white man, to the accompaniment of an incantation. These insignia and specifics he must not remove for three suns; nor could he be permitted to look upon the semi-divine Zalu Zako until whatever evil influence his foreign body might possess should have been exorcised by this powerful medicine.

To sit around half nude in such heat was no arduous undertaking, but to sleep without rubbing off the concoction was another matter; also the odour thereof was not pleasing to the nostrils of a white man. But Birnier accomplished the feat by smoking excessively and by marking with a pencil the various nostrums recommended by the amiable Burton, many of which were hardly less disagreeable than Doctor Bakahenzie's prescription.

That worthy's slaves had erected a hut for him nigh to the tent in the door of which he squatted, usually with Marufa beside him, throughout the day, with ever a contemplative eye upon his victim, an eye which Birnier was sure was eagerly seeking some excuse to plead that he had inadvertently rendered the magic impotent, and must accordingly have the ceremony repeated.

Amused by the ridiculous sight he presented, plastered over with this filth, Birnier made Mungongo, whom he had taught to operate a camera, take a photograph of him, which would entertain Lucille, as well as be of scientific interest. Bakahenzie and Marufa watched this performance from the fire with amazement, for they imagined that the camera was some kind of gun. When they heard the click, they grunted as if expecting the white man to fall dead. Birnier of course knew the universal native belief in the picture being the soul, or one of the souls. He summoned Bakahenzie and Marufa and showed them a photograph which, after some difficulty, they recognised as Mungongo.

"Eh," grunted a warrior, "indeed is Mungongo the slave of the white man, for hath he not imprisoned his soul?"

Mungongo laughed, yet he believed in the superstition as implicitly as any of his compatriots, for said he:

"It is a wise man who hath that which is his always within his hand, even as Moonspirit hath the soul of his favourite wife with him always, so that she may not be unfaithful unto him."

"Eh, he is wiser than the Banana Eater!" grunted the warrior in admiration.

Birnier's training to control his features was strained in the effort not to express surprise. He could not imagine from what Mungongo had derived this astonishing statement, until he recollected that the boy had seen a photograph of Lucille among his papers.

After this successful demonstration of his sophistication, Mungongo was anxious that Moonspirit give an exhibition of his magic to dumbfound the chief witch-doctor, desiring most ardently to work the gramophone, to operate which he had also learned. But on reflection, Birnier decided that it was not his policy to make his thunder too cheap.

Each evening as the last subtle violet quivered in the trees had Bakuma glided from the shelter of the undergrowth under the flap of Birnier's tent, where she had lain until the first tint of dawn on the foliage of the forest. Birnier had wished her to leave for some village until Bakahenzie had left the camp, but Bakuma had frantically pleaded to remain, knowing that the craft was seeking her throughout the country since Bakahenzie's latest interview with mighty Tarum.

But upon the third day as Birnier was seated reading philosophically at his tent door, the inevitable happened. A loud outcry arose and from the tangle of creepers started the lithe figure of Bakuma, who darted past him into the tent. For a moment there was silence. But Birnier guessed what the matter was. Bakahenzie emerged from the wall of green and cried out in a loud voice. Instantly the warriors around leaped to their feet, and broke out into great clamour.

Mungongo, busy with the cooking pots, rushed to Birnier's side, gesticulating wildly. Inside the tent crouched Bakuma. Towards Birnier advanced Bakahenzie and the warriors, whose dilated eyes and spears in their hands betokened that Bakahenzie had stirred their deepest feelings of terror and murder. Birnier smoked placidly, neither stirring nor permitting a sign of their presence to cross his features.

Mungongo, startled out of his confidence in Moonspirit, excitedly bade Bakuma go forth as Bakahenzie, stopping in front of the white man, broke into a harangue, bidding him to give up Bakuma whose sacrilege in breaking the magic circle, as he had said, had brought the terrible Eyes-in-the-hands upon them; that the welfare of the tribe depended upon her sacrifice to the angered Unmentionable One even as she had been doomed; and threatening that they would take the insolent white man, whose magic was as water, and sacrifice him as well, as was desired by the spirit of Tarum.

The longer he spoke the more excited he grew. Motivated by the sudden conviction that the sacrifice of Bakuma, whose action he had foretold so successfully, and the slaughter of the white would really restore to him his repute and remove at the same time the problem of controlling a superior magician who threatened to become his rival, Bakahenzie began to work himself up into the necessary state of prophetic hysteria. Cowering against the camp-bed Bakuma whimpered with terror; Mungongo incoherently begged Moonspirit to give up the girl.

Not a muscle moved upon Birnier's face; nor even did his eyes turn in the direction of the menacing crowd who with uplifted spears joggled each other around Bakahenzie. Birnier knew that it was a supreme test of nerve; knew that any attempt to snatch a rifle or a movement of any sort, would precipitate action on their side. He had no intention of surrendering the girl to a hideous fate, and also he saw beyond the incident that if Bakahenzie were to triumph over him now, not only would his prestige with the natives be gone for ever, but that his fate would be surely sealed. Slowly, exaggeratedly, as if he were alone, he killed a mosquito upon his bare right breast and lighted his pipe anew.

Bakahenzie advanced a step followed by the warriors. His voice had reached the falsetto timbre. Mungongo lost his head entirely and seizing Bakuma, began to drag her out of the tent. Birnier turned his head leisurely towards him. Said he very loudly:

"It is not seemly to rape a woman in my presence, O Mungongo. Let her be, for I will buy thee one."

Mungongo ceased to pull at Bakuma's arms and stared as if paralysed. Birnier saw the eyes switch in a terrified glance at the warriors behind him and heard Bakahenzie's yell to kill.

For one moment he thought that indeed the end had come. Before he could reach the rifle a dozen spears would be in his back. He sat motionless, the *Anatomy of Melancholy* still in his hand, and watched the gauge of Mungongo's eyes. Bakahenzie's voice rose to a screech. Suddenly Birnier wheeled round in his chair, snatched up the pencil and staring hard at them, began to sketch faces on the open page of the book.

At the sight the warriors ceased their shuffling dance, were arrested with the spears in their hands in as many poses. Bakahenzie's scream was stoppered as if by a hand upon his mouth. In the silence their heavy breathing rivalled the twitter and hum of the forest. Birnier sketched furiously, glaring portentously from the group to the paper. Bakahenzie took a step forward, a nervous step, and yelled, "Kill!" but his voice released those of the warriors. In one loud shout they cried:

"He bewitches us! He bewitches us!"

As Birnier bent his head to make another magic mark upon the magic book he heard the rush of feet.

"They have fled!" squealed Mungongo, still clutching Bakuma.

Birnier sighed and dropped his pencil as he glanced up. Bakahenzie and the warriors had disappeared, but by the fire squatted Marufa unconcernedly scratching his skinny ribs.

CHAPTER 16

Changed was the City of the Snake, the place of kings. Upon the site where had been the hive of huts wrapped in the green arms of the banana plantation, laboured under the incandescent sun gangs of prisoners under armed guards upon the building of larger huts laid out in streets, broad and geometrical, lined with correct ditches for drainage. Around the outskirts here and there remained charred posts.

Upon the hill of MKoffo was a palisade enclosing the barracks of two companies of the askaris and two guns. No brown cones peeped like candle-snuffers above the sea of green fronds upon the hills of the tombs of kings, but from the sacred hill of Kawa Kendi commanding the approach to the valley rose, black against the sky, the triangle of the roof frame of a large bungalow; around the crown of the hill was a stout palisade through which grinned in the sun the muzzles of a Nordenfeldt and a pom-pom; and outside upon a levee strutted rigidly four sentries night and day, a perpetual reminder to the passer-by below of efficient vigilance.

Within was a methodical formation of round huts dominated by a square one; at the far end, and in solitary grandeur beneath the Imperial flag upon a roughly-hewn flag-pole, was a green marquee tent, the temporary quarters of the Kommandant.

Under the tent verandah at the rear where were his private quarters sat zu Pfeiffer with a towel tucked around his neck upon which was scattered inch-lengths of hair. Sergeant Schultz sheared deftly with clippers like a reaper in a field of corn. When he had completed the final trimming behind the ears, he stood aside with the air of an artist viewing his work.

"Is that pleasing to your Excellence?"

Zu Pfeiffer ran a hand around his skull.

"Ya, that is better and cooler, sergeant."

With a professional air Schultz whisked around the Kommandant's neck with a light brush, untucked the towel and brushed him down. As zu Pfeiffer rose Bakunjala appeared with a broom of small branches and a pan and proceeded to sweep the earthen floor. Schultz neatly folded up the towel, placed it on the chair, and stood at attention.

"Is that all, Excellence?"

"Ya, sergeant. Take a cigar."

"Thank you, Excellence!"

The sergeant selected one, saluted and departed. Zu Pfeiffer lounged in a basket chair. The usual water bag and syphon were suspended at his elbow above sparklet and brandy bottles, and a box of cigars. Around him on the floor was a litter of papers, envelopes and documents. On his wrist sparkled the jewelled bracelet and between fingers, one of which bore the large diamond which had earned him his native name, was an official document bearing the Imperial Eagles.

As he read he smiled and patted his left moustache approvingly. Officially the authorities would not comply with his request made before leaving Ingonya for two more companies of askaris with white non-commissioned officers and two more guns; but unofficially he was informed that they would be supplied later and that the authorities were pleased. He picked up a private letter and re-read it. Then he smiled again, a sneering twist remaining at the corner of the mouth. Always he was informed by sympathetic friends and an agency of the whereabouts and doings of Lucille. On the 1st of August she had been due at Wiesbaden.

He threw the letter on the table with an irritable gesture and scowled as he drank. The arrival of the mail always brought vivid regrets for the glories and comforts he was missing by being condemned to war with "dirty swines of niggers." That was part of the penalty he had had to pay for being a gentleman in a land of dollar grubbers, yet a matter to be written up against the account of Lucille, the entzueckend Lucille. He must have been verrueckt, he reflected savagely. The delicate lips softened in ludicrous contrast to the brutal outline of a cropped skull. The blare of a trumpet disturbed his reveries, reveries which were apt to rankle until among his satellites went the word that the Eater-of-men was possessed by the demon once more.

After he had elegantly finished a small cup of cafe cognac and a cigarette, Sergeant Schultz strutted up, saluted, and at a nod from zu Pfeiffer handed a document to the Kommandant, a roster of the chiefs who had submitted with the approximate number of their followers. Officially there were five chiefs with some six thousand men who had nominally accepted the new ruler, each one of whom had to leave as hostage for his fidelity a son, who lived under guard in the village beneath the guns.

Zu Pfeiffer needed the extra companies and white men to establish stations at various points with the object of gradually extending the sphere of military occupation. Zu Pfeiffer left nothing, as far as he could foresee, to chance; his maxim was to conserve his force to the utmost, to attain his objective at the least possible cost in men and material. The policy of terrorisation was based on the reasoning that eventually schrecklichkeit saved both the conqueror and the conquered bloodshed and trouble; for if the enemy were not so impressed with the fact that all resistance was utterly useless, he would resort to the sporadic risings which would entail more slaughter on both sides. Zu Pfeiffer, acting on the teachings of the German masters, sought to make war psychologically as well as militarily, economically as well as geographically. Hence his dramatic step in the overthrow of the idol in person, and the care with which he planned to impress each chief and native with his omnipotence and magic. This system of the application of political science as well as of military science, of course, was sound, save for a temperamental error: the lack of sufficient imagination to realize the unknown quantity of chance, the inevitable mistake of military scientists who are loath to admit the artist to their counsels, exemplified by men of genius, such as Napoleon and Leonardo da Vinci, who were both mathematicians and artists.

In zu Pfeiffer's case, as in others of his type, the motivating principle was not bourgeois greed of material gain for himself; gain he could afford to despise in his wealth; such would have been contrary to the code of a gentleman. While he had not hesitated for a moment to destroy his rival, Birnier, he would not touch with one finger any of his goods; for that reason had he given permission to the corporal to take Birnier's equipment, so that he would not even be contaminated by the possession of them, a temperamental error again which had led to Birnier's escape.

The driving power in his caste and tribe was love of power to an excess masked with portentous solemnity under the cloak of benefiting this people and the peoples of the world; forcing them to have broad streets and sanitary arrangements, compelling them to laugh, to sing, and to be happy whether they would or no: an urge which is the curse of the world, the impulse to interfere in other folk's affairs, to teach them, to make them to know the true God, the right way of living, the right way of doing everything from the rising of the first sun of consciousness to that happy crack of doom when our planet tries to enforce its orbit upon some other planet.

Zu Pfeiffer pinched a cigar tip, lighted it meticulously and considered the roster.

"Sergeant, this man—what's the animal's name? Kalomato—has his son surrendered himself?"

"No, Excellence. The man says that he has fled the country."

"Where does he come from?"

"The neighbourhood, Excellence."

"That means that his son is with the rebels?"

"Probably not, Excellence. He is very young, they say."

"That does not matter. Sequester all the chief's property. If he won't give it up let the askaris deal with him. If that doesn't work, have him shot."

"Excellence!"

For such obstinate cases zu Pfeiffer had fallen upon the

custom of serving two purposes by handing over the victim to the mercies of his askaris which whetted their sadistic appetites and usually secured the desired revelation of the whereabouts of the hidden ivory or other goods under the torture of the burning feet, and divers other ingenious methods. Of late this practice had proved so satisfactory that the mere threat was usually sufficient.

"This man," continued zu Pfeiffer tapping the roster with his long nail, "his son is here?"

"Ja, Excellence."

"Has he paid the tithe due?"

"No, Excellence. He refuses."

"Have the son shot."

"Excellence!"

"Any report this morning?"

"Ja, Excellence. A Wamungo spy brings news that a white man entered the country from the south."

"Description?"

"They say he is a trader, Excellence, coming from the Kivu direction, but the savage cannot give any satisfactory description. It is the first white he has seen, he says."

"He won't be the last!" snapped zu Pfeiffer with a twitch of the left sentry moustache. "Saunders, possibly. If so he should be here shortly to report. Well?"

"The King and the few men left with him are in hiding, Excellence, in dense forest. They are demoralized and quarrel among themselves. Many are coming to surrender, for they say that you, Excellence, have eaten their god."

"Ach!" said zu Pfeiffer with satisfaction. "What did I tell you, sergeant?"

"Your Excellence was correct in every respect."

"Um! Pity I can't spare a company. That would settle them before they have a chance to reorganize. Ach, but they haven't the sense, the animals, to do that... Parade, sergeant."

Schultz saluted.

"Ready, Excellence."

Zu Pfeiffer rose, took up his gold-mounted sjambok, and the two walked around the big marquee to the front where between the orderly lines of huts those askaris not on duty were drawn up for inspection. The sergeant barked. Bayonets flashed as they presented arms. Another bark and they ported arms. Zu Pfeiffer walked down the line inspecting buttons, bolts, and rifles as meticulously as he had lighted his cigar. The fifteenth barrel he thrust away petulantly and flicked the askari's face with his sjambok. The muscles of the man's face twitched as the blow came and the eyes bulged, but he did not flinch.

"Twenty-five, sergeant!"

"Excellence!"

Zu Pfeiffer passed on. When the inspection was finished he

stood rigidly smoking, coldly watching Schultz dismiss the men. Then he stalked down the hill with Schultz slightly in the rear, followed by a big black Munyamwezi sergeant-major, towards the opposite hill, of MKoffo. But at the bottom of where there were some half-constructed huts he paused.

"The women, sergeant?"

"The large hut, Excellence. Two hundred as ordered."

"No women of chiefs?"

"No, Excellence. Those attending on the hostages are housed apart."

Zu Pfeiffer strode towards the hut indicated which stood near to the edge of a rased banana plantation. Two sentries without the fence presented arms stiffly and remained immobile. Within the compound were some sixty or more young girls, mostly having the black complexion of the slave type. The chattering and giggling ceased as the tall form of the dreaded Eyes-in-the-hands stood in the gate. A slight smile flirted his lips.

From the deep violet of the hut interior darted a young girl into the sunlight. At the sight of the white men she poised on her toes, one foot forward and hands extended as if about to whirl into a dance, staring with the curiosity of a fawn.

Tall for a native maid, the light bronze of her immature breasts revealed that she was of the Wongolo ruling caste. Around her slender neck was a circlet of bright blue beads. As zu Pfeiffer stiffened and stared she wheeled and fled into the hut.

"Gott im Himmel!" he muttered. "The body of Lucille in Carmen!"

"Who is that woman?" he demanded of Schultz.

"I don't know, Excellence," replied the sergeant and spoke to the black sergeant-major. "She is the daughter of the chief Bamana, Excellence, visiting these other women. I will have her removed."

"I will not have the sense of caste abused," said zu Pfeiffer, gazing into the hut. "That is not policy. Have her sent to the fort, sergeant, and placed under guard."

"Excellence!"

Zu Pfeiffer swung on his heels and strode out and up the hill of MKoffo. The inspection was more hurried than usual that day. Then he returned to the hill of Kawa Kendi to hold court in the big marquee tent. After a lunch and a long siesta in the heat of the noonday he strolled around the village superintending the rasing of huts and the staking out of the new village which was to rise upon the ashes of the old one, a concrete example of the wisdom and power of the new lord, Eyes-in-the-hands.

Under squads of askaris gangs of prisoners, criminal and political, bound by a light chain about each neck, laboured at clearing away charred stumps and debris, while other natives portered in saplings and loads of grass, each village which had submitted sending its allotted quota.

Trumpets blared. The keepers of the coughing monsters made magical dances with their fire sticks up on the hill of Kawa Kendi. The black, white and red totem of the conqueror fluttered to earth like a wounded bird. Night closed like a black lid placed upon the steaming cauldron of the sun.

After dinner zu Pfeiffer sat in his private tent at the rear of the marquee drinking brandy. Upon a camp table covered by a violet cloth was the portrait in the ivory frame at which he gazed as he smoked. The blue eyes and the feminine lips softened as sentimentally as any sex-starved Puritan virgin; perhaps not in spite of, but because of, a mediaeval code as senseless as the native system of tabu, for natural emotions suppressed find an outlet in some form.

From outside came the twitter and hum of the forest, the rhythm of frogs, the dim bleating of a goat and the distant wailing of the women's death lament. Zu Pfeiffer drank and smoked and stared at the portrait in the ivory frame. Once he slapped irritably at a mosquito which had escaped the double net over the tent door. A wave of emotion seemed to well within him. He looked as if he were about to blubber as leaning over the table he peered intently at the pictured face and whispered:

"Nur einmal noch moecht ich dich sehen,
Und sinken vor dir aufs Knie
Und sterbend zu dir sprechen:
'Madam, ich liebe Sie!'...

"Lucille!... Ach, Lucille!"

He drew himself back with a jerk, drank his brandy at a gulp and called angrily:

"Bakunjala!"

The flutter of sand preceded a gasped:

"Bwana!"

Zu Pfeiffer gave him an irritable command. Four minutes elapsed during which he gazed steadily at the portrait. He turned at the slither of feet. Bright blue beads glittered in the lamplight as the daughter of Bamana sank upon her heels.

CHAPTER 17

In his favourite seat by the door of his hut sat Zalu Zako waiting as patiently as only a native can to see the white man, symbol of a subconscious hope. The fact that Bakuma had not been found by the emissaries of the bloodthirsty Bakahenzie evoked a sensation of pleasure which was expressed merely in a feeling of well-being. Of her in person he thought consciously little; his attitude was much as a white lover who might discover his loved one to be a sister, and hence, by consanguinity, barred from him for ever, a terrible fact of fate; but, lacking the sentimental inhibition, Zalu Zako did not disguise the death wish because she was denied him. Desires are simpler in the savage, yet the driving motives are the same as in the "cultured" ex-animal overlaid with generations of inhibitions—tabus—which form complex strata making the truth more and more difficult to recognise. From that very obfuscation of motives arises civilisation.

Then from the blue depths of the humid green came a great outcry, answered by the ululation of the women in warning.

"Eyes-in-the-hands!" grunted Zalu Zako, voicing the perpetual fear of the camp, as he leaped for his gun which Moonspirit had sent him.

Above the medley of sounds arose an articulate shout:

"He has bewitched our souls! He has bewitched our souls!"

Zalu Zako paused and listened; replaced the gun and squatted, resuming his pose of dignity before the first man made entrance. For a few moments the shrilling of the women and the wild jabber continued. Then entered a slave followed by a warrior who, excitedly falling upon his knees, gasped out:

"He hath bewitched our souls! He hath bewitched our souls! Our spears were blunted by his magic! Our swords were turned by the wall of his soul! He is a mighty magician!"

"Of whom speakest thou, fool?"

As Zalu Zako put the question the tall figure of Bakahenzie stalked slowly into the courtyard. The warrior rose and fled at a command from Zalu Zako. Bakahenzie greeted him gravely and very elaborately took snuff in order to show how casual the matter was. When he had meticulously restored the cork of twisted leaves, he announced slowly:

"As I have prophesied the breaking of the sacred circle has delivered us into the hands of the false magician, Eyes-in-the-hands. The daughter of Bakala is even now at the camp of the white man, whom they call Moonspirit."

"Ehh!" commented Zalu Zako.

"The brother of Eyes-in-the-hands hath taken her in concubinage," continued Bakahenzie.

Zalu Zako made no response. Grimly approached Marufa and squatted beside them.

"Even as I have prophesied," commented Marufa, who never failed to seize an opportunity of suggestion.

"I bade him render up the Bride of the Banana; but she hath bitten his soul in his sleep. He held her in his arms. He breathed upon her so that she would not obey. The magic of this brother of Eyes-in-the-hands hath indeed rotted the livers of our people, for they fled like young jackals."

"Eh!"

Zalu Zako stared cautiously at the compound fence; Marufa regarded Bakahenzie's left knee with interest. For fully five minutes no word was said. Then Bakahenzie portentously:

"Tarum demands the brother of Eyes-in-the-hands, this Moonspirit, for if one be taken then will the other, Eyes-in-the-hands, wither away and the Unmentionable One will be revealed."

"Thou hast spoken!" assented Marufa.

But Zalu Zako continued to stare blankly at the fence. His mind was aflame for Bakuma. Bakahenzie had no suspicion of his passion, yet the fear of his enmity acted like a douche of water in spite of the fact that the implicit faith in the doctors had been weakened. But disbelief was not positive enough to stimulate action. However, from the news of Bakuma's proximity, he had gotten strength to doubt the efficacy of Bakuma's sacrifice to restore the kingdom, a strength which prompted him to say:

"Who is he that has said that Moonspirit be the twin of Eyes-in-the-hands? Enemies there are even among whites. If he be an enemy of Eyes-in-the-hands and he be a great magician, as they say, then through his magic may not Eyes-in-the-hands be slain?"

"He hath but young words," asserted Bakahenzie stonily.

"But Mungongo, the son of Marula, saith that—"

"Dost thou ask an infant to teach thee to hunt?" retorted Bakahenzie.

"Doth a warrior ask his women to mend his wounds?" added Marufa, putting in a gentle reminder that Zalu Zako was merely a chief and not of the craft.

"He hath been exorcised, let him be brought and put to the test before me," persisted Zalu Zako.

"That may not be," objected Bakahenzie, "for thou art not yet anointed."

"But that which is necessary has not yet been done," objected Zalu Zako obstinately. "If he have no magic and his heart be not white, then let him be doomed for the Feast of the Moon." And gaining courage, added the royal phrase: "I have spoken."

The three sat motionless. The silence twittered and hummed. The shadows swelled. Bakahenzie rose slowly and stalked away through the compound. Zalu Zako watched his departure without remark or expression. After an interval, Marufa also went.

Another person upon whom the news of the discovery had had a similar reaction was MYalu. Her proximity released the primitive desire to go forth and seize her. But such action was arrested by fear of the consequences from his fellows to whom the tabu was still real, and of the white man,

Moonspirit. MYalu could never overcome the fiat of the witch-doctors while he remained with them. Yonder—his decision to go with Yabolo and Sakamata was clinched, but—he would take Bakuma with him.

Straight to the hut of Bakahenzie, who seemed to be expecting him, stalked Marufa. Marufa squatted solemnly near to him. These catastrophic events had caused a general unrest which had weakened the discipline of superstition.

There are two types of magicians: those who are partially conscious hypocrites, and those who are gulled by their own fakes; for he who makes magic must be ever ready with an explanation of failure and very ingenious in the making. The fool, believing in his own medicine, is as much astounded at failure as the victim is angry. Bakahenzie and Marufa belonged to the first class; yet being of their particular mental development they were possessed of beliefs just as deeply as the most credulous layman. That the wizard, personally, of his own individual power could slay an enemy by incantation they did not believe; but that the spirit of the Banana or of other inanimate objects could do so, they believed most profoundly. Their creed was a form of pure animism; the storms, the winds, the lightning, trees, rocks, rivers had separate and conscious souls; other inanimate objects not included in an arbitrary list, had unconscious souls, each and every one capable of doing mischief or of good; hence the essence of religion in the act of imploring the good offices of the most powerful spirits, or in moments of exasperation of threatening them with dire punishments. Their hypocrisy lay not in disbelief but in pretending to the people that their intercession with the gods was infallible; they knew only too well that the said gods would seldom incline an ear to the magician.

Of course nearly every doctor had a slightly different dogma, usually based upon an incorrect deduction from a false premise. One doctor would place all his confidence in the spirit of the Banana—the most popular spirit; and another in the spirit of the river, because out of a dozen times that he had implored aid, five "miracles" at least had been vouchsafed, therefore, argued he, the spirit of the river is the true and most powerful god. The arguments of others were equally unsound as they were dominated by some hidden desire, much as reputable scientists, while rejecting phenomena accepted by the populace, cling fatuously to a belief in spooks in order to satisfy a subconscious desire for immortality, fear of death.

Hence the confusion in the heart of Bakahenzie. To him it appeared that the spirits had deserted him entirely; to him it seemed that perhaps these white men had indeed the true "magic," the art of controlling the spirits to their will. This terror had urged him to the destruction of the white man, Moonspirit. Now Zalu Zako had mutinied, and being unaware of the powerful impulse from which Zalu Zako had gotten this sudden strength, Bakahenzie attributed it to the magic influence of Moonspirit. At any cost, he argued, must Zalu Zako and the white man be kept apart.

But other pressing points were how to accomplish the slaughter of the white man, and what he should do now after the attempt to kill him had failed. Either Moonspirit would flee, which would be most happy proof to Bakahenzie that he was an impostor and no magician, or he would seek revenge immediately. No other action was conceivable to Bakahenzie. Therefore in such a case the obvious act was to strike the quicker. He contemplated his colleague without looking at him. What was his attitude? Bakahenzie, on general principles, was suspicious. If Marufa thought that by supporting the white man he might be able to attain Bakahenzie's overthrow and gain the position of chief witch-doctor, he would do it, even as he, Bakahenzie, would have done in his place. Therefore upon these matters did he talk very guardedly with Marufa, who was unusually reticent. However, after communing with himself in sphinx-like gravity, Marufa assented to the proposal that Zalu Zako be isolated in the godhood immediately.

So the slow rhythmic beat, which was the summons to the craft to assemble, throbbed in the clammy air. Before the humid shadows had lengthened a hand's breadth, were some twenty wizards, greater and lesser, fully dressed in the green feathers of the order, collected within the compound of Bakahenzie. Silently and woodenly they squatted in a half circle before the chief witch-doctor, each and every one excited by the marvellous stories circulated by the warriors returned from the camp of Moonspirit, stories which amply corroborated the tales of Mungongo. Those who supported Bakahenzie's party believed implicitly, because they wished so to do, the "reason" for the impotence of their united magic to be the breaking of the magic circle by Bakuma. But others who cherished personal ambitions for the head witch-doctorship were suspicious of each other and of Bakahenzie, each one according to his grade and consequent knowledge in the craft.

When the drum had ceased and they sat in impressive silence, Bakahenzie, squatting motionless on the threshold of his hut, began to mutter incantations and to rock from side to side. Now every one of the inner cult knew well enough that this performance was merely a ceremony prescribed by tradition and expediency; yet for that very reason and particularly for the benefit of the lesser wizards, they solemnly accepted it, grunting in chorus as heartily as the others to the chant of Bakahenzie. As suddenly as dramatically, Bakahenzie stopped with eyes staring upon another world and fell upon his back, to scream and to writhe realistically as practice assured him. Then when the mouth was flecked with foam, the spirit of Tarum spake through the rigid body which lay as in catalepsy with eyes inverted:

"Aie! Aie! I am the spirit of Kintu!
Aie! Aie! I am he who first was!
Aie! Aie! I am the banana from whom I was made!
Aie! Aie! The time of the nuptial draweth nigh!
Aie! Aie! But where is the bride of my bed?
Aie! Aie! Let her be found and prepared!
Aie! Aie! For my lips are athirst for her blood!
Aie! Aie! Let the son of the Snake be anointed!
Aie! Aie! Let him be ready to assist at my feast!
Aie! Aie! I have spoken, I, the father of Men!
Aie! Aie! I, Tarum, the soul of your ancestors!"

From the assembly came the low belly grunt of acceptance, for they were, by suggestion, infected with the induced hysteria almost as much as the superb actor himself; they believed; even the members of the inner cult were convinced for the moment that indeed the mighty spirit of their ancestors was speaking.

Slowly, with many prodigious grunts and twists, did Bakahenzie's soul return to his body. He sat up and after a long pause said impressively:

"What hath He said unto you?"

And Marufa, as solemnly, related all that He had said.

"Eh!" said Bakahenzie tonelessly, "it is even as I have prophesied. These indeed are the words of wisdom. Is it not so, O my brethren?" Again came the low grunt of assent. "Let us obey, that these foul spirits may pass and the Unmentionable One return unto his children!"

Then, according to custom, all save those of the inner cult arose and went forth silently. In the heart of Yabolo, as he squatted as expressionless as the others, was satisfaction, for he saw, or thought he saw, that Eyes-in-the-hands would be pleased with the destruction of a man who might possibly become his rival; and on that principle imagined himself introduced by his relative, Sakamata, to Eyes-in-the-hands as the slayer, or initiator of the slaying, of his rival, Moonspirit. That Zalu Zako should be anointed King-God suited him as well as the other wizards and for the same reason. Therefore Yabolo for once raised no objection to the behests of Bakahenzie.

Already from the encampment rose the excited voices of the warriors who had been informed of the decision of the assembly of wizards. But the shadows were long. The forest was even more thickly peopled with spirits than their own park-like country. One of the inner cult of five suggested that the attack be made at dawn; but Bakahenzie, still baited by uncertainty regarding the reality of the magic of Moonspirit and the possible influence of Zalu Zako now that he had apparently developed a will of his own before they could shut him up in the godhead, was for immediate action, and insisted that they call together the warriors and make special magic to protect them from the forest demons. Yabolo, as anxious as Bakahenzie, became his ally in urging that this be done. But Marufa was not at all of this way of thinking. While the fate of Zalu Zako was quite immaterial, his attitude to Moonspirit was much the same as the young man's, but prompted by a different motive; a power possible to utilize for his benefit. But he said no word, listening indifferently apparently to the throbbing of the drums summoning the warriors. When the inner circle broke up he stalked solemnly to his own hut, but when he was within he took from a gourd a special amulet, slipped through a hole in the palisade behind the hut, and disappeared into the forest.

CHAPTER 18

Meanwhile the object of Bakahenzie's political perplexities was also holding a council of war. Mungongo and Bakuma were divided in opinion. The former had recovered his complete confidence in Moonspirit. After the repulse of the greatest magician and his warriors he became filled with a martial ardour and strongly advocated advancing upon the village immediately. Birnier smiled and considered. As a matter of fact the plan was not so utterly insane as it appeared. Did he follow up swiftly upon the heels of the terror-stricken warriors the probability was that the whole camp would be infected by the spirit of panic and bolt. However, he could not see any object to be attained by stampeding the village. Mungongo, ever eager for a miracle, urged that Moonspirit should take upon him the spirit form and descend upon them at night. To his disgust Moonspirit refused, so Mungongo retired to the fire and consoled himself by another vivid description of the powers of his master—growing every day!—to Bakuma, who sat and listened dully with ever an anxious eye and ear upon the forest trail.

Bakuma was obsessed by terror inspired by the fact that Bakahenzie had discovered her presence; the inherent awe of the witch-doctor which had been temporarily allayed by the presence of the white, was revived, as well as the

Charles Beadle

inevitability of her doom. Only the strict injunctions of Moonspirit prevented her fleeing through the jungle to take refuge in some distant goatherd village. She was convinced the wizard would soon find out where she had gone; for she was persuaded that Bakahenzie had discovered her former hiding place by magic divination, maintaining as proof that although she had been as usual completely hidden in the undergrowth, Bakahenzie had walked directly to her.

Birnier foresaw that the situation might become serious. Bakahenzie's attitude was one of suspicion based, he guessed correctly, on professional jealousy. The finding of Bakuma had probably been more of an excuse to assail the possible rival and thus to satisfy this subconscious death wish. Now, reckoned Birnier, Bakahenzie would probably be more exasperated than ever at the triumph of the said rival's magic. He would therefore, knowing the strength of the driving force of religious conviction, endeavour to play upon the emotions of the tribe by advocation of the efficacy of appeasing their fallen god by the sacrifice of the girl, and so work them up to an exalted state of fanaticism to attack in force; an additional stimulant to such action on their part would be the unconscious satisfaction in slaying the "brother" of the one who had invaded their country, Eyes-in-the-hands.

Another point was that the more a person is scared the less easy it is for him to forgive, hence the greater resistance to the overtures of amity. Beyond the partially formed idea to overset zu Pfeiffer's petty sovereignty was the strictly professional one of studying from the most intimate viewpoint possible a system of primitive theology of a most complex and illuminating kind. The main object to be attained therefore was resolved by the best method calculated to win the friendship and confidence of all concerned, particularly of Bakahenzie. To Birnier, who was not as yet conversant with the system, Bakahenzie seemed of less importance than Zalu Zako, the King-God, or potential King-God. Yet apparently he could not hope to approach Zalu Zako without overcoming the opposition offered by Bakahenzie. To give up little Bakuma to the sacrificial orgy was unthinkable; such an act would have appeared to him tantamount to sacrificing the girl to attain his own ends.

For precaution he placed two of his men as pickets in the jungle to give warning of any surprise, although he did not consider that they would be likely to renew the attack that day; then, as usual when in difficulties, he retired to his tent for a smoke. As he browsed upon his estimable friend Burton, his eyes caught a paragraph upon cures for love melancholy recommended by the amiable doctor.

"Lemnius, imstit. cap 58. admires rue and commends it to have excellent virtues, to expel vain imaginations, devils and to... Other things are much magnified by writers, as an old cock, a ram's head, a wolf's heart borne or eaten, which Mercurialis approves: Prosper Altinus, the water of the Nile; Gomesius, all sea water, and at seasonable times to be sick... the bone in a stag's heart, a monocerot's horn..."

He glanced up to see Bakuma squatting disconsolately by the fire listening to the hundredth repetition of his wonder working according to Mungongo. The outline of her rounded back and hunched shoulders, the bronze hands clasped beneath the chin and the misty brown eyes apprehensively regarding the trail was a sculpture of melancholy. He smiled as he reflected that the devils and witches of Chrysostom and Paracelsus were as real to them as the forest spirits and the magic of Bakahenzie to this girl. After all some of these concoctions sounded as if they should most certainly appeal to Bakahenzie and his brethren of the craft. He wandered off into a reverie, wondering why it was that superstition is so hard to eradicate from the human mind. In Birnier was a strain of humorous melancholy which appreciated the comedy of human marionettes made to dance to the legion of devils and bugaboos invented by themselves, and as a stimulant to the dominant scientific absorption was the knowledge that upon him and his fellows depended their only hope of release—which was the greater reason that Bakahenzie should slay him, he added whimsically, did he but know it!

Moved by the ever-present curiosity to know what was going on inside other people's minds, he called Bakuma and Mungongo to him, observing the sprightly action of the boy moved by his faith in him for his good in contrast to the dull movements of the girl in her lack of confidence to make for her good. And when they were come to him and were seated on the ground at his feet he said to Bakuma:

"Wherefore hast thou the black bird within thy breast, O Bakuma?"

She gazed up at him with the pathetic pleading of a gazelle.

"Do not birds seek the broken twigs for the building of nests, O Moonspirit?"

"Truly, but why are the branches of thy tree rotted and broken?"

"When the axe of the peasant pecks at the roots of the tree dost thou think then that the sap runs the more swiftly, knowing?"

"A devil hast told thee this thing, O Bakuma. When the sun was but a man's height did not a jackal break out of the forest seeking to devour, and yet the chicken was neither hurt nor taken. Are these not white words?"

"Truly, O Moonspirit," acknowledged Bakuma reluctantly.

"Was not then the magic of Moonspirit more potent than that of thy wizards?"

"Thy words are white," she admitted.

"Wherefore then hast thou ashes in thy mouth?"

Bakuma dismally contemplated Birnier's booted leg.

"Eh!" grunted the sophisticated Mungongo, "to those who live on the mountain the crocodile is not!"

"Open thy breasts unto me, O Bakuma," said Birnier.

"Clk!" she gasped, making a little gesture of hopelessness. "When the sun shines are not the flowers open? But when the night hath come where are the flowers? The deer feed on sweet pastures, but when the shadow of the lion falleth upon the grass hath not a great cloud come over the world?"

"But thy lion hath fled, O Bakuma!"

She gazed at the white man with curious wonderment at the stupidity of one failing to comprehend the simplest problem. She sighed and then as if with much patience for another's shortcomings:

"Thou hast strong magic, O white man," said she, "magic that makes the magic of Bakahenzie to fall as water. Yet was the daughter of Bakala not found by divination? Was the daughter of Bakala not revealed to be the bride of the Banana by divination? There shall be made magic that the voice of the one shall be obeyed. Eh! Aiee! Aie!"

The brown eyes welled opals which splashed upon a bronze breast. As Birnier watched her, pity stimulated a desire to relieve this symbol of self-torture, and he thought of a favourite passage in the "Anatomy":

"Ay, but we are more miserable than others, what shall we do? Beside private miseries, we live in perpetual fear and danger; for epithalamiums, for pleasant music, that fearful noise of ordnance, drums, and warlike trumpets still sounding in our ears; instead of nuptial torches, we have the firing of towns and cities; for triumph, lamentations; for joy, tears."

"Well, Bakuma," said he in English, smiling covertly, "we'll see if we can't get you the nuptial torches!"

Bakuma gazed at him perplexedly with big eyes.

"Already Moonspirit begins the incantation of mighty magic," explained Mungongo solemnly.

"Eh!" murmured Bakuma expectantly.

Birnier smoked and pondered. The walls of the forest were growing closer in the beginning of twilight. The soul of fear, reflected Birnier, dwells in the unknown. Reveal the god in the machine and the mystery dies. To Bakuma he said:

"Listen, O Bakuma, I would speak heavy words to thee. When thou puttest the seed of the gourd into the ground then within half a moon there appears the plant of the gourd; is it not so?"

"Truly," answered Bakuma disinterestedly.

"Is that then magic?"

"Eh!" commented Bakuma, as in astonishment. "Nay, how could that be? Does not the soul of the plant grow even as a child grows?"

"Good. Turn thine eyes to me." Bakuma watched the operation of striking and lighting a match with indifference. "Then is this fire which I make done by magic?"

"Truly."

"And thou, Mungongo, what thinkest thou?"

"Moonspirit tickles the souls of my feet!"

"H'm." Birnier repressed a smile. "Thou knowest that my words are white?"

"Truly."

"Then I tell thee that this is not done by magic."

"Ehh! Ehh!" chorused the twain.

"This thing on the end of this thing which you call a magic fire twig is made of—of—is made of several kinds of—of earth found in the—earth, and when—and when—" He sought frantically for native words which were not, "the two are brought together—as one strikes a spear—" Birnier hesitated, finding himself as perplexed as a psychologist endeavouring to explain the abstract working of conscious-ness in concrete words. "When one strikes a spear upon a rock there is an eye of fire, is it not so?"

Mungongo's eyes dimly reflected a growing horror.

Bakuma stared.

"The magic of Bakahenzie," murmured Mungongo.

"Already is his soul bewitched," muttered Bakuma.

"Is it not so?" persisted Birnier.

"Aye," admitted Mungongo, moving uneasily and speaking as if humouring a dangerous lunatic. "It is the eye of the angry spirit of the rock."

Birnier saw his danger and made another effort.

"Even so. Also thou knowest that thou canst make fire by the rubbing together of two sticks. Is that then magic also?"

"Truly," continued Mungongo in the same tone. "Can the spirits of the souls of the twigs be summoned without the incantations by the Keeper of Fires?"

"O my God!" groaned Birnier, sotto voce, and he abandoned the effort to explain combustion. "Thus is it then with these that ye call the magic fire twigs."

"Even as we have said," asserted Mungongo triumphantly.

Birnier lapsed into silent defeat. Bakuma began to edge away. As Mungongo rose came a stifled scream from Bakuma who sprang to her feet and dashed towards the tent; then as if recollecting that her saviour had been bewitched by Bakahenzie, fled into the gloom beyond. Mungongo had seized a spear stuck in the earth near to him. As appeared the wizened figure of Marufa, who saluted as he squatted in the native manner, Birnier recollected that he had been with Bakahenzie and wondered what he wanted. Mungongo replaced his spear and came to the tent.

"Greeting, O son of MTungo!"

Marufa mumbled the orthodox return.

"Thou hast need of Moonspirit?" demanded Mungongo, some of his officious confidence in Birnier returning.

"Doth the leopard go to the goat pen to seek nuts?" grumbled the old man. He tapped out snuff slowly and grunted.

Presently said Marufa:

"Moonspirit is the brother of Eyes-in-the-hands?"

"Nay," answered Birnier, wondering at the persistency of this idea. "Eyes-in-the-hands is of another tribe ten moons distant from Moonspirit."

Marufa grunted. Another long pause. Then:

"The magic of Moonspirit hath blunted the spears of Bakahenzie?"

"Even so," said Birnier modestly.

"The son of Maliko maketh much magic that the bride of the Banana be taken from the white stranger."

"The monkey makes many faces and much noise, but does he eat up the leopard?"

"The bite of the spear is more deadly than the bleat of a goat," retorted Marufa.

"Doth the wise man eat the heart of a goat to gain courage?"

"The louder the lion roars the less teeth has he!"

"But only the fool opens his mouth to see how many he has!"

"The wise father examines the grain of the tusks before he sells his daughter."

"But the wise man sees the daughter before he offers the tusks!"

"Ugm!"

Marufa took more snuff and contemplated the interior of the tent where a native was lighting a lamp. Birnier reflected. Evidently Marufa had come with an object and had inferred that he had something to bargain about. What was it? Also he wanted to be sure that he was setting his trap at the right pool. Birnier decided that he was probably acting on his own initiative and willing to conspire against Bakahenzie. An impulse to experiment upon him as he had upon Mungongo and Bakuma was repressed, for from the previous effort he had cemented the conclusion that it was impossible to explain rational phenomena to irrational minds; that as ever the adventurous champion of reason would be either regarded as insane or inspired; that which is not compre-hended is divine or ridiculous. However, through Marufa might come a suggestion for the tactics of campaign to gain the good-will of Bakahenzie or Zalu Zako and the attainment of his scientific object—as well as to give Bakuma the torches he had promised her. Whether I will or no, he reflected smiling in the dark, must I be either a magician or a fool. Fools get nowhere; witch-doctors do here as elsewhere. He saw that in order to influence these peoples or any others, he had perforce to work in terms of their own understanding, as the early Christian missionaries practised in their conversion of the Teutons, the Scandinavians and the Britons. A nucleus of a plan had been given by Mungongo's impetuous suggestion. He decided to develop it. But through Marufa, who first of all must be impressed with the fact that Moonspirit was the greatest magician the world had ever seen. So therefore he called to the native within: "O Bakombi, put out the light." And to Marufa: "O wise man, thunder has not always lightning. Behold! I am part of that which is and is not!"

"Clk!"

A click of astonishment was squeezed from Marufa by the chance mystic phrase which was interpreted by him as referring to the Unmentionable One.

Then taking out his metal box of vestas Birnier moistened one. As he rubbed around his eyes Marufa, who was expecting a miracle, observed the growing phosphorescence in stoical calm, while Mungongo, delighted at the long deferred proof of his boasts, grunted admiringly.

But when a glowing skeleton hand, which Birnier had prepared behind his back, hovered over the old wizard's head, he grunted and made a slight convulsive movement.

"Have no fear, O my friend," came Birnier's voice, "the spirit loves my friends and destroys my enemies."

That belly grunt had registered the degree of impression that Birnier sought. So he lighted the lamp, bade the excited Mungongo to bring out the phonograph, a machine adjusted with the recording cylinders as well as the reproduction, and after a successful demonstration of magic, discussed with Marufa a certain scheme to which the old wizard, quick to see the possibilities, afforded many invaluable suggestions.

CHAPTER 19

When Zalu Zako was notified of the verdict of the Council and the words of Tarum the sense of the inevitable returned, extinguishing the spark of rebellion that had been kindled by his passion for Bakuma. To Bakahenzie, or to the wizards separately, or collectively, he had had the strength to voice his own desires, but to the veritable voice of Tarum was no resistance dared. He was bidden to preside by right and precedent at the anointing of the warriors. He did not make any feint at refusal, for his will was crushed, as it had been weeks before by the doom of godhood and celibacy.

Beyond the fact that Bakuma would soon be forbidden to him for ever, he did not think; desire was strangled. Even the recollection that Bakahenzie had stated that Moonspirit had taken her gave him no reaction. To him as to his brethren, while in physical love is bound up the control of the universe, because it is vaguely apprehended as a creative force, it is of no importance to the individual lover unless he be guilty of breaking the sexual tabu: if the girl is not a consenting party to the illicit union then she is free; if she is, then it is death to both of them, for as every one knows, such criminal action endangers the balance of the burden of the world upon the shoulders of the King-God. Thus it was that the words of Bakahenzie had produced no reaction against Moonspirit in the mind of Zalu Zako; indeed, if the words were true and he could yet obtain Bakuma, she might have a son by the white which would obviously bring the marvellous power of white magic to his successor, the next King-God; and possibly, had mused Zalu Zako, dimly straining at such a radical thought against the influence of the priesthood, make the king more powerful a magician than the witch-doctors themselves.

But he obeyed the mandate and took his place as bidden. Bakahenzie had caused preparation to be begun immediately for the ceremony of making enchantment against the spirits of the night. In the circle of cleared ground, where sat the temporary Council of Elders, big fires were lighted as the dark wall of the forest drew in upon them. Bakahenzie squatted before a big calabash, specially reserved and enchanted for the making of magic, in which a mess of certain herbs whose spirits were violent haters of the demons of all trees, rocks and streams, were to be released from the vegetable bondage by stewing that they might be distributed among the warriors for the night assault. These warriors, some fifty chosen from the followers of Bakahenzie and Marufa, sat on their hams within the circle of fires, uneasily casting glances behind them at the deepening sepia, from whence arose the nocturnal chant of the spirits of the forest. In order to insure no interference from malign animals, Bakahenzie caused to be brought a pure white goat whose throat was cut and bled into the cauldron; for as any one knows, that soul which is white must necessarily fight well against anything that be black. Yet in spite of this potent magic the warriors grew unquiet; they felt, rather than thought, that if the magic of their witch-doctors had failed against one white why should it succeed against another like unto him? And their faith thus weakened, doubts regarding the efficacy of the same magic against spirits of the forest bred as mosquitoes after rain.

Charles Beadle

Bakahenzie remarked the uneasiness, but the stronger grew his need to restore the waning confidence in his powers by removing the white; the blood desire had now been transferred from Bakuma to Moonspirit as the most effective demonstration possible to him.

The fires smouldered and flickered yellow tongues upon the greens of the warriors' bodies and the blues of the wizards' head-dresses. Faint blue vapour swirled around the scarlet feather above Bakahenzie's graven face as he muttered incantations and stirred the cauldron. Then as the drums throbbed and the warriors grunted rhythmically to Bakahenzie's song of enchantment came a squawk as of a parrot. The chant ceased. Branches rustled. Every head quirked automatically towards the sound. Came a low belly grunt of terror as if an invisible hand had punched them in their solar plexus.

Just in the shadow line where the glow of the fires faintly tinted and greened the curves of his bronze body against the sepia of his feathers, appeared the figure of Marufa, his spear lifted on high as he cried out in a loud voice:

"Greetings, O people of the Banana, I bring you tidings of him who is and is not, of him who was lost and yet is come. 'Behold, I show you a sign!'"

Against the gloom his left arm and hand glowed with a strange light. An unanimous "Ehh!" rose from the assembled warriors and wizards alike.

"Raise your ears!" continued Marufa, "that the Voice may speak unto you!"

In the silence came a subdued click and commenced a high-pitched voice in the dialect:

"Aie! Aie! I am the spirit of Kintu!
Aie! Aie! I am he who first was!
Aie! Aie! I am the Banana from whom I was made!"

Whites of eyes glimmered like butterflies in starlight. Nothing was visible. The voice appeared to rise from every direction. The new miracle petrified the limbs of all.

"Aie! Aie! My soul is defiled and my children enslaved!
Aie! Aie! My face hath been scratched by an alien claw!
Aie! Aie! I send you the revenge which is white!
Aie! Aie! I send you the One who is bidden!
Aie! Aie! Let that One arise who is I!
Aie! Aie! The mighty One who will blot out the curse!
Aie! Aie! I have spoken, I, the Father of Men!
Aie! Aie! I, Tarum; the soul of your Ancestors!"

A faint whirr as of wings was drowned in the automatic grunt of acceptance squeezed from all the warriors and the wizards by the sacred chant, except those of the inner circle. In dread sat the warriors of the terrible magic of their doctors which they had once doubted. But the minds of Bakahenzie, Yabolo, and the other two master craftsmen were stunned. The phenomenon of the glowing hand had they never seen before, but they recollected the stones of Mungongo. Even was Sakamata, sophisticated to the wonders of Eyes-in-the-hands, impressed and bewildered. Dormant awe for the Unmentionable One was awakened in every one of them. Zalu Zako felt that his doom was upon him; that the Unmentionable One was about to call him to his duty, which invoked fear for the sacrilege he had committed in entertaining such radical thoughts in the immediate past. But in Bakahenzie was a streak of suspicion; how was it that Marufa was thus chosen as the divine messenger? Yet perhaps the veritable god was, or gods were, speaking! Doubt held him silent.

"O my brethren, would ye that we seek the voice of the Unmentionable One?" cried Marufa.

"Ough! Ough!" grunted the wizards.

Marufa stalked slowly to the nearest fire, muttering a spell. From his loin cloth he took the three digital bones of an enemy and proceeded to discover the whereabouts by geomancy. And behold! the fingers pointed in one direction which all could see. Oblivious to the tight indifference of Bakahenzie the old man rose and began to gyrate, mumbling incantations, towards a thicket of grass on the fringe of the undergrowth, holding aloft the magic bones in the glowing hand. Anxiously the assembly watched the skinny figure, half bent, glide out from the glow of the fires into the blue shadows. A small log collapsed, throwing a red gleam upon the form poised upright before the clump of grass as Marufa cried out:

"Let him who-may-not-be-mentioned speak that his children may hear!"

Immediately commenced a high voice chanting:

"Take up, O Marufa, the wise, the pod of my soul!"

Then in the sight of every man Marufa bent upon his knees, muttering, and arose unharmed. Save for the slow turn of each head the better to follow the progress of the magician no limb nor muscle moved as in silence Marufa bore the like of which had never before been seen; a thing like unto a stone, having an ear almost as large and as erect as an angry elephant, the colour of a lion yet hairless. "The pod of the soul" Marufa placed within the circle of the fires so that all should see. More incantations did Marufa make, sitting fearlessly; he caressed it as a young man caresses a maid and came forth again the voice of Tarum:

"Rejoice, O my children, for he that is bidden shall come!
Rejoice, O ye warriors, for he that shall lead you shall
come!
Rejoice, O ye wizards, for he that is greater than ye shall
come!
Rejoice, O ye women, for he that fertilizes shall come!
He shall eat up your enemies as a lion eateth buck.
He shall make your dead to be seen and your phantoms to
talk!
He shall give to your women to have sons of your breed!
He shall give you that which was slain on the hill!
He that walks in a flame in the night!
He that is whiter than the flesh of the baobab!
He shall come forth bearing that which ye seek!
He shall come forth bearing that which is yours!
Hear me, my people, and give voice to my word!"

"Ough! Ough!" came the chorus of assent.

Not a limb nor a hand moved among the concourse of
warriors and wizards until a new voice, deep, as one who
commands, cried out:

"Let the son of Kawa Kendi, the son of MFunya MPopo, the
son of MKoffo, move not; neither he nor Marufa, the son of
MTungo! Unto ye others we say unto you, depart that we
speak in peace with this our son and priest!"

And simultaneously appeared in the gloom of the undergrowth three pairs of eyes as luminous as the glowworm,
vaster than any human; and beside the souls of the dead
King-Gods were terrible hands. Warriors and wizards, all
save Bakahenzie and Zalu Zako, literally leaped for the
forest and village in one convulsive bound and grunt. Zalu

Zako had remained upon the ground, green with terror. Bakahenzie stood upright, his scarlet feather fluorescent in the fire-glow. The anthem of the forest was only broken by the rustle of branches and the breathing of Zalu Zako and Bakahenzie. A harsh voice cried:

"Begone, Bakahenzie, son of a dog! Lest we take thy soul to be with us!"

The eyes appeared to float nearer; hands pointed menacingly. Bakahenzie boggled; hesitated; then the dignity of his pose melted into the graceful bounds of a fleeing leopard. Even for the professional ghost manipulator, such a phenomenon of the spirits, with whom he was supposed to be on familiar terms, was demoralizing. But half-way through a thicket of undergrowth, where he could no longer see the horrific eyes, his courage began to return.

To his ears came a new voice chanting:

"Sweeter than warm honey is the scent of my man!
Fiercer than scorpions is the grip of his hand!
Whiter than a spear flash is the gleam of his teeth!
Smoother than river stone is the feel of his chest!
Bakuma rejoices!"

Peering through the interstices Bakahenzie could see the gleam of the fire upon the bangles of the Son-of-the-Snake and the blue flash upon his spear as he melted into the forest wall.

CHAPTER 20

The actual sight of spirits from ghostland, of which hitherto they had only heard, had been too much for the nerves of the tribe already overstrung by the overthrow of the idol and the magic and slaughter of zu Pfeiffer; the warriors had fled like scared poultry to the jungle, up trees, in the undergrowth and in their huts, where they cowered among their women and slaves, reading awful omens and portents in every sound of the forest.

The phenomenon had been just as startling and awe-inspiring to Bakahenzie as it had been to his most ignorant dupe. His belief in ghostland was implicit, but now he had seen what, professionally, he was supposed to see and converse with on familiar terms. As Zalu Zako disappeared he continued to listen intently. Above the slight rustle of the bushes as the Son-of-the-Snake moved through the undergrowth rose a feminine laugh. Bakahenzie's liver was squeezed by that sardonic chuckle; for, as is well known, female demons are much more malignant than the male. For the space of a chant he remained crouching there, curiosity and the dread of revealing his terror to his fellows tugging at his feet and fear of the demons clutching him around the waist. Save the anthem of the forest no further sound of the ghosts was audible.

Cautiously rose Bakahenzie, wriggled out of his nest and with as much dignity as maybe, strode back to the fire. From the village came a slight whimpering. With satisfaction Bakahenzie noted that no one else was in sight. For another space he sat with unquiet eyes and ears upon the forest. Then gathering courage as nothing happened, he pondered upon what attitude he should assume.

Yabolo stalked from round a hut and squatting calmly beside Bakahenzie, nonchalantly proceeded to tap out snuff and offered some to Bakahenzie, who grunted acceptance and sniffed with even greater indifference. Motionless they continued to sit and silently. Bakahenzie wondered whether Yabolo knew that he, too, had fled, and Yabolo, who did know, waited for the first move on Bakahenzie's part to retort.

Yabolo, indeed, who had been as panic-stricken as Bakahenzie, was more suspicious in view of the accounts he had heard of the magic of Eyes-in-the-hands. Who knew but this vision might not be another manifestation of Eyes-in-the-hands? And more slowly a similar idea began to occur to Bakahenzie, save that he had in mind the incident of Moonspirit's magic in the face of his bravest warriors. The calmer he became the more was he inclined to accept this explanation of the apparitions; such was infinitely more comforting to him than the conception that they had been in truth spirits from ghostland. As the doubt grew the wisdom of propitiating this powerful Moonspirit became apparent; yet was present the dread of loosing what remained of his autocratic power. The problem now was to enlist the white and discover some means of controlling him and his magic.

But to both men the vital question was, what had become of Zalu Zako? There were two alternatives: if the visions had been genuine ghosts, then undoubtedly Zalu Zako was dead;

but if they had been produced through the magic of a white man, then, Bakahenzie argued, Zalu Zako and Marufa must be in league with Moonspirit, and Yabolo opined that Zalu Zako had been captured by Eyes-in-the-hands. To the latter the effect was to strengthen the determination to go over to Eyes-in-the-hands. If the first possibility was correct the greater need had he of strong magic if real ghosts were taking to walking abroad visibly, and the other case merely proved beyond question the invincible magic of Eyes-in-the-hands. But to Bakahenzie the reaction was slightly different, for his elemental reason took him a little farther than Yabolo by pointing out that in all his wide experience never had spirits taken demons' shape, so that the suspicion that they had been due to Moonspirit became more plausible, and was supported by the recollection of Marufa's unexplained absence and sudden reappearance on familiar terms with the spirits.

The longer he pondered on the strange actions of Marufa the more he was persuaded that that wily colleague was acting upon sound information, and the tangle of his affairs made him so desperate that he decided to gamble upon that assumption: for magician Bakahenzie began to realize that Marufa had somehow scored a point and that now was approaching the crux which would determine whether he won back or lost for ever that which was the essence of life to him.

Meanwhile the two puzzled plotters sat motionless and silent as if mutually agreeing that no question regarding each other's late movements had better be asked.

Accordingly to the depth of his superstition returned each witch-doctor. When they were come, without one word of explanation, Bakahenzie lifted his voice in a high falsetto, bidding the lay warriors to return to hear the voice of the elders. Reassured by this command which carried far on the still air, they began to emerge from hut and undergrowth. The first to arrive was MYalu, angry to find the whole assembly of wizards apparently sitting as if they had never moved, engaged in mystic incantations. MYalu had not fled far and from his cranny had seen the flight of Bakahenzie and the departure of Zalu Zako, but he dared not betray the doctors. He squatted sullenly and waited while the remainder of the warriors, of whom many had also seen the general stampede, filed to their places.

When all were assembled Bakahenzie looked up from his spell and bade them to listen to what message the faculty— for obvious policy's sake he included the whole of the ghosts—had received from ghostland by the three spirits, emphasising the vision of the magicians as proof positive of the terrible power of the craft. By reason of the sin committed by one who had broken the magic circle, as they all knew, said Bakahenzie, had this wrath of the Unmentionable One come upon them, permitting the incarnation of a demon, Eyes-in-the-hands, to work his will upon them and to make them slaves, as were their dogs the Wamungo; and so in the depth of their tribulation he, Bakahenzie, whose magic had been rendered impotent by the betrayal of the Bride of the Banana, had invoked the spirits of the three, as they all had witnessed.

"Ough! Ough!" grunted the warriors in assent, although many of them were sorely puzzled to know why the doctors themselves had fled. Yabolo began to grow restless in his mind. To allow Bakahenzie to steal all the thunder and condemn the possible source of political power to the level of an evil demon was contrary to his policy, but he gave no physical sign save to become engrossed in his snuff box.

Then Bakahenzie continued with a long harangue maintaining

the necessity of the consummation of the Marriage of the Banana and announced that Zalu Zako had been taken by the spirit of his forefathers in order to prepare magic for the eating up of the terrible Eyes-in-the-hands; that as the voice of Tarum had said, Zalu Zako would return with "That which was slain on the hill—that which ye seek, that which is yours." Although Bakahenzie was not sure to what these words had referred, yet he was sagacious enough to know that if Marufa had engineered that scene, then there must be some plan at the back of it, and in any case knew, as any white medicine man, that words in mystic phrasing are always soul-satisfying to the credulous who interpret them in terms of their subconscious desires. Then with political prudence he avoided any reference to uncomfortable topics, by dismissing the assembly before any pertinent questions could be asked.

But when Bakahenzie had retired to his hut, presumably for the night, as Marufa had done before him, he girded himself with an amulet containing the gall of an enemy killed in battle and a short stabbing spear and sallied forth through a hole in the fence to brave the spirits of the forests in his need.

In the village generally sleep was not entertained with enthusiasm by any save those women and slaves who knew not of the great happenings. In the hut of Yabolo were MYalu and Sakamata. From the old men MYalu received much consolation and advice, but no information as to why the wizards had bolted as fast as the laymen from ghosts invoked by their own magic. Sakamata confirmed authoritatively Yabolo's suspicion that the phenomena had been produced through the magic of Eyes-in-the-hands, urging that they lose no time in going to him to make submission. Yabolo had already decided on that course, but MYalu refused to give a definite decision as to when he would go. He sat sullenly, saying no word, and eventually departed to his own hut where he dismissed his wives and continued to brood.

The fear and rage aroused by the anointing of the warriors for the capture of Bakuma had been dissipated by the general panic produced by the ghosts. Afterwards MYalu had unconsciously hoped, because he so desired it, that the pursuit of the Bride would be abandoned; hence Bakahenzie's renewal of the chase had angered and frightened him anew. As all the rest of them, he wondered and pondered upon the fate of Zalu Zako and Marufa. Marufa, as he well knew, had a black heart and two tongues; therefore was he suspicious of any manifestation with which the son of MTungo could be connected. Zalu Zako was wealthy; perhaps he had bribed Marufa to make magic in order to enable him to escape the doom of the king-godship and to flee to another country with Bakuma under the protection of Moonspirit. A lover's jealousy is as powerful a driving force as ambition. In this case it drove even MYalu to defy the spirits of the night, for at the hour of the monkey he too stole away into the gloom.

So it was that as the patterned roof of the forest was etched in the timid green of dawn peeped MYalu through the gate of the zareba of Moonspirit to discover the gaunt form of Bakahenzie squatted by the embers of a fire within a deserted compound. Bakahenzie's quick eyes, on the alert for ghosts or any moving thing, saw him; so coldly MYalu advanced and sat beside him, grunting the formal greeting.

MYalu noted the age of the spoor about the compound, the tent peg holes newly pulled. Now was he sure that Marufa and Zalu Zako were in league with Moonspirit. Wrath smouldered in his broad chest. At length spoke Bakahenzie casually:

"The Bride of the Banana hath been taken away." Bakahenzie

paused as if weighing his words, and added: "But the feet of spirits are heavy on the land." MYalu grunted. Bakahenzie had an idea and to MYalu was born another about the same instant. Said Bakahenzie, who wished to know the whereabouts of Marufa, Moonspirit and company: "If the Marriage of the Bride be not consummated then will the power of Eyes-in-the-hands prevail." And after a long pause: "Who will seek the Bride?"

MYalu remained silent, revolving his own notion in his mind. There remained with him still many traces of the awe and belief in the power and knowledge of Bakahenzie, and so his words threatening the triumph of Eyes-in-the-hands assured and strengthened his purpose; for he thought that if he could accomplish his plan then would Eyes-in-the-hands surely triumph as Bakahenzie predicted. Thus it was that he said:

"O master of Wisdom, give unto me a mighty charm against the evil eye of traitors and will I and those that follow me seek the Bride and bring her so that which is bidden may be, that the children of the Banana may triumph."

MYalu rose. The two started on the return to the village. On the road Bakahenzie sought to flatter MYalu by pretending to take him into his confidence, adjuring him to secrecy and informing him that he would cause it to be known that MYalu, the son of MBusa, would bring back the Bride of the Banana. MYalu assented gravely. Just before reaching the village his keen eyes noticed a slight trail from the regular path. Broken, twisted and crushed leaves and strained branches indicated the recent passage of two or three people through the undergrowth.

With difficulty, for the Wongolo are not forest people, he followed the spoor in a semi-circle towards the village and a footprint in the slime revealed the track of Zalu Zako or Marufa coming from the fires. MYalu grunted, but he said nothing to Bakahenzie or anybody else. That the vision had been caused by Moonspirit's magic he had now no doubt, and his estimation of Moonspirit's power increased to the point of terror; yet the smouldering jealousy and desire for Bakuma drove him dreadfully on.

Before the sun was two spans high MYalu left the village with some two hundred of his followers anointed against magic and spirits. The track from Moonspirit's camp was like an elephant's path. Through the steamy heat they followed all day until they came out upon a river near to a village upon the border of the forest. The headman of the village was away with his chief; but women, children and slaves remained. Zalu Zako, in the company of a white man called Moonspirit, Marufa, the wizard, and a girl had arrived, had taken three canoes and had left up-stream within a hand's breadth of a shadow. MYalu took all the canoes available and started in pursuit, leaving the rest of his men to follow as soon as they had procured other canoes from the nearest village.

The river was small but deep and flowed swiftly between the vast curtains of the overhanging trees. When the dungeon of the forest was glooming to night they saw the gleam of a fire. Swiftly and silently they landed, surrounded the camp and uttering the war yell, rushed.

But Moonspirit, Zalu Zako or Marufa they found not—only Bakuma with some dozen Wamungo carriers. Even the dismal squawk of a Baroto bird could not damp the relief and joy of MYalu. Next morning he despatched a secret messenger to Yabolo, making a rendezvous at a certain village and with a weeping Bakuma in his train set out to seek the rest of his fortune at the camp of Eyes-in-the-hands.

CHAPTER 21

In the village of Bakahenzie was discontent.

The desertion of Sakamata, Yabolo, and three chiefs, had corroborated his suspicions of the unfrocked priest. That Sakamata had been preaching open sedition he had known, yet Bakahenzie was in the situation of many a president or prime minister; he had feared to put his own position in jeopardy by having the offender removed expeditiously. This treachery, which synchronised with the time when MYalu should have either returned or sent a messenger, implied another grave error. All the information he could gather was that MYalu had returned through the village by the river with the girl Bakuma, some prisoners and some of the white man's equipment, on his way to the north-east; but no one apparently had seen Zalu Zako, Marufa nor the white man.

Bakahenzie was at a loss to discover a plausible theory to account for MYalu having kidnapped Bakuma, who could not be of any political importance to him in going over to Eyes-in-the-hands, but would rather prejudice him seriously with the rest of the tribe for the sin of sacrilege in taking the Bride of the Banana. Shrewd judge of his compatriots though he was, the possibility of a love motive never occurred to Bakahenzie. A dominating passion in an individual for any particular female was rare in the native world; attractive wives or concubines were chosen and bought as one buys a goat or an ox. Bakuma, in her capacity as a sacrificial victim, was to him merely a good-looking girl, well selected by Marufa for the orgy of the Harvest Festival.

Bakahenzie was distraught. He feared that he had not the authority to prevent further desertions; he did not know how far Sakamata's propaganda had permeated; he could not guess what Zalu Zako, Marufa and the white man were going to do. As many a wise statesman before and after him he adopted a policy of "wait and see." To provide an exciting distraction to keep his constituents amused and from thinking too much, he borrowed another political tactic of abusing some one vigorously. He called a meeting of the faculty and the warriors. There he solemnly denounced MYalu as a traitor and accused him of the crime of having abducted the Bride of the Banana, and consequently as the cause of the continuance of the misfortunes of the tribe.

The move was successful, inasmuch that it afforded discussion and absorbed wrath for two whole days. Various chiefs proposed as many plans. But none was taken. Everybody was discontented and quarrelsome, as fearful of Eyes-in-the-hands as he was of his tribal god; many were impressed by the propaganda of Sakamata and Yabolo and the impunity with which Yabolo and Sakamata and company had quietly gone over to the enemy. Meanwhile Bakahenzie squatted in oracular silence, murmuring incantations that were prayers to the Unmentionable One interlarded with promises of the things he would accomplish for the said Deity, with solemnity and sincerity, for he felt that the result of Marufa's intrigue with the magician Moonspirit would mature very shortly. What that would be he had no notion; only he strained every nerve to be alert when the crisis came to snatch from Marufa the advantage that wily old man had gained.

On the third day two more chiefs followed in the wake of Yabolo. Bakahenzie made no comment, but he realised that before long, unless the unknown happened, he would be unable to retain any of his followers; realised that his one chance lay in procrastination. In his despair he began to contemplate an alliance with Marufa, even if he had to take a subordinate role—which would at any rate give him his only ally, time, to help checkmate his colleague.

On the next day yet another chief and his men departed. Bakahenzie knew that they were like a herd of goats and that to stop the stampede he must adopt desperate measures. To quell the restlessness which murmured ominously throughout the camp he called another meeting as soon as the news had come of the last desertion. While the drum tapped out the summons Bakahenzie sat muttering his most impressive spells alone, endeavouring to discover a plausible excuse for some sort of excitement to distract the public mind.

Slowly and sulkily the remainder of the brethren of the craft and those lay chiefs that were left, assembled within the circle of fires. Squatted in the prescribed order they eyed the figure of Bakahenzie in his red and green feathers mumbling incantations with doubt and disfavour. Indeed Bakahenzie seemed to them the symbol of the fallen god and a past regime; impotent and as mistaken as they were. In each and every one of them were suspicions and fears growing like weeds in tropic rain that he had made an error in not propitiating the new god in time, an impulse which required but a few hours' growth to propel them out to the north-east after Sakamata and the others.

As they watched in silence Bakahenzie was aware of the state of their minds towards him and grew the more perplexed in his search for an entertainment sufficiently stimulating to postpone the effects of their discontent. Sapiently he decided that any more messages from Tarum would be unwise in the present atmosphere. An idea of a revelation by divination to appoint a substitute for Bakuma as the Bride of the Banana and thus thrust forward a reason for a feast, as there was now no Yabolo to object, was abandoned because such an orgy was exclusive to the craft and would serve to exasperate the lay chiefs.

His resource suggested a method. Suddenly he uttered a piercing yell and fell sideways as in the manner of one about to receive a communication from Tarum; but instead of the habitual seizure and cries and groans he lay rigid and silent. The divergence from the usual distracted the doubts of the audience.

The fires flickered and danced to the insectile anthem as for twenty minutes or more he lay there as one dead. But at the first flutter of inattention among the doctors he sat up with closed eyes and called out in a loud voice:

"That which is and must be, shall be!"

Intuitively he had followed the precept of witch-doctors the world over of saying nothing at all in such a way that as many interpretations may be deduced as there are listeners. Each and every doctor and chief accordingly saw in these mystic words, as Marufa had done in the chance phrase of Moonspirit, that which he was most urged to do. Bakahenzie had accomplished his temporary object. Once more he cried out:

"Let the children of the Banana be as the wild-cat at the fishpool that that which I have prophesied may come to pass!"

The charging of the air with the familiar suggestion of magical doings gripped the audience and forced from them the conventional grunt of assent. Bakahenzie began again to mutter incantations. He had, he knew, averted the immediate danger for at least another sun, or perhaps two. Now was there only to wait and see. But Bakahenzie, as all great men, had the distinct vein of luck that follows the bold. Even as they squatted there, thoroughly worked up for the reception of a miracle, came a rustle among the leaves. Every head turned as one to see once more the mystic gleam of eyes in the gloom as the voice of Marufa cried:

"Let there be a new fire!"

From the cavern of the undergrowth emerged a white man bearing upon his shoulders a burden which, as he staggered into the gleam of the fires, was seen to be in form and in shape that of the burned idol. Then did Bakahenzie leap to his feet and in one stroke recover his lead and fetter his most dangerous enemy by proclaiming in a loud voice:

"Behold! The bearer of the Burden of the World even as Bakahenzie hath prophesied!"

And as Birnier set down the idol, from warrior and wizard, with the chief witch-doctor's declaration, "That which is and must be, shall be," echoing in their ears, came the deep grunt of acceptance of the new King-God of the lost Usakuma, the Incarnation of the Unmentionable One.

CHAPTER 22

In the humid heat of the forenoon the small hills of Fort Eitel, as zu Pfeiffer had renamed the Place of Kings, in the centre of the rased banana plantations, resembled scabby pimples upon a shaven patch of a green head seething with a verminous activity.

Across the ford of the river came a puckered-faced Bakuma in the train of carriers and slaves of MYalu, who with Yabolo was coming to make obeisance to Eyes-in-the-hands, under the protection of Sakamata. To Bakuma there was no joy in the prospect of the sight of her old home; the bitter taste of the oleander was in her mouth as she trudged despondently with downcast head.

But the breast of MYalu was filled with the song of the cricket. The terrors that had haunted him throughout the journey, of being overtaken by the magic of Bakahenzie or his emissaries, for the sacrilege of stealing the Bride of the Banana, began to evaporate at the approach to his village where now dwelt a new god more powerful than any, from whom he was about to gain protection, honours, and incidentally the ivory, which his anxious eyes pictured still within his hut. But when they broke from the outer banana plantation a mighty grunt was punched from the chests of Yabolo and MYalu at the vision of the half-completed street of large huts in the midst of desolation.

"Eh!" quoth Sakamata, "is not the way of the mighty one more wonderful than he who is gone? Behold, he maketh a city like unto that of his people, a city of gods!"

But MYalu had no admiration to spare, for to him the alleged beauty thereof was fogged by the fact that his own huts were but blackened ruins. The next moment MYalu, in spite of his native dignity, started as one of those uniformed keepers of the coughing monsters barked at them magic words.

Sakamata replied. Yabolo and MYalu stiffened as they observed the cringe of the shoulders as he fumbled hastily within his loin-cloth and presented a piece of hard substance, the colour of blue clay with magic marks upon it. The demon grunted at them to proceed as if talking to a slave. Followed in file the rest of the caravan. As Bakuma passed the uniformed demon standing with the sword and gun with seven voices upon his shoulder, leered, and grunting in a strange tongue, stepped forward and spun her round by the shoulders. Bakuma cried out in terror and the carriers gasped fearfully. MYalu and Yabolo wheeled. MYalu's facial scar twitched with rage as he raised his spear. But Sakamata clung to his arm as the soldier, grinning, raised his rifle in their direction. Bakuma ran on. The man laughed and turned his back to them, calling out something that the Wongolo could not understand.

"Eh!" commented Sakamata indignantly, "the dog hath eaten poison grass! We will tell his words to Eyes-in-the-hands and he will be beaten until he stales."

MYalu, slightly mollified by this promise of revenge, strode on in silence, bewildered and resentful, wondering at these strange things in the camp of the new god. In a large open space resembling a public square, was a big unfinished hut: the guest house, Sakamata informed them, for those who sought an audience with the Invincible One. As they squatted on the floor waiting patiently until the sun was two hand's-breadth above the hill for the appointed time, food and beer were brought to them by a Wamungo slave. Zu Pfeiffer was careful to foster the class distinction. Sakamata duly held forth upon the generosity of Eyes-in-the-hands, the wonder of his works and presence; but his words were received in unsympathetic silence, for the incident on the road had wounded the dignity of both chief and witch-doctor; raised dim fears and forebodings.

At length a strange sound rang out on the still hot air. The signal, Sakamata explained, that Eyes-in-the-hands would receive his guests. Leaving Bakuma squatted in the lethargy which appeared to be habitual to her now, the three slowly mounted the sacred hill, marvelling greatly at the black triangle of the roof of the new temple, gazing with veiled suspicion at the gleaming brass fittings of the coughing monster in the great gate, and eyeing uneasily the double lines of uniformed devils, their bayonets flaming in the sun, who were drawn up outside the green palace of Eyes-in-the-hands.

On each side of the tent door stood the two tallest men in the companies, coal-black forms which towered above the slighter build of the Wongolo, as rigid and as silent as trees. Through this terrifying guard walked Sakamata leading his two compatriots, already startled and impressed. Immediately within Sakamata fell upon his knees. Before them at the end of the tent sat zu Pfeiffer in the full dress of his regiment, plumed helmet, blazoned uniform and sword; and beside him, erect, the two sergeants Schultz and Ludwig in full parade uniform. Above them was a blaze of red, white and black and in the midst another splash of colour. But before this vision had penetrated their brains, had risen the voice of Sakamata bidding them to kneel likewise. Bewildered and awed they obeyed. Then came a voice saying:

"Rise, approach, O chiefs!"

Accordingly they arose and following Sakamata, advanced and squatted, their eyes dominated and held by those myriad gleams of magic "eyes" on hands and wrists. Then the interpreter, standing at attention, spoke this harangue tonelessly:

"Greeting and welcome, children of the Banana! Eyes-in-the-hands who is known to the people where the sun rises as the Eater-of-Men, hath come from afar, the messenger of a greater than he, the Lord of the World, the Earthquake, the World Trembler, who eats up what he pleases, whose eyes see all things, whose sword slays all things, whose breath is the rain, whose voice is the thunder, whose teeth are the lightning, whose frown is the earthquake, whose smile is the sun, whose ear is the moon, whose eyes are the stars, whose body is the world! Look upon one soul of him which he hath sent that ye may worship and know him!"

Zu Pfeiffer raised the jewelled hand above his shoulder as the man ceased. From out the medley of colours to the unaccustomed native eyes grew slowly the form and face of a white man as strangely clothed as Eyes-in-the-hands, covered with amulets and charms upon his breast. For four minutes by his wrist-watch, zu Pfeiffer sat silent and as frozen as his sergeants; then secretly he pulled a string.

"Ehh!" grunted Yabolo and MYalu involuntarily, for before them appeared even, as Sakamata had related, the two souls of every person present. Stunned at such a manifestation of magic, they slowly turned from one to the other. As silently as they had appeared did the visions vanish.

"O son of MYana, tell the tale of the possession of these thy friends and allies," commanded zu Pfeiffer.

Sakamata obeyed. But as he recited the approximate number of MYalu's followers, the number of his oxen and goats, the number of fine tusks and small, the number of wives, concubines, and children, and slaves, the eyes of MYalu grew unquiet. Had he known that he would be required to render an account he would have computed at half the actual amount, whereas, in order to impress Sakamata with his importance, he had exaggerated to almost double what he had ever possessed. Then as Sakamata proceeded to perform the same service for Yabolo, relating, by arrangement with his relative, about one-third of his possession, MYalu observed in a corner a man making magic upon a table, a native clerk keeping tally; for zu Pfeiffer kept an exact record of every chief's alleged possessions, as given by Sakamata and corroborated—by silent consent—by the said chief, so that when afterwards any discrepancy with the said list was discovered, the chief was proven a liar and subject to the punishment of further confiscation as such, and served as well to enhance the reputation for omniscience of Eyes-in-the-hands.

At the end of the recitals of property, MYalu was told, not asked, to bow his head to the ground in token of allegiance. He obeyed in bewilderment which changed to rage when he was informed that the third of his property must be rendered to the august being before one sun's delay; that he was to be ready at a summons to produce a given number of warriors; and that his small and only son was immediately to be placed in the "village of sons of chiefs" as guaranty of obedience and good behaviour.

In a mist of fright, anger and awe, he sat motionless. Sakamata proceeded to relate the doings of Zalu Zako and those who had remained faithful to him. Zu Pfeiffer had fairly precise information from spies of the movements of the Wongolo since the return of Sergeant Ludwig, who had burned the village of Yagonyana, but shortage of men and the serious disadvantage of traversing and fighting in the forest had prevented him from sending another punitive expedition. Also had he heard of a white man who had passed through the country. Sakamata, native-like, eager to placate, asserted that he had actually seen the white man who was called Moonspirit, and from the same motive, ever wishing to flatter, announced positively that he had no magic at all, was dark and small and a trader, the only kind of white man other than the military at Ingonya of whom Sakamata had ever seen.

Zu Pfeiffer stroked his left moustache and reflected. He had at first thought that the man might possibly be Saunders, a trader who was in his pay, but now decided that he was probably some new trader or hunter from the Tanganyika district. He instructed Sakamata that he was to send a messenger to this white man and command him to come to him immediately. Then waving the imperious jewelled hand, he dismissed them. But noticing the sullen countenance of MYalu, he drew Sergeant Schultz's attention, ordering him to mark the man and if the tax was not forthcoming quickly, to have him given fifty lashes. Silently Schultz saluted.

So it was that MYalu, sulky, smouldering with anger against Sakamata, for he felt that he had been betrayed into a trap, followed Yabolo out into the sun. Not only had he not gotten back his ivory left in the village, but he was ordered to pay much more than he actually possessed.

But when he had descended the hill to the guest house he

came to the weeping and wailing of his people, who informed him that Bakuma had been taken away by three of the demon keepers of the coughing monsters.

CHAPTER 23

Upon the site of Birnier's old camp in the forest was a high palisade built from tree to tree. Inside of the gate beside a small conical hut burned the sacred fires tended by Mungongo; before a green canvas tent stood the new idol, which differed from the original in having a better perspective and proportion of features and body, yet lacked the master touch of expression given by the subconscious fingers of the native artist.

Against the wall were stacked uniform cases to make a table, upon which were a hand-mirror and toilet articles; above a photograph of Lucille was pinned upon the canvas. Upon the camp bed, screened by a mosquito net, lay the new King-God, Moonspirit, the magic book in his hands.

"Kings, princes, monarchs, and magistrates seem to be most happy, but look into their estate; you shall find them to be most cumbered with cares, in perpetual fear, agony, suspicion, jealousy: that as he (Valer. i. 7, c. 3) saith of a crown, if they but knew the discontents that accompany it, they would not stoop to pick it up. Quem mihi regem dabis (saith Chrysostom) non curis plenum?"

The Incarnation of the Unmentionable One smiled, put down the book and glanced across at the photograph.

"And yet they still talk of the advantages of a monarchy!" he commented.

The original plan concocted with Marufa and Zalu Zako in the forest when making the new idol was that Birnier should become chief witch-doctor and Zalu Zako be anointed King-God, with Marufa as the power behind the throne. Although Zalu Zako desired to escape the yoke, his protest was enfeebled by the sense of fatality, and had been utterly squashed by the promise of Marufa, at Birnier's suggestion, that the sex tabu would be lifted from the godhead. But the negligence of Marufa in allowing the white man to carry the idol, arranged with the idea of investing Moonspirit with greater prestige according to the prophecies already announced by Tarum, had permitted Bakahenzie to make his *coup d'etat*—thrust the godhood upon the white and recover his own position.

Birnier in truth had little option of refusal as well as little time for reflection upon a situation the possibility of which had not occurred to him; for Marufa was completely out-manoeuvred by his rival, and the certainty of escape from his doom offered by Bakahenzie revived the image of Bakuma in Zalu Zako and bought his partisanship instantly.

With Napoleonic swiftness to grasp the advantages gained Bakahenzie drove the lay chiefs from the sacred presence, which he surrounded by a bodyguard of the awed brethren; expelled the household from Zalu Zako's compound and hustled the incarnation, bearing the new god, into holy isolation.

Bewildered by the rapidity of the moves Marufa and Zalu Zako were separated from Moonspirit. In the general confusion, not knowing exactly what was happening, Birnier complied with what he believed to be the regulations regarding gods. But when he perceived that he was about to be left alone he clutched Mungongo and refused to part with him. Bakahenzie, compelled to avoid any delay before consolidating his position, instantly shut up Mungongo in the same web by declaring him the Keeper of the Sacred Fires and so disposed of any agent outside the tabu or craft. As soon as this was accomplished and a dance to celebrate the lighting of the new fires commanded, the wily chief witch-doctor approached Marufa who, realizing that he was hopelessly outwitted, was only too eager to make the best terms possible.

Birnier had known that the King-God was never allowed to be seen by the populace except at the Harvest Festival, yet he accepted his isolation philosophically, lured by the expectation of the secrets he was about to learn, although his curiosity led sometimes to the vision of a god peeping through a fence.

While the drums summoning the council of chiefs and wizards were muttering through the moist air, to Birnier, squatting on the floor of Zalu Zako's hut with Mungongo beside him, came Bakahenzie to instruct him in his role. To whet his curiosity still more he learned that from the moment of appearance in the gate of the sacred enclosure for the ceremony of the lighting of the royal fires, every movement of body and speech was regulated as rigidly as the etiquette of the Court of Spain. At a signal from the chief witch-doctor was the King-God to leave the hut and appear from behind the idol; with arms in a certain position was he to approach and squat at an exact spot. To Mungongo was given charge of the two fire sticks, newly consecrated.

As the chief witch-doctor retired the chanting began. Interested to know what was about to happen Birnier obeyed in the spirit of a game. So in the warm darkness they

Charles Beadle

squatted, these two, listening to the chanting, cries and groans to the accompaniment of the drums and lyres and the perpetual twitter of the forest. At last came a violent howl from Bakahenzie which Mungongo declared was their cue.

Around the circle of the fence to avoid the eyes of the audience ran Mungongo to the temporary Place of Fires. Feeling as if he were once more playing in an amateur dramatic club, Birnier stalked with portentous dignity from the hut, past the idol, and took his seat upon the enchanted place. Without the palisade and within another squatted in correct order the lines of wizards and chiefs, Zalu Zako retaining, rather by prestige of his former holiness and indecision as to what his status really was, his position at their head.

Upon his haunches before a large calabash upon a fire Bakahenzie finished the mumbling of incantations over the sacred ingredients, and leaping to his feet began a wild dance to the throb of the drums and the diaphragmatic chorus of the assembled cult... Swifter and swifter spun the chief witch-doctor. The glow of the fire tinted his whirling bronze body with flecks of green and red as he gyrated in and out of the shadows. Suddenly he threw a handful of herbs upon the fire which was immediately enveloped in a cloud of smoke, into which with a screech Bakahenzie disappeared... The drums and grunting ceased. Then in the swirling column of blue appeared his figure holding something in his hands. To the wild outburst of drums and groans he sprang towards the King-God elect and anointed his breast and shoulders with a pungent compound, and leaped away into another dance, while Mungongo plied the two fire sticks. When the spark was blown upon the dry tinder and the first flame flickered Bakahenzie dropped flat before the gate as from the wizards went up the great shout:

"The fire is lighted!"

And from the mass of warriors and folk confined to their huts behind the outer palisade the phrase was echoed in a mighty wail, startling monkeys and parrots into as wild an acclamation of the new King-God.

Bakahenzie, rising to his haunches, began a chant in honour of the new King, a chant based upon the song composed by Marufa and repeated on the phonograph, but developing even stranger merits and attributes. Until the first glimmer of dawn through the forest roof squatted Birnier, as motionless as etiquette demanded, listening to the strange psalm of praise with avid interest and observation.

Suddenly, amid a furious clamour of the drums, Bakahenzie, Marufa, and one other of the inner cult of the five who had not deserted, led the body of the doctors in a rush into the sacred enclosure, seized upon the startled King and hustled him to the base of the idol where, yielding to the whispered instructions of Marufa, he took the idol once more upon his shoulders and guided by Bakahenzie, walked out of the gate and through the village to the yelling and screaming of the wizards, some of whom, according to precedent, ran about screeching and rattling hut doors, pulling thatches and howling ferociously in search of any sacrilegious peeper.

As he tramped on with his load Marufa yelled in his ear that he must carry the Burden of the World no matter what happened to him, for if he let the idol fall then would he be killed upon the spot to save the sky from falling too. Wondering what this meant and where he was going, the cut of thongs upon his legs surprised him into a halt. Immediately a terrific cry went up:

"The Bearer of the World stumbles! Aie! Aieeeeeeeee!"

Despite the furious flogging the intellectual interest in this strange conception distracted his mind from the pain of the blows; also his bare back was protected by the idol and his leggings and trousers deadened the lashes. A moment more he hesitated. But he was unarmed and had voluntarily taken on the adventure, so he would see it through. As he broke into a shuffling run, for the idol fortunately was lighter than the previous one and he was a more powerful man than Kawa Kendi, another howl of joy and relief echoed throughout the village.

So along the old forest trail he travelled as fast as he could, assisted slightly by wizards' hands as he crawled over clumps of undergrowth. The intensity of the whipping had decreased as soon as they were out of the village but throughout an occasional vicious whack testified to the presence of some devout doctor. Thus it was that the white King-God came to his throne and sat in state upon his bed to smile at the reflections of a melancholic philosopher.

So far so good, reflected Birnier, although the enforced isolation and strict curtailment of his actions had already begun to be irksome; yet to attain so difficult a goal sacrifice must be borne, he argued philosophically.

The royal larder, he noticed with thankfulness, was kept well stocked. Every day appeared a slave who left just within the entrance chickens, bananas, milk and fresh water, and sometimes a young goat. All such provisions which he had happened to take into the forest with him and so had escaped MYalu's marauding hands had been placed in his tent with other cases, as containing no man knew what mighty magic.

For three days he had been left utterly alone. Sounds of drums and chanting from the distant village had reached them on the still air, but what they were doing he could not discover. No layman was allowed to come near the sacred enclosure. While he strolled, taking a smoke and constitutional around and around his "pen," as he put it, several of the lesser wizards appeared and stood at a distance from the gate to stare at him. When addressed they made no reply. On the second occasion he began to be irritated, but he kept his temper and went to cover in his tent, muttering: "Why the devil don't they bring me some buns?"

On the fourth day patience began to fray. He had no notion of knowing how long this quarantine was going to last. He was on the point of going to find out, but Mungongo pleaded so earnestly that they would instantly be killed if they did, that he desisted. So Birnier retired to the tent to seek consolation from a record of Lucille's voice.

Birnier attempted to cross-examine Mungongo to find out what was the object of this isolation, but beyond the fact that strangers were never permitted to behold the King-God, even lay natives, without special magic, which was only made once a year at the Harvest Festival, lest evil be made upon his person and so endanger the world, Mungongo did not know; merely, that so it was. What power over the head witch-doctor the King really had, Mungongo had no notion. The King-God was the most powerful magician known, asserted Mungongo. Did he not make rain and bear the world upon his shoulders? When Birnier unwisely denied this feat, Mungongo looked pained and began a remark, but balked before the name Moonspirit to ask the name of Birnier's father.

At the mental image conjured up of a handsome white-haired planter and ex-owner of many slaves Birnier smiled, but he knew the tabu regarding the ban upon the names of the dead and that he, presumably, having ascended into the divine plane, was therefore classed with the departed. He recollected that the old man, who belonged to a cadet branch of a royalist family, had been called "le Marquis," of which he was excessively proud. Birnier translated into the dialect the nearest possible rendition of the title: The Lord-of-many-Lands.

"The son of the Lord-of-many-Lands," continued Mungongo satisfied, "doth but tickle the feet of his slave."

On the fifth afternoon, while the god was engrossed in a cure for love madness which, he reflected, might be of service to zu Pfeiffer, came a voice without crying:

"The son of Maliko would speak with the Lord, the Bearer of the World!"

Birnier glanced across at the photograph of Lucille.

"Some job I've gotten!" he remarked as he rose. In the gate sat Bakahenzie. Birnier was conscious of an idiotic impulse to rush forward to greet him as an old and long lost friend. But remembering the dignity of his godhood he remained in the tent doorway, bidding the chief witch-doctor to advance.

Birnier retired backwards and sat beneath the net, for the mosquitoes were as thick as they are on the bayou Barataria. Mungongo, possibly to prove his erudition, sat upon one of the cases containing much magic, at which Bakahenzie from the floor in the doorway looked askance. Birnier was keenly anxious to know what was happening regarding the fortunes of the tribe, hoping that with the restoration of the Unmentionable One that they would return to their allegiance. According to etiquette he remained silent, waiting for Bakahenzie to open the conversation, until, realizing that he was a god and that the chief witch-doctor was doing the same thing, reflected swiftly and desiring to make an impression, repeated Bakahenzie's mystic phrase which he had overheard whilst hiding in the jungle previous to the denouement:

"That which is and must be, shall be!" Bakahenzie grunted his acknowledgment of the profundity of the statement. "He who would trap the leopard must needs dig the pit!" Another uncompromising silence urged Birnier to force the pace a little: "O son of Maliko, what say the omens and the signs of the evil one, Eyes-in-the-hands?"

"When shall the Unmentionable One return unto the Place of Kings?" demanded Bakahenzie.

"The Holy One returneth not unto the place appointed until that which defileth is removed," retorted Birnier.

Bakahenzie took snuff and appeared to consider. Then he glanced around the tent as if in search of something.

"When will the voice of Tarum speak through the pod of the soul?"

Mungongo looked expectant and stood up. But Birnier ignored him.

"The fruit doth not fall until it be ripe. He would know what hath been done by his slaves for the baiting of the pit for the unclean one."

"Would the magician that cometh from the sea make pretence that an elephant is a mouse?" inquired Bakahenzie.

For a moment Birnier was perplexed; then he realized that the chief witch-doctor inferred that he, as King-God, mocked his priest by pretending that he did not know all things.

"Doth the chief witch-doctor make magic for the curing of the scratch of a girl of the hut thatch?" he retorted. "Lest thy heart wither like unto a fallen leaf, know then that the soul of Tarum hath made words for the return of the Unmentionable One to the Place of Kings, but that his children may not be as the dogs of the village who are driven, he wills that you prepare the pit for the trapping of the defiled one." Bakahenzie's eyes stolidly regarded the tent wall. "O son of Maliko, hast thou sent forth the sound of the drum throughout the land that the children may know of the Coming?"

"When will the voice of Tarum speak through the pod of the soul?" demanded Bakahenzie insistently.

Birnier sat motionless in the native manner. Irritated by this childish tenacity to apparently a fixed idea, he yielded to an impulse which was almost a weakness.

"O son of Maliko," said he, "thou art a mighty magician!" Bakahenzie grunted modest assent. "Even as I am." Another grunt. "Give unto me thine ears and thine eyes that I may reveal unto thee that which is known to the mightiest of magicians." Commanding the delighted Mungongo to bring out the phonograph, he continued: "Thou hast heard of the mighty doings of the unclean devourer of men, Eyes-in-the-hands. I have magic the like of which man hath never seen. Is it not so?"

"Ough!"

"Yet will the son of the Lord-of-many-Lands make thee to see that which is, is not!"

"That which is, is not," repeated Bakahenzie, whose professional mind was pleased with the phrase.

In the desire to explain rationally the mystery of a phono-graph and despairing of any attempt to describe the laws of vibration, Birnier sought for a likely simile. Encouraged by the almost imperceptible fact that he had awakened Bakahenzie's visible interest, he plunged on: "Within this piece of tree is there nought but many pieces of iron such as thy spears are made of. Thou knowest that there are places by the river and in the rocks where a man may speak and that his words will be returned to him. Is it not so?"

"They are white words, O son of the Lord-of-many-Lands!" returned Bakahenzie. "For the spirits of the river and the rocks mock the voices of those who have not eaten of the Sacred Banana" (the uninitiated).

"But they mock thy voice as well," protested Birnier.

"Are there not goats in ghostland who bleat at the wizard and the peasant?"

"By the Lord!" murmured Birnier, although the mask of his face did not change. "Ghostland is full of goats if one were to credit some of the most modern witch-doctors! Still demonstration...

"Thou seest, fellow magician," he continued, "the pod of the soul of mighty Tarum, his ear like unto an elephant, his colour like unto a lion!" Birnier got out of the mosquito net and knelt beside the phonograph in front of Bakahenzie. Taking off the trumpet and cylinder carrier he opened up the inside, revealing the clockwork motor, wound it up, stopped it and released it. "Thine eyes see that my words are white. These things are but as pieces of metal of thy spears. Is it not so?"

"Ough!"

Birnier closed the machine, adjusted the trumpet and put on the cylinder of Marufa's record.

"Aie! Aiee! I am the spirit of Kintu!
Aie! Aiee! I am he who first was!"

chanted the machine.

Birnier, noticing that the desired astonishment was registered by an almost impalpable start, stopped the machine and changed the record.

"Rejoice, O my children, for he that is bidden shall come!
Rejoice, O ye warriors, for he that shall lead you shall come!
Rejoice, O ye wizards, for he that is greater than ye shall come!
Rejoice, O ye women, for he that fertilizes shall come!"

Birnier allowed the machine to run through the chant until the end:

"He shall come forth bearing that which ye seek!
Hear ye, my people, and give voice to my word!"

The machine whirred and stopped. Birnier turned to Bakahenzie.

"Thou hast seen, O my brother magician, that my words are white?"

"Ough!" assented Bakahenzie.

"Thou hast seen, O my brother magician, that at the will of my finger upon that which is made but of spear-heads that the voice of Tarum hath spoken, the voice which is but the mocking voice of Marufa amid the trees of the forest?"

"Ough!"

"Dost thou not know that he who knows the ways of rocks, who can make pieces of spear into that which will say and do that which he wills, is a greater magician than he who must needs go unto the rocks to be mocked?"

"Thou art the greatest of magicians, O son of the Lord-of-many-Lands," responded Bakahenzie in a burst of eloquence. "For thou hast entrapped the spirits of rocks and spears to do thy bidding."

"O God!" sighed the professor, "what is the use of language?"

CHAPTER 24

A favourite panacea for the results of a stupid action is the sentiment of martyrdom. When MYalu persisted in bitter reproaches to Yabolo and Sakamata the first retorted that the punishment was the result of having committed the sacrilege of kidnapping the sacred Bride of the Banana. Then MYalu considered that not only had he been trapped by one of his own people whom he had deserted, but to add insult to injury he felt he was not understood. Neither Yabolo nor Sakamata, as Bakahenzie, could comprehend a chief and a warrior making such a fuss over a girl. That the confiscation of MYalu's property was an insult they both agreed, but biassed by both fear of Eyes-in-the-hands and their own interests, they were disposed to pretend that after all such a small matter as the abduction of a girl could be overlooked when committed by the follower of such a powerful god and magician, as expedience is so often the father of a dispensation. Yet nevertheless in Yabolo, if not in Sakamata, whose hatred of the tribal craft was deep in ratio to the degeneracy of his native code, the outrage upon Bakuma as the Bride of the Banana, while an act of dangerous sacrilege when performed by a Wongolo, violated the half suppressed traditions and kindled a spark of bitter resentment ready to flare up against Eyes-in-the-hands or Sakamata; but being a diplomatist, he concealed that anger, even from himself to a certain degree.

Upon MYalu's arrival in the guest-house to find that Bakuma had been taken, his passion had nearly led to his instant destruction, for he had desired to run amok among the grinning askaris. Afterwards, when the efforts of his friends and the hungry points of bayonets had cooled his ardour, he had wanted to rush straight to Eyes-in-the-hands who, according to Sakamata employed as master of ceremony at the daily audiences, would instantly restore Bakuma to him and visit a terrible punishment upon the evil-doer. But the august presence could not be approached so casually: petition must be made in orthodox form and the royal pleasure awaited meekly.

According to the words of the Son-of-the-Earthquake, as zu Pfeiffer was officially designated by his men, who placed the actual name under the tabu in token of the acceptance of the magic purple, came a guard to take away MYalu's first-born as hostage to the village of the sons of chiefs. Seething with red rage MYalu mutely followed Yabolo to the place appointed for their housing. Then on the following afternoon at the time of audience MYalu waited in the broiling heat for three hand's-spans of the sun without being summoned to the green temple. And thus it was for three days.

But upon the fourth, when MYalu squatted in the general hut in company with Yabolo, Sakamata, and other renegade chiefs, smouldering with bitter resentment, came the pulse of a distant drum, the furious tattoo and long pause, tattoo and long pause, which accompanies the mighty shout at the coronation of a new King-God, "The Fire is lighted!" news that had throbbed from that point within the forest from village to village to the slopes of the Gamballagalla and to the Wamungo country. The perceptible effect upon that circle of bronze figures was a scarcely audible grunt, yet nevertheless the message was like unto a live ember dropped in the dry grass of the cattle country.

That morning one of the renegade chiefs had brought in two others to make their allegiance and received as reward for his fidelity a remittance of one-third of the tax levy upon his property, a policy adopted by zu Pfeiffer calculated to encourage the recruiting of his followers by establishing a reputation for lavish generosity to those who obeyed him, in contrast to his merciless severity to the recalcitrant ones.

An hour later MYalu was summoned from the sweating throng squatted before the line of demon keepers through the giant ebon guards to audience with the Son-of-the-Earthquake. At the entrance as bidden he knelt, for he knew that he would be compelled did he refuse. A white flame was in his heart, but yet the magnificence of the son of the World Trembler and his satellites, the terrible ghosts of the distant white god, with amulets and charms upon his breast, had awed and subdued MYalu. Then came the voice of Sakamata relating that the chief MYalu, son of MBusa, made complaint to the Son-of-the-Earthquake that his slaves, the keepers of the coughing demons, had taken a girl named Bakuma, daughter of Bakala, and that he craved restitution of his property. While this was being translated by the corporal interpreter, MYalu watched the magic flame in the mouth of Eyes-in-the-hands, marvelling greatly at the smoke which emerged. Then said the interpreter:

"The son of the Lord-of-the-World, the Earthquake, the World Trembler who eats up whom he pleases, whose eyes see all things, whose sword slays all things, whose breath is the rain, whose voice is the thunder, whose teeth are the lightning, whose frown is the earthquake, whose smile is the sun, whose ear is the moon, whose eyes are the stars, whose body is the world, saith that when the son of MBusa (MYalu) bringeth three chiefs of the same rank to sit at the Feet then shall the daughter of Bakala return unto him, but in the meantime shall her girdle remain untied. He hath spoken!"

As he finished zu Pfeiffer made the signal of dismissal with his jewelled hand, but MYalu with the throb of that distant drum in his ears, cried out in protest, saying:

"The words of the Son-of-the-Earthquake are like unto spears made of grass!"

The interpreter boggled at the translation of the sentence. Zu Pfeiffer saw a ripple of insubordination. He rapped out an order to have the man taken away and given fifty lashes. Instantly the guards surrounded MYalu, who submitted in sudden misgiving, and led him away to receive the punishment.

Zu Pfeiffer gave orders that the girl Bakuma should be found and called the next case, Kalomato the elderly chief who had had all his property sequestered until he should deliver his eldest son as hostage. He was a slight withered old man with a white tuft of beard and at the hands of the askaris, after considerable endurance, had screamed his submission. Now he hobbled into zu Pfeiffer's presence with the aid of a stick. Pompously the interpreter recited the list of the titles of the august one, and then dwelt upon the wondrous benefits to be obtained at the magic jewelled hands, and demanded that the old chief "eat the dust" and obey the royal mandate.

But the sharp eyes gazed steadily from their wrinkled sockets with a curious gleam in them as he mumbled that "his soul had wandered" (he had dreamed) "and had met the spirit of Tarum, who had forbidden him to obey the white god."

"The shenzie" (savage—used contemptuously) "longs for more fire for his paws, O Bwana," translated the interpreter into Kiswahili.

"What does he say?" demanded zu Pfeiffer.

"He says, Bwana, that he hath dreamed that his god hath told him that he must not obey you. Indio, Bwana."

"Tell him that I slew his god, as every man knows."

"The Son-of-the-Earthquake bids thee to know that he hath eaten up thy god as he eateth up thy warriors when his wrath is aroused. Eat dust that thy beard grow yet longer; stretch thy tongue and thou shalt be eaten entirely and all that is thine!"

"The Fire is lighted," mumbled the old man.

"What does he say?" demanded zu Pfeiffer sharply.

"He attempts to make magic against thee, Bwana," replied the interpreter who knew not the meaning of the phrase.

"Take away the animal," commanded zu Pfeiffer.

The old man was accordingly led out to the further attentions of the soldiery. But during that afternoon zu Pfeiffer became conscious of a subtle air of defiance, a restlessness and exchanging of glances, so that the demon which Bakunjala had once seen so vividly came back to roost somewhere beneath the immaculate uniform.

Neither he nor his sergeants nor their men could speak the Wongolo tongue fluently, so that for interpreter he was compelled to employ one of the corporals. To employ any newly subjected race or tribe as soldiers or in any responsible capacity is unwise, for ties of blood are liable to lead to treachery; to trust to the idiosyncrasies and personal values of any native interpreter is equally impolitic. Zu Pfeiffer and his party were as unaware of the meaning of the phrases exchanged as they were of the message in the throbbing of that distant drum. Between the conqueror and the subjected tribe was a wall denser than any steel; the same wall of tabu of the craft that Birnier was finding so difficult to penetrate.

Every attempt to persuade any of the witch-doctors to disclose the secrets of their craft through the interpreter was doomed to failure; even had zu Pfeiffer been able to speak the dialect as well as Birnier he would never have accomplished it. Yet he tried the impossible. The answer was invariably a mask of ox-like stupidity or the retort that he, being a mighty magician, must needs know that he did but "tickle their feet"! At length, irritated by this persistence, he had Sakamata put to the torture and had for his pains a story in which the idol as the first man was the father of the tribe whom the people believed to have been eaten up literally, so that the conqueror had become the father of the people, having the idol inside him, and the chance that the tale had a faint resemblance to an account by a Frenchman of the superstitions of a West African tribe, convinced him. Implicitly he believed the ingenious yarn invented by a wily witch-doctor to save his hide and the perquisites of his job by placating the white man, the trap into which most white chroniclers have fallen. This conviction, which flattered his sagacity and lulled any suspicions, strengthened his arm in the delivering of punishment and reward.

CHAPTER 25

In the camp of Bakahenzie was the low mutter of the drums by day and night. The village had straggled farther through the forest in each direction save that of the sacred enclosure. Already were some five hundred warriors there and more were pouring in every day. Busy were Bakahenzie and wizards, great and small, in the preparing of amulets of the hearts of lions, livers of leopards and galls of birds, and the brewing of potent decoctions to be smeared with parrot feathers upon the warriors old and young against the evil eye and the spirits of the night. And dispensed by Bakahenzie and Marufa, from whom had come the original idea, was a special and rather expensive charm against the coughing monsters, which was made by, and invested with, the magic of the King-God himself, a can key. That morning had there been a special meeting of the craft and the chiefs before the sacred enclosure, where they had looked upon the sacred form of the King-God and heard the magic elephant's ear give them instructions and a prophecy. Around and about a hundred fires, flickering mystically in the moist cavern of the forest, shuffled and chanted the warriors invoking the aid of Tarum, the spirit of their ancestors.

On the threshold of his hut squatted a sullen Zalu Zako. He had discovered that he had escaped from the river bearing him to the pool of celibacy to find that the bird had been captured by another. Although he had known that before attaining his desire he would have had to extricate Bakuma from the net of the tabu, yet, lover-like and human, that task unconsidered had seemed as easy as stalking a buck in a wood. But the joy of his own release had been dissipated as a cloud of dust by a shower by the news of MYalu's abduction of the girl and his desertion. Zalu Zako was so obsessed by chagrin at this wholly unexpected appearance of a rival that he was inclined to regret that he had ever thought of the move by which he could escape his late doom and rescue Bakuma at the same time. The illusion of nearness to the desired object had served naturally to whet his appetite; the balked love motive dominated him almost to the exclusion of political affairs. What his official status was now that all precedent had been broken Bakahenzie did not know and had not decided, and Zalu Zako cared less.

Though his faith in most of the tribal theology was unshaken, he did not believe in the sanctity, or the necessity, of the marriage of the Bride of the Banana, because he had a defensive complex of desire for her that inhibited that belief. Towards MYalu, Zalu Zako's natural reaction was revenge. The matter was how to accomplish that end. To reveal to Bakahenzie that he was the lover of Bakuma would be tantamount to admitting sacrilege in having a passion for the Bride of the Banana.

As Zalu Zako was unable to get at the person of his rival the most logical method to his mind was by witchcraft. To obtain some relics of the body of MYalu proved easy, as his wives and slaves being forced to flee, had been unable to burn the deserted hut, thus leaving in the customary place in the thatch some of the hair and nail clippings. Also to find an excuse for the cursing of MYalu was still easier. So at a meeting of the chiefs he rivalled Bakahenzie in denunciation of the absconding chief, insisted that a mighty magic be made against him and produced the necessary corporeal parts upon which to work. So it was that Bakahenzie and Marufa, a quiet watchful Marufa, brewed the magic brew and condemned MYalu by the proxy of his nail clippings to die, a process that took root in a very firm conviction in the mind of Zalu Zako and the others that die MYalu would.

After this satisfaction of the first fierce instinct Zalu Zako was more at liberty to consider other matters, which resulted in an effort to quicken the collective will to recover the tribe's country and possessions, symbolised in Zalu Zako's mind by the delicate figure of Bakuma.

The ceremony of the lighting of the new fires he had attended perfunctorily. To have regret or pity for the white man, Moonspirit who had taken over his doom, never occurred to Zalu Zako, for to him as to Bakahenzie Moonspirit was a mighty magician who, if competent to effect the magic he had already displayed, was capable of looking after himself; moreover, as he had recalled the Unmentionable One, he stood as the incarnation of the tribe, the god, therefore beyond human consideration.

Bakahenzie's chief regard was, of course, to unify the tribe once more and to rouse those who had submitted to Eyes-in-the-hands to rebellion, which was but a projection of his desire, as that of all patriots, to consolidate his own position and to regain his lost prestige. He had had no need to command that the news be sent abroad. At the ceremony of the Lighting of the Fires the drum notes had been picked up by the nearest village and sent ricocheting across the length and breadth of the country, rippling through the Court of the Son-of-the-Earthquake.

Bakahenzie's confidence had increased tenfold since, by his clever coup, he had locked up the white magician in the godhead. He believed that Moonspirit was the mightiest magician the world had ever seen, a demi-god; for had he, Bakahenzie, not seen these wondrous miracles with his own eyes? Had not he, Bakahenzie, captured and tamed this marvellous power to his own ends?

So absolute was this confidence in the powers of the white that Bakahenzie was perfectly sincere, as Mungongo and Bakuma had been, in asserting that the "son of the Lord-of-many-Lands" was pleased to pretend that "an elephant was a mouse," that he "tickled their feet." The only doubt raised in his mind at that interview was whether he could persuade this powerful being to destroy the usurper "out of hand," as it were, or even whether Moonspirit could do so; for it was quite reasonable to him to suppose that even a god, in fighting another god, might have to do battle for the victory.

Not in spite of, but because of, this firm faith Bakahenzie took more precautions than ever before to surround the captured god with the toughest fibres of the tabu to keep him in isolation. Obviously such a valuable prize demanded special precautions. He promulgated an ordinance, in the amplitude of his regained power, that no lay man nor any wizard save the inner cult, whom he dared not forbid, were to approach within sight of the sacred enclosure. In the jungle of his mind lurked the fear that the new god might be seen to leave the sacred ground and thus render the penalty of death imperative according to the laws of the tabu upon a god who jeopardised the tribal welfare as MFunya MPopo had done by his failure to bring rain. The belief that he could control a force which he admitted was infinitely greater than he, and of punishing it if it did not behave, was not at all inconsistent to the native mind, nor more illogical than many theological ideas of whites.

At the last interview Bakahenzie had tried to persuade

Birnier to permit him to speak into the mighty ear of the magic box; in effect an attempt to gain complete control. But Birnier, when he at length had realised that Bakahenzie's mental development was little greater than Mungongo's, and keenly aware of the isolation to which he was to be subjected, as well as the purpose in the witch-doctor's mind, had resolutely refused. Bakahenzie had accepted the intimation that the god would not work miracles through any other mouth than that of his incarnation, and after a long cogitative silence had departed without further comment.

But of course he came back again next day, as Birnier had known that he would. Birnier hinted at the expected initiation into the "mysteries" of the craft, particularly of the Festival of the Banana and the other ceremonies connected with his role as King-God. But Bakahenzie's gaze, fixed upon an object on the toilet table, did not quiver. Birnier repeated the inquiry more bluntly. Said Bakahenzie:

"The fingers of the son of Maliko are hungry to touch the magic knife of the son of the Lord-of-many-Lands."

"Damn it," muttered Birnier. "That's my favourite!" But he handed the razor to Bakahenzie, saying: "Is not the porridge pot free to all brothers?" Gravely Bakahenzie slipped the safety razor into his loin cloth, mumbled the orthodox adieu and departed.

Although devoted to Birnier as much as ever, Mungongo was bound just as much by the articles of the tabu as any other native; in fact, since his appointment to the high office of Keeper of the Fires, he was if possible more terrified by the bogies of their theology than before. Put one foot out of the sacred ground he would not, for he was convinced that immediately he did so, the ghosts of the dead kings would instantly strangle him. Birnier attempted to persuade him to get into communication with Marufa, but that wily gentle-man, grieving over the failure of the coup he had aided Birnier to make, and for the moment completely under the domination of Bakahenzie, who, he knew, had him watched every moment of the day and night, would never approach the Place of the Unmentionable One. Nor dared Zalu Zako break the tabu placed by Bakahenzie. To Bakahenzie and not to Birnier he owed his escape from the dreaded godhood. One who had released him might quite reasonably have him back again if annoyed. The few wizards who came to gaze at the imprisoned god like children at the Zoo, as Birnier had commented, were deaf to any remark, instruction, or plea of the Holy One. So it was that Birnier began to realise that the functions of a god were so very purely divine that he would never be allowed to interfere in human affairs at all except by grace of the high priest, and possibly he was not the first god who had found that out.

This jungle of secrecy and the denial of any active part in the organising of the tribe began to irritate Birnier. Yet he perceived clearly enough from his knowledge of the native mind that a premature effort to force either confidence or action would end in disaster. Patience and perseverance alone would bring success; and the moulding of the material through forces which already controlled it. He must play the witch-doctor to the full. Working upon this hypothesis he determined to control Bakahenzie through "messages" from the spirit of Tarum. The trouble was to find out whether Bakahenzie would obey him or not and to what extent.

So in the early hours of one morning Bakahenzie's watchers in the forest shuddered as they heard more of the mysterious voices of the Unmentionable One making wondrous magic within the temple as Mungongo chanted, at Birnier's prompting, the god's instructions to his high priest and people. The form of the chant was not correct as Mungongo's memory was very unreliable, but as Birnier remarked to the portrait of Lucille, "I don't suppose Maestro Bakahenzie is such a stylist as he would have the public suppose." Afterwards, to Mungongo's delight, who was never tired of any manifestation of Moonspirit's magic, he put out the light and lay upon his bed within the temple listening to the voice of Lucille pouring out the passion of "Mon coeur s'ouvre a ta voix," in *Samson et Delilah*, to the sleepy ears of the monkeys above the figure of the idol limned against the moon-patterned roof of the forest.

But scarcely had the moist ultramarine shadows turned to mauve than the voice of Bakahenzie hailed the god most punctiliously from without. However Birnier happened to be sleepy, and the chance of the early hour presented such an opportunity to gain prestige that he sent the Keeper of the Fires to inform the High Priest that the god was not yet up and that he must needs wait. And wait did Bakahenzie, like unto a graven image at the gate until the sun was four hand's-spans above the trees. When Birnier had breakfasted upon broiled kid, eggs, banana and weak tea, Bakahenzie was summoned to the august presence.

Wondering what new idea Bakahenzie had gotten into his head Birnier solemnly talked the usual preliminaries, intending to announce in the best manner that Tarum had a message for the son of Maliko; but to his astonishment Bakahenzie forestalled him by demanding to know when the god would speak again.

When Mungongo had gravely placed the machine at his feet Birnier set the record. The chant bade the son of Maliko to summon the wizards and the warriors of the tribe to the abode of the Unmentionable One; to send to those who had fallen into the power of Eyes-in-the-hands instructions that they were not to reveal by word or deed that the

Unmentionable One had been pleased to return, but to wait like a wild cat at a fish pool until a signal was given through the drums, when they were to smite swiftly at every keeper of the demons and to flee immediately to their brethren in the forest; that they were on no account to kill or wound Eyes-in-the-hands nor any white man that was his, lest their powerful ghosts exact a terrible penalty and refuse to be propitiated; that when these things had been done would the spirit of Tarum issue further instructions.

In composing this message Bernier had sought to gain the advantage of a surprise attack and to secure the massacre of as many of the askaris as possible; to save zu Pfeiffer and his white sergeants from the fate which would await them should they fall into the hands of the Wongolo; to minimise the loss of men which would occur were the tribe to attempt to face the guns; afterwards to lure zu Pfeiffer away from his fortifications and the open country, in order to compel him to fight in the forest where he could not ascertain what force was against him; and in the meantime to slip round and establish the idol in the Place of Kings, which act would consolidate the moral of the tribe as well as cut the line of zu Pfeiffer's communications with Ingonya.

As Bakahenzie listened gravely and attentively, Birnier keenly watched his face. Although the mask did not quiver, a half suppressed grunt at the end persuaded him that Bakahenzie was duly impressed, but he made no comment. After regarding Mungongo solemnly putting away the machine Bakahenzie remarked casually:

"In the village is a messenger from Eyes-in-the-hands who sends thee greetings."

This was the first news that Birnier had received since his ascent to the godhood. He had expected that sooner or later zu Pfeiffer would hear of the presence of a white man, but he was rather startled at the inference that zu Pfeiffer knew who he was. He made no visible sign as he waited. Bakahenzie took snuff interestedly and continued:

"Eyes-in-the-hands bids thee to go unto the Place of Kings to eat the dust before him."

Bakahenzie regarded him with keen eyes. Birnier considered swiftly. From the latter part of the message he gathered that zu Pfeiffer was not aware of his identity. His opinion of zu Pfeiffer's character suggested certain psychological possibilities. His policy was to lure him away from his fort; to destroy his military judgment. Therefore to cause him at this juncture to be violently disturbed by a personal emotion might tend to confuse his mind. Enmity—fear—might equally serve as the lure required. In spite of committing a breach of native etiquette Birnier could not resist smiling. He reached for the "Anatomy" and as he scribbled two words he said to Bakahenzie solemnly:

"O son of Maliko, say unto this man of many tongues as well as many eyes, 'that the jackal follows the lion that he may feed upon his leavings; that the voice of the hyena is loudest when he eateth offal.' And shall the slave take unto him that which is mighty magic, such magic that when Eyes-in-the-hands doth but touch it shall he trumpet like unto a wounded cow elephant. Bid him to mark that my words be white!"

And when Bakahenzie had gone Birnier turned to the portrait on the wall and remarked as he indulged in the luxury of a grin: "Say, honey, but if that doesn't make him mad, I'll—I'll eat my own manuscripts!"

CHAPTER 26

In a corner of one of the half-completed huts in a half-completed street of the new village of the Place of Kings squatted Yabolo and other chiefs. As Sakamata was up in the fort serving Eyes-in-the-hands they could talk freely, yet in low tones and with wary eyes for the interstices of the unfinished wall. More than one chief had been thrashed but none as high in rank as MYalu; moreover, those that had been severely punished had been taken in fair fight or had attempted to escape, whereas MYalu had done nothing that they considered to merit punishment. The growing detestation and hatred smouldering within all of them against the new ruler had burst into flame at the first hint of the news vibrating upon the moist air. Later had come another drum message bidding them await new words of Tarum, and forty-eight hours afterwards the messenger sent by zu Pfeiffer to summon Moonspirit, who squatted in the group, whispered word for word Birnier's message on the phonograph, adding further instructions from Bakahenzie that the signal should be another message upon the drums: "The Fire is lighted."

Warm banana wrapped in leaves, which a slave had brought in, was placed before the chiefs while the messenger related the gossip of the village in the forest. Later, while lolling through the mid-day heat waiting for the time of audience, he produced from his loin cloth the magic charm which the son

Charles Beadle

of the Lord-of-many-Lands, the King-God, had sent to Eyes-in-the-hands and repeated the prophecy that he should trumpet like unto a wounded cow elephant, eliciting many grunts of admiration and awe. Then he inquired for Sakamata and MYalu, and upon hearing the account, reported that they were both traitors and had been condemned to die by the magic of Bakahenzie and Marufa.

Each and every chief felt that he had been betrayed by Sakamata. Even Yabolo, his relative, particularly because his visionary schemes had come to nought, was against Sakamata. Sakamata had heard the message of the drums, "The Fire is lighted." But of the details of the return of the Unmentionable One and of the new King-God he knew nothing, although every other Wongolo man, woman, and child, knew it. The terror of the tabu, of the power of the Unmentionable One, was more overwhelming than his fear of Eyes-in-the-hands, wizard and ex-member of the inner cult though he be. The Unmentionable One had returned, a miracle! In a thousand signs of birds and beasts, twigs and shadows, Sakamata saw omens of evil. He knew that he was an outcast, that his fellows were plotting; that they knew something that he did not; yet he dared not tell Eyes-in-the-hands lest he be killed on the instant, not by Eyes-in-the-hands but by the mystic power of the Unmentionable One.

Farther down the line, in a small hut, lay MYalu motionless. His mind was a whirling red spot of rage and pain, obliterating the image of Bakuma, his ivory, and everything. From the base of the spine to his neck he was criss-crossed with bloody weals administered with a kiboko (whip of hippopotamus hide) by one of the black giants who formed the door guard at the tent of Eyes-in-the-hands. More stimulating to his anger even than the excessive pain was the indignity, that he, MYalu, son of MBusa, a chief, had been flogged like a slave before all men! Could he have gotten free he would have leaped upon zu Pfeiffer, god or no, and torn him to pieces with hands and teeth. But he could scarcely move. Never had such an act been conceived by MYalu. The native dignity and reserve was shattered. He lay upon his belly and glared with the eyes of a maddened and tortured animal.

The yellow glare in the open doorway was darkened, but MYalu did not stir. The figure of Yabolo, a short throwing sword in hand, moved towards him and squatted down, muttering greetings. MYalu made no response. Yabolo repeated the message from the spirit of Tarum.

"Let thy spear be made sharp, O son of MBusa, that we may make the jackal who would command the lion to eat offal!" MYalu grunted. "The son of Bayakala saith that it will be soon, so that thou mayest yet eat of thy defiler ere thou art gone to ghostland." MYalu turned his head. "The son of MTungo and the son of Maliko," explained the old man, "have made magic upon the parts which thou didst foolishly leave within thy hut."

Again MYalu merely grunted and turned away his head. But that dread news had quenched the white flame of anger. The spirits were wroth; even had they caused him to eat the dust before all men. Conviction in the efficacy of the magic for which he would have bought Marufa to make against Zalu Zako was as absolute as his faith in the death magic made against him by the two powerful witch-doctors, and intensified by the miraculous return of the Unmentionable One against whom he had committed sacrilege. He recollected the cry of the Baroto bird on the night on which he had kidnapped the Bride of the Banana. The spirit of Tarum was wroth. The mighty new King-God of the Unmentionable One was about to eat up all the enemies of the land. MYalu was convinced that he was doomed; certain that Yabolo knew that he was doomed; that every man knew that he was doomed.

For ten minutes the figures, squatting and lying, remained as motionless as bronzes. Then MYalu rose to his knees and said calmly: "Give me thy sword, O son of Zingala."

Silently Yabolo handed him the sword which MYalu placed beneath him and laid down again. So quietly he died.

From the sacred hill blared the harsh cry of the yellow bird, as the natives called the trumpet, announcing that the august presence was in audience. But instead of the usual crowd of immobile figures squatted almost under the shadow of the pom-pom within the gate of the fort, sat only the messenger. Sakamata, knowing that something portended and yet not exactly what, was so scared that his skinny limbs quivered as if with an ague. Although he desired to warn Eyes-in-the-hands in order to save himself, he dared not attempt to do so lest the august one visit his anger upon his person; vague ideas of redeeming his treachery by delivering Eyes-in-the-hands over to his countrymen were stoppered by terror of the wrath of the Unmentionable One.

So it was that the pomp of the Son-of-the-Earthquake and the glory of the soul of the World-Trembler with many charms upon his breast was reserved for the humble messenger who entered escorted by Sakamata. After bowing in the prescribed manner the messenger squatted at zu Pfeiffer's feet and addressed himself to the corporal interpreter.

"The son of the Lord-of-many-lands, that is the King-God of the One-not-to-be-mentioned, sends greeting to the son of the World-Trembler, called Eyes-in-the-hands, and this message: 'Say unto the man of many tongues as well as many eyes that the jackal follows the lion that he may feed on the leavings; the voice of the hyena is loudest when he eateth offal!'"

"What does the animal say?" demanded zu Pfeiffer, impatient of the native preamble.

"He says, Bwana," said the interpreter, "that the white man is sick and cannot move, but that he will come as soon as he is well."

From the folds of his loin cloth the messenger was dutifully extracting something wrapped up in a banana leaf, which he handed to the interpreter as he finished the message:

"And by his slave he sendeth that which is mighty magic; such magic that he who toucheth it shall trumpet like unto a wounded cow elephant."

"He says, Bwana," continued the interpreter glibly, "that he sends to the mighty Eater-of-Men a small present," and with the words the corporal guilelessly proffered the small package. Zu Pfeiffer took it and tore off the covering...

Then was the magic of the new King-god of the Unmentionable One made manifest to all men, and particularly a group of chiefs hiding in a small thicket beneath the hill, for indeed did the Son-of-the-Earthquake trumpet like unto a wounded cow elephant at the sight of an ivory disc on which was written:

"Amantes—Amentes!"

CHAPTER 27

All day at Fort Eitel had been stir and bustle, the blare of
trumpets and the barking of sergeants, white and black. Long
lines of women and slaves streamed in from the surrounding
countryside bearing loads of corn and bananas. In the half-
made parade ground at the foot of the hill of Kawa Kendi,
half a company of Wongolo whom zu Pfeiffer had
conscripted from the chiefs, stumbled and ran in awkward
squads. In the hut of the Wongolo chiefs squatted Yabolo
among the rest, silently observing the preparations for the
punitive expedition which Sakamata had informed them was
being prepared in response to the insolent challenge of the
white man who had allied himself with the "rebels." But over
them, as well as every Wongolo in and about the place, was
a sullen air not of defiance but of expectant listening.

In the mess hut a nervous Bakunjala prepared the table for
dinner, the whites of his eyes rolling at every sound of zu
Pfeiffer's voice from the marquee adjoining. Never in his
experience, nor in that of other servants or soldiers, had the
demon so utterly possessed the dread Eater-of-Men as since
the receipt of some terrible magic sent to him by the white
man. Opinion was divided as to whether this white man was
the one who had been arrested and sent to the coast with
Corporal Inyira or whether he was a brother; some said that
the magic leaf which the messenger had brought was the soul

of the white man, others maintained that it was the incarnation of Bakra, which explained why the Eater-of-Men was so entirely possessed. Had he not screamed? they demanded, which clearly proved, as everybody knew, the dreadful agony as the ghost entered into the body.

Even the white sergeants were frightened of their chief. They had been seen talking together secretly, doubtless discussing what medicine they could give him to exorcise the demon. Had he not been commanded by this demon to leave the safety of the fort where they had the guns on the hills, and to go into the forest where, as anybody knew, their eyes would be taken from them so that they could not see to kill the dogs of Wongolo? They were all conscious, native-like, that something was brewing among the Wongolo, but what it was exactly they did not know. Two men had had fifty lashes that morning because they had not saluted the totem—flag— correctly; and a Wongolo chief had been shot because he had not brought in the amount of ivory commanded. None dared to warn the Eater-of-Men. Some one had said that the "leaf" was the soul of the idol come to lead the Eater-of-Men to destruction. This idea took deep root among the Wunyamwezi soldiers, for although they had delighted in the slaughter and rapine under the leadership of the Eater-of-Men, yet always had there been an uneasy feeling of sacrilege in destroying an idol.

In the half of the marquee reserved for the Kommandant's private quarters sat zu Pfeiffer in his camp chair with the inevitable stinger at his elbow. Erect by the door stood Sergeant Schultz taking details for the disposition of stores and troops during the absence of the punitive expedition. Never had he in four years' service seen the lieutenant as he was now. Although Schultz could speak Kiswahili fluently he knew no word of Munyamwezi, else he might have been disposed to agree with Bakunjala and his friends. As it was he thought that the Herr Lieutenant had gotten a touch of the sun or was drinking too heavily or perhaps a bit of both; for to his mind the act of dividing up their scanty forces and leaving their fortified positions to enter the forest, with no chance of keeping open the line of communication, appeared to be military suicide.

He deemed it his duty to bring this point of view to his Kommandant's notice, but he was uncomfortably aware of zu Pfeiffer's headstrong character.

"What time does the moon set, sergeant?" demanded zu Pfeiffer.

"About three, Excellence."

"Good. Then at five precisely the column will move. Warn Sergeant Schneider."

"Ya, Excellence."

"You will transfer the remainder of your men and the Nordenfeldt as soon as we have gone."

"Ya, Excellence."

"That is all, sergeant."

Zu Pfeiffer dropped his head wearily on to his hand. Schultz remained rigidly by the door. Zu Pfeiffer glanced up peevishly.

"I said that was all, sergeant," he exclaimed tetchily.

"Ya, Excellence."

"Herr Gott, what are you standing there for like a stuffed pig?"

Schultz saluted.

"Excellence, it is my duty to remind your Excellence that according to regulation 47 of..."

"To hell with you and your regulations, damn you... Will you leave me alone!" The last was almost a plea.

"Excellence!"

Schultz saluted briskly and went. Again zu Pfeiffer's head dropped on to the cupped hand and he gazed at the portrait in the ivory frame... Against the blue twilight of the door appeared a tall figure in white.

"What in the name of—" began zu Pfeiffer.

"Chakula tayari, Bwana," announced Bakunjala timidly.

"I don't want any chakula," said zu Pfeiffer. "Wait. Bring some here."

"Bwana!"

Bakunjala fled, to reappear almost instantly with a covered plate, which he placed on the table as bidden and vanished. Zu Pfeiffer regarded distastefully his favourite dish of curried eggs. Then he bawled irritably:

"Lights, animal!"

"Bwana!" gasped Bakunjala appearing in the doorway with the lamp.

But zu Pfeiffer pushed the plate away to stare at the photograph of Lucille. The stare turned to a glare, and then as if mutinying against his god, as Kawa Kendi had done when summoning rain, he suddenly snatched at the frame and flung it upon the floor with an oath, grabbed up a fountain pen and began to write.

Indeed zu Pfeiffer was half insane with anger which he was disposed to vent upon Lucille by proxy as the source of yet another trouble and possibly official disgrace. He had not had a notion that Birnier could have survived the gentle hands of the corporal until without warning came that ivory disc with "Amantes—Amentes!" scribbled upon it, which not only inferred that Birnier had escaped, but that he was near to him and intended to champion these native dogs against the Imperial Government in the person of himself.

The message had been made the more insulting by the note of exclamation at the end implying derisive laughter. It had, as Birnier had calculated that it would, struck zu Pfeiffer upon the most tender spot in his mental anatomy, evoking a homicidal mania which dominated his consciousness. To be cheated, to be swindled, to be sworn at, cursed, even to be beaten was sufferable to a degree, but to be laughed at—zu Pfeiffer's haughty soul exploded like a bomb at an impact. For a time he had been absolutely incoherent with rage. His one impulse had been to rush out and tear Birnier limb from limb. Well might the listening natives believe in the mighty magic of the new King-God, that it should make the Son-of-the-Earthquake to trumpet like a wounded cow elephant!

Then out of the dissolving acrid smoke of wounded pride begin to loom arbitrary points. First, that Birnier would have complained, as he once had threatened to do, to Washington, which would infuriate the authorities in Berlin; and secondly, that he would have written to Lucille revealing the attempt he had made upon the life of her husband as well as the things he had said. How Birnier had escaped was immaterial, but the particular fate that awaited Corporal Inyira was decided but futilely; for the bold son of Banyala and his merry men were footing it to the south of lake Tanganika, scared by day lest the long arm of the Eater-of-Men should overtake them and haunted by the terror of seeing another illuminated ghost by night.

As the jewelled hand glittered in the lamp-light came the mutter of a distant drum on the moist darkness; zu Pfeiffer, abnormally irritable, raised his head, scowled, and muttering that he would have to issue an order to have the drums stopped, bent again to the uncongenial task of finishing the report due for headquarters before he left. The drum ceased; began again and was answered by another drum seemingly nearer at hand.

Five or ten minutes elapsed. As zu Pfeiffer took up a fresh sheet of paper a shot rang out followed instantly by yells. Zu Pfeiffer with an oath sprang to his feet, snatched at the revolver hanging above his camp bed and rushed out as a fusillade of shots mingled with wilder cries. The gruff coughs of the corporal in charge of the guard competed with the sharp barks of Sergeant Schultz. Zu Pfeiffer, bawling for a sergeant, ran to the great gate where the pom-pom was stationed. On the opposite hill red flashes of rifle fire darted downwards. Came another outburst of yelling. Forms of askaris scurrying to their places round the fence brushed by him on every side.

"Sergeant Schultz!" shouted zu Pfeiffer.

A figure in white appeared beside him in the darkness.

"Excellence!"

"Put the gun on them! Quick!"

At the bark of the sergeant the gun crew, already at their post, deftly manipulated the machine which coughed angry red bursts of flame into the darkness. The cries and howls ceased as suddenly as they had begun.

"Cease fire!" commanded zu Pfeiffer.

In the resulting stillness muttered shouts and cries from somewhere in the village below were punctuated by odd shots from the other hill.

"Sergeant Ludwig!" yelled zu Pfeiffer.

"Excellence!"

"Report!" snapped zu Pfeiffer.

"An unknown body of natives attacked and killed the sentry on the eastern gate, Excellence," came Sergeant Ludwig's voice from the gloom. "They entered and were repulsed according to instructions. That is all, Excellence."

"Losses?"

"None other, Excellence."

"What about the lower guards?"

"I do not know, Excellence."

"Take a platoon and investigate. We will cover you with the gun."

"Excellence."

The mutter of his orders was drowned in the excited jabber of the askaris.

"Didimalla!" came the dreaded voice of the Eater-of-Men. Instantly there was silence. "Report!" commanded zu Pfeiffer to Sergeant Schultz.

"A body of natives attacked upon the western gate, Excellence. They were repulsed."

"Losses?"

"Two men killed and three wounded."

"Ugm! Where's the interpreter?"

"Bwana!"

Cloth creaked as the man saluted in the dark.

"Where is Sakamata?" demanded zu Pfeiffer in Kiswahili.

"Here, Excellence," replied Sergeant Schultz. "He was running away. I had him arrested."

"Good. Bring the animal to my quarters."

"Excellence."

The sergeant and the interpreter, with a trembling Sakamata between them, followed zu Pfeiffer to the tent. As he entered he picked up the portrait in the ivory frame and replaced it carefully on the table and sat down.

"Ask the shenzie why he has not informed us of this attack?"

The interpreter put the question to the terrified old man who mumbled that he had not known anything about it.

"Ugm!" grunted zu Pfeiffer. "Send for a file of men, sergeant, and—No!" Zu Pfeiffer rose. "I'll get the truth out of him. Stand aside, corporal!"

The corporal obeyed with alacrity as jerking his revolver downwards zu Pfeiffer pulled the trigger. The shot took off two of Sakamata's smaller toes. The corporal grinned in appreciation. Zu Pfeiffer experienced a shadow of the pleasure he would have had in mutilating Birnier.

"Pull him up!" commanded zu Pfeiffer. "Now ask him again!"

For a moment or two Sakamata, scarcely conscious of any pain in his fright, could not comprehend what was said; at length he mumbled and muttered. The interpreter lowered his head to listen.

"Well?"

"He says, Bwana, that he does not know anything; that they will not tell him, but that he has heard that the god has come back."

"The god! What god?"

"The god which these shenzie (savages) had here before the Bwana came."

"The idol!" Zu Pfeiffer ripped out an oath. Then glaring questioningly at the shrunken figure on the floor considered.

"Tell him he lies. How does he know that the idol has come

back if they will not tell him anything?"

Again the interpreter jabbered at Sakamata who mumbled back.

"He says, Bwana, that his words are white. That they have not told him, but that he has heard the message of the drums. 'The Fire is lighted!'"

"What is that?"

"I don't know, Bwana."

"Ask him, you swine pig!"

"He says that whenever there is a new king that they call out those words, meaning that he is come."

"Ugm!" Zu Pfeiffer took out a cigar and lighted it as he considered. I believe the animal is right, he reflected. That swinehund American has done this! He turned sharply to Sergeant Schultz: "Post double guards; bring me Ludwig's report and take this thing away and have it shot."

"Excellence!"

The party went out. Zu Pfeiffer sat smoking fiercely. A single shot rang out. Presently came Sergeant Ludwig in person.

"I have to report, Excellence, that the investigation infers that the attack was only made with the purpose of freeing the sons of chiefs, for the picket has been slain but all the others are unhurt save three wounded."

Zu Pfeiffer swore mightily, but he dismissed the sergeant

with an admonition to have his troops ready for inspection at four-thirty. He drank a brandy neat and sat on, staring at the darkness. Then suddenly he exclaimed and wheeled to the abandoned report.

"This is an undeniable overt act," he muttered, seeing what he considered an opportunity to neutralise the suppositious complaint which Birnier had sent to Washington; and taking up his pen began a formal accusation against Birnier, as an American subject, for having violated the international laws of the Geneva Convention by aiding and abetting rebels of his Imperial Majesty.

CHAPTER 28

Sergeant Schultz's gloomy foreboding of the inevitable result attending the refusal to follow the teachings of his national preceptors was justified.

Zu Pfeiffer, crazed with wounded pride or magic, according to the white or black point of view, had held rigidly to his schedule; precisely at four-thirty he had inspected the expedition and marched at the first streak of dawn. Schultz removed to the other hill, leaving twenty-five men and a gun under a black sergeant. Afterwards he visited the village. The bodies of five of the picket were lying in the sun mutilated. Not a native of any sort was to be seen or heard. He sent out scouts. A village a couple of miles away was deserted too. He wished to burn the huts and plantation to clear the ground around the fort but he dared not do so without orders. Muttering to himself he returned and posted double sentries.

Throughout the day and the moonlight not a sound of a drum or the voice of a native disturbed the moist heat. He slept for a while and then took to pacing upon the levee outside the fort. He was aware of a restlessness among the men. About midnight a nervous sentry fired at a moving shadow in the village. Erratic shots followed; flickered and ceased at the sergeant's angry order. The trees seemed to whisper mockingly. The sergeant decided that it must have been a prowling jackal or hyena; but the incident made him irritable.

In ordinary circumstances he would have posted picket sentries as provided by the regulations, but he could not spare any of his fifty men, for in the case of an attack they would never regain the fort. The moon sank as if reluctantly, seeming to hesitate upon the fringe of banana fronds at something that she alone could see. But the night creaked slowly on. Schultz knew that the favourite hour for an attack was just at the first glimmer of dawn when the spirits are making for their homes and the light is deceptive.

He was standing in front of the Nordenfeldt when a sentry's keener ears caught a peculiar whispering rustle. As Schultz turned his head to listen, the whisper grew in volume to the sound of a hail-storm—the patter of bare feet on sand. Faint light on spears rippled round the base of the hills. Schultz sprang inside the barrier barking at his men to open fire. He deflected the muzzle of his gun and began pumping nickel into the advancing mass of yelling figures...

The rush carried the fort; for the defenders were out-numbered by fifty to one. Schultz fell under a dozen spear thrusts. The askaris were massacred to a man before the sun rose inquiringly beyond the sacred hill of Kawa Kendi.

When all the bloody acts of war were done and the triumphant yelling quietened, there came from across the river a pulsing trickle of sound in the sizzling heat, which was answered by a thundering crash of spear against shield and the "Ough! Ough!" of three thousand warriors gathered upon the hill to do homage to the Unmentionable One.

Across the river, at the ford where Bakuma had sung her swan song, came the procession led by the craft in full panoply. In the van stalked Bakahenzie, grave and solemn as befitted the high priest. Around him capered with untiring energy a group of lesser wizards whose duties were as those of professional dancers, having dried bladders and magic beads fastened to their ankles and wrists. Then behind Marufa a litter was borne by sacred slaves doomed to perish after performing their holy office, in which, swathed entirely from the public gaze, was Usakuma, the Incarnation of the Unmentionable One. In another litter, as securely screened, was the son of the Lord-of-many-Lands, endeavouring to endure a perpetual bath of sweat in the sacred cause, peeking professorial eyes through the interstices, scribbling in a notebook. Behind again marched Mungongo bearing a smouldering brand of the Sacred Fire; then Yabolo, reinstated in office for a reason that any politician will understand. After him came more litters bearing the magic "things" of the Incarnation of an Incarnation, the King-God.

As they splashed across the river, like troops of bronze gazelle, women and girls dashed eager to gather of fertility from the water enchanted by the passage of the Bearer of the World.

So they came through the banana plantation and up the wide street which the Son-of-the-Earthquake had planned. The chant quavered like a dragonfly in the sun and the chorus of the warriors replied with the rhythm and the profundity of gargantuan frogs. Then as Bakahenzie stepped upon the incline of the hill, burst from the women the cricket song which is made tremolo by the rapid beating of the fingers upon the lips, as from the drums went out the message over the land that the Unmentionable One had indeed returned to the Place of Kings, the City of the Snake.

Ten minutes later a half-stewed god, as exhausted as any emperor after a state parade, was permitted to emerge from the litter and to recuperate within the cool of the unfinished house that was to have been the bungalow of the Kommandant. No one else save the Keeper of the Fires, Bakahenzie and Marufa, were within the stockade which ringed the fort. Outside rose the mutter and rumble of the warriors and the cries of the women. The huddled lines of huts which had been barracks were already in process of demolition at the hands of the slaves, and the square within the fort was cleared of the slain askaris by the simple process of heaving the bodies over the palisade. The idol remained within the litter until the consecrating of the defiled ground should be performed by Bakahenzie and the craft.

No Wongolo nor any wizard, not even Bakahenzie, would touch the enchanted coughing monsters; but as the holy slaves were already doomed they were set to pull and to push the Nordenfeldt from the embrasure beside the entrance across the levee until it toppled over and rolled half-way down the hill, where it was allowed to stay, surrounded from morning to night by a crowd of women and children and idle warriors.

The thirst which afflicted Birnier rendered him oblivious of his godhood and of the sacred office of Mungongo who was dutifully busy upon his knees blowing up the sacred fires from the ember which he had carried; so that at a summons to bring water he was both embarrassed and awed, for the presence of the High Priest intensified his natural terror of breaking any of the meshes of the tabu. At the second imperative demand Bakahenzie soothed the angry god by commanding a slave to run to fetch water from without. But even then Birnier had the parched felicity of waiting while the High Priest solemnly exorcised the gourd of water which, as all food, could not be permitted to pass the lips of the King-God without the prescribed incantations.

However, within quite a reasonable time the sacred prisoner was accommodated with the possession of his goods, magic and culinary. The bungalow of the Kommandant, Birnier gathered, was to be converted into the temple after the ceremony of purification, and the idol was to stand in front in the place occupied by its predecessor at the coronation of the late Kawa Kendi.

All that day were Bakahenzie and Marufa and the wizards working hard at the various ceremonies of purification of those who had slain, the consecration of the Holy Hill, and the exorcising of the evil spirits attached thereto by the residence of the Son-of-the-Earthquake. Meanwhile Birnier and Mungongo were left to themselves within the enclosure to listen to the chanting and thrumming of the drums. Birnier had much to do in compiling his notes and reflections; Mungongo nothing save to prepare their meals and attend the Sacred Fires.

Exactly what had happened Birnier did not know and could not extract from Bakahenzie, who adopted his usual effective method of ignoring every direct question. Before they had left the place in the forest he had informed Birnier that the commands of the spirit of Tarum through the magic ear had been performed, but with what restrictions, modifications, or embroideries, Birnier had no means of ascertaining. His definite knowledge was that Zalu Zako, together with other chiefs and a vast crowd of warriors, were to remain in the forest where zu Pfeiffer was to be led into ambush by the power of the magic which he had sent, the American flag, an idea which certainly tickled Birnier's sense of humour considerably, particularly as it appealed to him, if successful, as an ideal case of poetic justice.

That zu Pfeiffer's fort had fallen was obvious, although what the disposition of his forces had been and of how the assault had been carried, Birnier had no idea. But of one thing he was reasonably sure, and that was that his analysis of zu Pfeiffer's reactions and the psychological effect upon the natives of having the idol reinstated in the Place of Kings, had been entirely correct. After all, as he admitted with a smile, zu Pfeiffer's system of native psychology had been based on the same fundamental principles as his own except that he had not reckoned with the unknown quantity, the equal intelligence working against him and able to discount his moves, plus heavier artillery in the form of an emotional broadside, the possibility of which rather naturally had never occurred to him.

An item which worried Birnier was that he had no means, and could hope for none apparently, of discovering whether and to what extent his orders through the phonograph had been carried out regarding the treatment of the white men. Their fate at the hands of the Wongolo, particularly after the merciless massacres inflicted by zu Pfeiffer, would scarcely bear imagining. From the fact of the instant and apparently easy success of the assault on the forts, he did not doubt that zu Pfeiffer, who had been foolish enough to be lured into dividing his forces, was doomed to defeat. In this instance he would not have any of the advantages of his triumphal entry into the country; would not be able to accomplish a surprise attack, and the weakening of the native moral by massacre and the downfall of the idol; in fact he had these very forces against him: for the success of their first venture, their overwhelming numbers in the forest, the exaltation of fanaticism excited by the restoration of their tribal god, practically tacked a label of suicide upon his military actions.

During that day Bakahenzie, evidently too busy with the duties of his office, did not come near to him. But that evening, in order to ensure as far as possible obedience to his orders through the mouth of the oracle, Birnier caused

Mungongo to chant further instructions into the phonograph commanding that the Son-of-the-Earthquake was to be brought alive to receive judgment from the Unmentionable One through the Incarnation, the son of the Lord-of-many-Lands. Whether this would work or not Birnier of course could not know. Already had he discovered that nobody could control the complicated machinery of the native tabu any more than any one statesman could manage always any vast political machine; indeed he, as many others, might more than conceivably be ground up by the gargantuan engine with whose starting lever he had played. All he could do had been done; nothing remained but to adopt Marufa's favourite maxim: "wait and see."

In the evening Mungongo, who had at length been persuaded to project his eyes beyond the sacred ground even if he would not his feet, reported that much chanting and drumming indicated that the warriors, or a great number of them, had departed, evidently to reinforce the troops of Zalu Zako or with the object of taking zu Pfeiffer in the rear: a fact which made Birnier a little uneasy lest the news of the fall of the station might bring zu Pfeiffer to his senses and cause him to return, in which case the position might prove to be somewhat uncomfortable.

However, the night passed to the soft thrumming of the drums. At dawn appeared Bakahenzie as solemnly as usual. He began by demanding that the "pod of the soul" of Tarum should be prepared to listen to him. Birnier observed a slight increase in the domineering manner and realized more keenly that unless he checked that tendency the worthy High Priest would become altogether unmanageable.

Birnier commanded Mungongo to bring forth the instrument and reproduced for Bakahenzie's benefit the oration of the previous night. Bakahenzie listened solemnly, grunted acquiescence, and again made his request. Birnier refused abruptly. Again Bakahenzie grunted acceptance which caused Birnier to speculate upon what move the wily doctor had in mind. However, after the usual starting of false trails, he announced that the consecration of the idol would take place that day and began to instruct the new god in his divine duties. That there was something unusual in the form, either exaggerated or curtailed, Birnier gathered from Bakahenzie's method of expounding the rites; and the solution came in the announcement, just before leaving, that as soon as the Son-of-the-Earthquake had been "eaten up," that he, Bakahenzie, would summon the craft and the people to the Harvest Festival.

The form of the statement again drew Birnier's attention to the fact that Bakahenzie was assuming the reins of power far too fast for his satisfaction; that unless he contrived to put on the curb he would never attain the goal of a beneficent agent nor be able to satisfy his professional curiosity.

However, when he had gone, Birnier began anew to question Mungongo regarding the reputed ceremonies of the festival, but beyond the fact that it was an occasion allied to the Christian-Pagan festival of a kind of thanksgiving for the harvest and sacrifice to the god which involved the ceremony of the marriage of the Bride of the Banana, Mungongo knew nothing.

In the afternoon Birnier was required to preside at the consecrating of the ground and the setting up of the idol. But all he had to do was to squat silently in front of the new temple and before Bakahenzie and the group of the cult, while the concourse of the other wizards and the few chiefs that were not away grunted a belly chorus upon the levee without. The ceremony was disappointing as ceremonies go, for beyond the stewing in the great calabash of a magic concoction with which to anoint the hole for the feet of the idol, the doorposts of the temple and the House of Fires, to the accompaniment of the usual chanting and drumming, it was ended by a dance, with Bakahenzie as the premier danseur.

After his evening meal of boiled chicken, goat flesh and milk, Birnier squatted in the doorway of his new quarters smoking. He had no lights as his store of carbide was finished. Before leaving for the forest to carve the Incarnation of the new Unmentionable One, he had had the forethought to despatch a messenger to a certain village on the great lake to intercept his carriers with goods and the mail for which he had sent after escaping from the noble son of Banyala; he had already informed Bakahenzie of the coming of a fresh stock of magic and impressed upon him that great precaution must be taken to ensure that it came directly to him, lest contact with strangers should offend the spirits. Bakahenzie had assented in his usual non-committal manner, a manner that was beginning to get upon Birnier's nerves.

As he smoked, staring up at the great moon over the sinister head of the idol framed in the green light, he observed that the day after the next would be the full moon, the Harvest Moon, the time of the yearly festival. Then, by a coincidence which sometimes seems to have a telepathic basis as explanation, he heard a curious soft sound from apparently behind the hut. Mungongo, squatting near his Sacred Fires in the immobile manner of the native, heard the sound too. Again a sibilant whisper, almost like the hiss of a snake, brought a "Clk" of astonishment to Mungongo's lips. He rose swiftly and disappeared behind the hut. Another muffled exclamation of astonishment aroused Birnier's curiosity. He followed, to find Mungongo leaning over the palisade as if speaking to some one.

"Ehh!" murmured a familiar voice. "'Tis Moonspirit!"

With a grunt of horror Mungongo turned upon Birnier and began to push him away, gasping: "She is accursed! If the evil of her eyes rest upon thee thou art sick unto death!"

"The devil take you!" muttered Birnier, angry at the touch of force; then recollecting that the tabu forbade alien eyes to gaze on his sacred body upon which the world depended, he realized that Mungongo was trying to save him. He held him off by the arms, saying: "Be quiet, thou fool! Hath not my magic shown thee that I am above all magic?"

Mungongo appeared to consider that there was some truth in the statement and at any rate it gave him something to think about. He stood passively but as if momentarily expecting Birnier, magic or no, to melt before his eyes. Bending over the fence Birnier saw the slender form of Bakuma crouched against the earth.

"What dost thou here, O little one?" he whispered, for of course he knew nothing of her fate after the abduction by M'Yalu.

So horror-struck at her own temerity in approaching the person of the King-God was she that she dared not raise her eyes as she stuttered:

"A demon hath driven the bird of my soul into the net of thy wrath."

"Still the black wings in thy breast, O Bakuma," said Birnier, trying to soothe the child. "Come thou within and show thy father thy bosom."

"Ehh! Ehh!" gasped Bakuma, quivering in greater panic

than ever.

Aware of the danger Birnier stooped, took her by the arms and lifted her over the palisade, remarking the violent trembling of the frail little body whose limbs seemed like candles.

"Come thou," said Birnier, moving towards the hut.

But she cowered where he had dumped her, covering her eyes with her hands so that she gazed not upon the sacred body. Mungongo stood like a tree, the whites of terrified eyes glimmering in the moonlight. Birnier picked up the girl and carried her into the hut, followed by a quaking Keeper of the Sacred Fires.

"Go, thou fool," commanded Birnier, "and watch that none approaches!" Mungongo gasped. But he obeyed. "Now, little one," continued Birnier, "bare thy bosom that I may know how to make the magic of healing."

Squatting on the threshold, her emaciated arms still covering her eyes, Bakuma strove to obey. At length she faltered out the story of her double abduction. The capture by the askaris had made but little difference to her, for, as she phrased it, the beak of her soul was like unto the mouth of the crocodile. Her captor had thrust her into a hut in the village together with some other female captives, but as the man had had to continue his military duties, night had fallen before he returned, by which time she had bribed some of the women, whose captivity was not as loathsome to them as the pride of their race should have made it, with a powerful charm which Birnier had given her, a nickel-plated razor-strop. She had escaped. But more fearful of her doom as the Bride of the Banana than she was of MYalu or the askaris, she had hidden in the forest, living upon wild fruit and roots. Then had she heard the drums announcing the return of the Unmentionable One, and aware that Moonspirit had gone into the forest to seek Him, had guessed that he was triumphant. Away in the jungle she had heard the sound of the rejoicing at the homecoming of the King-God; had hesitated, and at last she had come to Moonspirit, in spite of his divinity, in the fluttering hope of aid, driven by a demon to break another tabu, the same demon which urges so many to break magic circles—the subconscious love motive.

Poor kid! commented Birnier to himself as he regarded the pitiful cowering form. We haven't gotten the nuptial torches for you yet, but we will, by God!... Give me thine ear, O little one... But as he talked to her, soothing the terror by promises of mightier magic, came Mungongo crying in a terrified whisper that Bakahenzie was claiming audience. At the back of the next room of the bungalow, built upon a plan of the one in Ingonya, was a bathroom, and into that was Bakuma hurried and bidden to lie as quiet as a crocodile.

CHAPTER 29

Bakahenzie had come to announce that the certain magic "things," which a messenger had brought from the white man's country, had arrived. Although he could not expect an answer to his letter to Lucille in Europe, there might be others; and such an event as the receipt of a mail once in six months is apt to be exciting. Birnier forgot his role for the moment, leaped to his feet preparatory to rushing out to meet the runner, but a grunt from Bakahenzie and an alarmed cry from Mungongo were just in time to prevent him from jeopardizing the stability of the world and all that he had won by violating the tabu by stepping beyond the sacred ground. Other gods and emperors have indeed wrecked empires through a lesser aberration. Even realization of the penalty was scarcely enough to hobble his impatient legs, for the very suggestion of what the mail represented melted the fetters of this native world as wax in the sun.

Indeed more effort of will was required to return to his god-like throne upon the camp-bed, and to amble through the etiquette which discussion of such an important matter demanded, than to carry the idol on his back through the forest and bear the sound thrashing to boot. Then as a further test, Bakahenzie slowly developed a dictum that the magic things could not be permitted to enter the sacred enclosure until they had been disinfected from the multitude of evil

Charles Beadle

eyes through which they must have passed. At that the god came near to swearing or weeping, he did not know which.

But as he fumed inwardly he recollected that at any moment Zalu Zako and his troops might return; or if the battle had gone the other way, then zu Pfeiffer; in the former case the excitement would still further delay the goods and mail, and the latter event might entail the complete loss. As well as the growing irritation caused by Bakahenzie's interminable list of tabus was the necessity of proclaiming, or rather gaining, his authority before he could be of any assistance either to Bakuma, the white men or himself. Indeed he had been waiting the arrival of these goods to secure the subjection of Bakahenzie to his will. He determined that the trial should be now. Merely to demand would, he felt, arouse the obstinacy of the chief witch-doctor, who would never, unless compelled by force or cunning, give up the reins of power which to him was the *raison d'etre* of his life. Birnier must attack through the line of least resistance. With the carriers bearing the mail was a case of "imprisoned stars" (rockets) and a special cinema outfit, so that Birnier felt that he could afford to explode the last manifestation of magic which remained to him. After a judicious interval, he said to Bakahenzie:

"O son of Maliko, is not my tongue the tongue of the Unmentionable One?"

"He who knoweth all things knoweth that which is white," retorted Bakahenzie.

"Verily. Therefore do thou cause to be brought that which is come, that which the fingers of the Unmentionable One are hungry to touch. Thou knowest his power of magic. Therefore are the evil eyes of the multitude but dry leaves in the wind of his breath."

"Indeed thy words are white, O son of the Lord-of-many-Lands."

"Depart then that the hunger of His fingers may be appeased."

"The drums speak not yet of the eating up of Eyes-in-the-hands. Hath not the ear of the spirit of Tarum spoken upon these matters?" inquired Bakahenzie in his favourite dialectical manner.

"The spirit of Tarum hath naught to say to thee," replied Birnier, "but the fingers of Tarum will to make thee to itch even as his fingers."

Birnier called to Mungongo who brought and placed at his feet a fairly powerful electric battery. Bakahenzie eyed the box; curiosity was keenly awakened. He stared interestedly when Birnier raised the lid. Taking the handles he said:

"These, O son of Maliko, are the hands of Tarum made manifest. He wishes that thou shouldst feel the itch of his desire!" and with the words he clapped one handle to the belly and the other at the base of the spine of the chief witch-doctor. Bakahenzie convulsed as he was compelled to do. Swiftly Birnier applied the shock to the shoulders, holding the handles there as he remarked to a violently trembling Bakahenzie: "Behold! the itch of the fingers of Tarum!"

But as he lowered his hands towards the spine again, Bakahenzie moved rapidly and with no dignity.

Solemnly Birnier replaced the handles and closed the lid, and said quietly:

"Thou hast felt, O brother magician, that the fingers of

Tarum do itch indeed?"

"Truly!" responded Bakahenzie with a celerity as unusual as the quaver in his voice. "Indeed thy words are white, O mightiest of magicians. What are indeed the evil eyes of savages against the power of thy magic, O son of the Lord-of-many-Lands!"

And contrary to all precedent Bakahenzie rose and left. Within a quarter of an hour his voice announced that slaves with the magic "things" were without the palisade, and called upon Mungongo to go to the gate to fetch them as strangers were forbidden even to look upon the King-God. Birnier, by the light of a torch, opened the mail, sent a wad of letters and a sheaf of telegraph slips on to the floor, and snatched a long green envelope scrawled in French characters:

Monsieur le Curateur du Jardin des Plantes.

For a moment he stared at it perplexedly, for there was no stamp or cancellation.

"What in the name—" he muttered as he slit it open.

Entebbe,
Aout 13, 19—

Mon petit loup, what have you been doing? Ou est tu? Comment et pourquoi? Oh, I am cross with you, with Monsieur le Professeur! Why do you write me so ridiculous a letter? I laugh, but always I laugh, so what good is that to you? I will not reply to your letter, mon vieux—jamais. But I will tell you so that you may know why I am here. Yes, parmi les animaux!

Birnier winced at the phrase which seemed to come back at

him like a boomerang from the lips of zu Pfeiffer.

I am to go for vacation to Wiesbaden with some very terrible peoples. Oh, on me degoute! I have an engagement for the winter in Berlin as before. I have engagement for Paris—eh! but—pouf! Figure me on the charming *Mauretania* and I am sitting on the deck where you once made yourself so ridiculous. Rappelle toi? I am sick—No, mon vieux, pas du mal de mer! I should not be for everybody to look at. Oh, no! I am sick, I tell you. Je reve de mon petit coco parmi les sales animaux! Je me dis: Zut! il est fou! il est tape! Mais en moi meme je l'adore! Tout de suite I tell a creature who brings me my books, my fan, un espece de tapette, je m'en vais la, moi! He ask me where? I tell him I go to look for mon amant in Afrique Centrale! Mais oui! He thinks I am mad! I tell him so and I laugh! How I laugh. But he is right, yes, je suis folle—de toi!

Alors I come to Marseilles and I catch a boat to Mombassa. Ouf! Je vais mourir a cause de mon petit loup! La mer rouge! Quel cauchemar! Enfin I still arrive what of Lucille is left and I ask for you, for Monsieur le Professeur Americain, but no one knows you. On the boat I have attached to myself trois mousquetaires Anglais. Tous les trois sont droles! They bring me on the ever so funny little train to here. Entebbe. Les Anglais sont tres polis, tu sais! Monsieur le Gouverneur stop drinking whisky politely to tell me that Monsieur has been and has gone! Quelle horreur! You have gone but three days! Pense tu! I ask myself what have I done that the bon Dieu should be so unkind. Then quel malheur! I remember to myself that I commence to come to you on *Friday!* You laugh! Yes, I laugh too but—Quien sabe? I commence to come to you on a Friday and you are gone three little days!

Then my good friends, les trois mousquetaires, send for me a what they call a runner—the red peas—C'est drole! but the little pea black he did not find you. He brings a message that you had gone to some place with a terrible name.

Then come the two most ridiculous letters. I will *not* reply to any such ridiculous letters—jamais!

Birnier scowled. Two letters? he muttered. What letters?

You must come now. Immediately. I want you. I will wait here for you. You must leave your ridiculous animals as I have left mes affaires for you. Come to me. I wait for you.

Lower down on the same page, but written with a thick pen, the letter continued:

Again I have read your absurd letter. Tu es fou! You make such a noise because this foolish young man is jealous of mon mari and make you to go round the detestable country, which you like so much, instead of straight through to the ridiculous place you say you want to go.

Birnier smiled grimly.

Peuh! Ecoute, mon cher, it is true I have met the young man in Washington. Mon Dieu, are there not plenty of young men in Washington, Paris, Berlin? He fell in love with me. Mon Dieu, they are as thick as the blackberries! Perhaps I tease him pour faire la blague! Pourquoi pas? I give him a photograph and I sign it, just as I sign plenty for amusing friends. But then he become too ridiculous. He has no sense of humour comme tous les Allemands. He wishes to fight all my friends, tes compatriotes si sombres et graves! Figure toi! Then he make a challenge and naturellement it is not the custom in thy country. Mon pauvre petit Dorsay refuse and this person become crazy wild, as you say, and he strike him with his cane in the street. Quelle horreur! Quel scandale! He run away of course. The Embassy help him. Qui sait? That is the last I hear until I receive this ridiculous letter, together with thy ridiculous letter. I send him to you. How drole that you two should meet all among les animaux. It is so funny that he did not kill you, this monstre allemand! Tu es en cross encore avec moi? Zut! mon vieux it is not my fault that everybody goes mad after me except mon petit mari! Leave the ridiculous garcon where he is. But why do I talk so much about a cochon? Because you are ridiculous! Tant pis pour toi! Now sois gentil and come to me *immediately*—unless you love your sales animaux plus que moi! If you do not come I will never never, jamais de ma vie, give you one single baiser again! No! Mille baisers! Mais comme je te deteste!

LUCILLE.

CHAPTER 30

Forty-eight hours later, the furious drumming, chanting and screaming heralded the return of the victorious troops of Zalu Zako. Birnier from his gaol on the hill watched the bronze flood pour like a stream of lava out of the plantation and flood the village, spears flashing silver points in the slanting rays of the sun. But what had happened to zu Pfeiffer and the white sergeants? No sign of them could he see. Waves of sound lapped continuously around the temple.

The long mauve shadow of the hill ate up the village. Fires began to flicker amid the huts and away in the recesses of the plantation. The lowing of cattle added to the general clamour. As the western sky was still ablaze with incandescent colour stole the cold green of the advancing moon in the east.

"Mungongo, what are thy brethren about to do?"

"It is the Festival of the Harvest, as I have told thee, O son of the Lord-of-many-Lands."

"But they have not the Bride?"

"Nay." Mungongo glanced apprehensively towards the temple where in what was to have been a bathroom, was

Bakuma hidden. "He-who-may-not-be-mentioned demands but blood. The Bride is the food of the wizards. But to each warrior is every woman his bride this night."

"Why didst thou not tell me this thing before?" demanded Birnier, who knew that such was one of the customs of primitive tribes in all parts of the world and in all ages.

"Thou didst not ask me," retorted Mungongo, to whom the affair was such a matter of course that it was not worth mentioning.

"Do they make sacrifice?"

"The Bride is married to the Banana, but of the manner of her nuptial know I not. Am I a wizard?"

The divine king grimly watched his subjects. In the growing light flitted gnomes around the huts in and out the sepia caverns of the plantation. As a banana front was etched in sepia against the great moon, the ocean of clamour was cleft by the high treble of the tribal troubadour. At the bottom of the wide street appeared dancing figures. As they approached, Birnier could distinguish Bakahenzie, Marufa and Yabolo in the van, dressed in full panoply, whirling and leaping with untiring energy. Behind them shuffled and pranced a vast mass of warriors, behind whom again several hundred women shrilled and wriggled in the mighty chorus. The rhythm of the drums increased to the maddening action impulse of the two short—long beat:

Pm-pm—Pommmmm!   Pm-pm—Pommmmm!   Pm-pm—Pommmmm!

The treble solo of the chant darted above that throb and grunt like a mad bird skimming the turbulent tops of a dark forest.

Pm-pm—Pommmmm!   Pm-pm—Pommmmm!   Pm-pm—
Pommmmm!

The rhythm seemed like a febrile pulse within Birnier's
brain, dominating him with hypnotic suggestion to action.
An urge to scream and to yell, to dance and to leap, plucked
at his limbs. Resurgent desires from he knew not what
subconscious catacombs, wriggled and struggled furiously
within him. The great moon scattered blue stars upon the
spears as if upon the green scales of some leviathan
squirming in delirious torment.

Control the twitching of his muscles to that rhythm Birnier
could not. He had to fight to resist the waves of hysteria
permeating the air. He glanced at Mungongo. The whites of
his eyes were rolling. Birnier cursed the insistency of the
drums and the orgiastical grunts. Forcibly he kept up a
running fire of psychological explanations: "Annihilation of
inhibitions... dissociation of personality... triumph of the
subconscious animal," as a wizard muttering incantations
against evil spirits. He felt dizzy. "God, I'm drunk with
rhythm!" he exclaimed.

The priests were entering the large gate of the outer
enclosure. In the village and on the opposite hill the people
resembled a swarm of black locusts. The drums ceased.
Bakahenzie and Marufa and Yabolo ran straight towards him
screeching. This was the cue.

Birnier walked back slowly. In awful silence they began to
push the idol. The wood creaked protestingly. Slowly the
mass slid on to Birnier's back. He gripped it and began to
walk to the entrance. As he passed Mungongo the Sacred
Fires shot up yellow tongues. A sound like a moan rose
dripping with screams and grew into a continuous thunder of
noise. The drums rippled a furious tattoo. The three wizards

dashed before him, leaping high in the air. Birnier shuffled a dozen yards to the left and turned. He stopped.

Upon the ground, just within the outer gate in view of the multitude beyond, green ivory in the moonlight, was the naked figure of a white man. Above him pranced Bakahenzie in whose hand gleamed a knife.

The training of his life enabled Birnier to throw upon the screen of his mind the essential points more rapidly than conscious thought. Bakahenzie, as well as the others, was in an abnormal state of excitement. There was no time to employ "magic" rockets or anything else. He swung the idol upon one shoulder and ran forward. He saw the blue eyes move and the bracelet wink in the moonlight as he stepped over the bound form. He bent, balancing the image upon his shoulders, and seized zu Pfeiffer by the arm.

The throb of the drums and the roar of the people who knew not but that this act was in accordance with the rules, continued. The priests remained motionless: expectant. Bakahenzie stood rigid as if paralysed by the unexpected: the knife was a blue snake in his hand.

Half blinded with sweat, with his muscles cracking, Birnier staggered on with the heavy burden, dragging the nude body after him. Hours seemed to pass, each second of which might bring a spear in his back before he reached the place before the temple. He slid the idol into the hole and turned.

From the tumult of sound the screech of Bakahenzie shot up like a snipe from a rice field. The other wizards sprang with him. The moonlight kissed a spearhead beside the stone figure of Mungongo by the Sacred Fires. Birnier leaped, plucked the spear, caught zu Pfeiffer in his arms and raised him shoulder high that all might see.

At the entrance of the enclosure Bakahenzie and the other two were arrested by astonishment. Lowering the body to the base of the idol which leaned sideways in a drunken leer, Birnier lifted the spear and brought it down accurately between zu Pfeiffer's left arm and breast, and dropping swiftly upon his knees to cover his actions, slashed his own left forearm. Then he jumped to his feet and held the blooded spear aloft as he cried aloud:

"The god hath taken his own!"

Bakahenzie was the first to see that the white breast of the victim was indeed deluged in blood; perhaps the veneration engendered by "the fingers of Tarum" moved beneath the blood lust.

"The god hath taken his own!" he repeated in a piercing scream. Marufa echoed the shout. As they turned the cry was ricocheted beyond the farthest hill.

"The god hath taken his own!"

CHAPTER 31

The reflection of a shaft of moonlight through the half-completed thatch upon zu Pfeiffer's "magic" mirror, which the natives had not dared to remove, set afire the sapphires upon his bracelet as he sat rigidly in a camp chair in a suit of pyjamas. Upon the bed lay Birnier, nursing his bandaged left arm. Now and again the thrumming, chanting and the shrilling of the saturnalia without rose into discordant yells like a gust of wind whipping tree-tops into fury.

Zu Pfeiffer appeared taciturn and suspicious. Perhaps the slackening of his will, tautened to meet death as his caste demanded that he should, and the confrontation of the object of his violent hate, had completely unnerved him. When Birnier had dragged him within and cut his bonds, he had grunted curt, official thanks for the rescue. As sullenly he had hesitated at the offer of the pyjamas, but as if deciding that he could not retain any dignity in his own bloodied skin, had accepted them, as well as a sorely needed drink of water.

The reaction after the crisis, and possibly the influence of the general hysteria in the air, had distorted Birnier's vision of things. He was very conscious of a neurotic desire to laugh unrestrainedly. Thus it was that for nearly half an hour the two men remained in the gloom in silence. Birnier had a psychological comprehension of the highly nervous tension of his guest. For he had long ago realized that the only solution of zu Pfeiffer's crazy statement that he was engaged to the wife of a man to whom he was speaking, indicated a form of insanity.

A psychological law is that natural emotions must have an outlet; if they are repressed they are apt to cause a state of mental disease which in an aggravated form may lead the patient to the asylum, but in the incipient stage are as common as jackals in Africa. Zu Pfeiffer was suffering from such a case of mild psychosis. Brought up under an iron code which did not permit his instincts to react, the repressed emotions bubbled out in the form of a deification of his Kaiser and the adoration of Lucille, both states being absolutely apart from all reason, indeed approached to a state of dissociation of consciousness. The desired unattainable is projected into the dream plane, the realm of myth. Such a case is the historical one of the man who, keenly intelligent upon every subject mentioned, startles the visitor by the demand for a piece of toast, gravely explaining that he is a poached egg and that he wishes to sit down; or as Pascal, who ever had beside him the great black dog. To attempt to rationalise with such an one was merely to excite the insane part of him. So it was that Birnier determined to ignore the subject entirely, perfectly aware that the sullenness of the man sitting in the camp chair opposite to him was caused by an exaggerated terror that he would insist upon speaking of the one subject which should be tabu.

The associative suggestion of Lucille diverted his mind until he became immersed in thoughts of her. A queer vision of a well-fed tiger playing with a kid entered his mind. More conscious than ever of her attraction by reason of the intensified sense of her wrought by her letter, he glanced surreptitiously at the rigid form in the chair and a wave of pity mixed with a half conscious pride that she belonged to him, rose within him. Then Birnier started as he was brought back to a realization of the passing of time by a harsh voice that told of creaking nerves:

"Herr Professor, what is your pleasure to do with me, if you please?"

"I beg your pardon!" Birnier sat up. "Er—naturally I shall endeavour to get you away as early as possible. It would be as well if you took advantage of the present—er—saturnalia to escape. I cannot do much. I can provide you with a gun and food. As you are not injured you should be able to get a reasonable distance from here by morning; for the rest I am afraid you must fend for yourself. I wish that I could do more, but I'm afraid that my power is not yet sufficient to ensure any help from the natives."

An inarticulate sound emerged from zu Pfeiffer's mouth. Birnier's eyes caught the sheen of the photograph upon the wall. Escape! Lucille! Almost involuntarily he stretched out a hand and took Lucille's letter from the table. Again came zu Pfeiffer's voice:

"I thank you, Herr Professor, but I cannot accept—for myself." Birnier stared at him. "I wish you to understand that for myself that is impossible." The tall figure seemed to straighten in the chair. "But as I have the honour to serve his Imperial Majesty I am bound to preserve to the best of my ability my body in order to answer for my culpable negligence which has resulted in the loss of my two companies. Most distinctly, Herr Professor, I wish you to know that I accept your offer in order to place myself before the Court Martial that awaits me."

Birnier almost gasped. That this anomaly of a man, who was capable of cold-blooded murder at the prompting of an hallucination, and who now appeared equally capable of the utter annihilation of self at the service of his Imperial Master, meant what he said, Birnier did not doubt. Yet it was not anomalous. Logical in fact; the capability of supreme sacrifice for either of his idols.

"I understand you, Lieutenant," said he courteously. "I—" The two letters in his hand crackled. Before he could master the mean desire he had handed the second letter to zu Pfeiffer with the words:

"Forgive me, I have here a letter which it is my duty to return to you."

The sapphires winked as zu Pfeiffer held up the letter in the shaft of moonlight. There was a suppressed grunt as of pain. Zu Pfeiffer rose stiffly and walked to the door. His tall figure was silhouetted in profile against the green sky and as Birnier watched he saw a gleam as of crystal upon an eyelash. Birnier, ashamed of his sole vengeance, turned away.

But as if revenge were recoiling upon him came in the wake of that satisfied primitive instinct a surge of longing for Lucille. Lucille! Lucille! God! how he desired to see those eyes again! Feel those lips and hear the gurgle of her laughter! Sense the perfume of her hair as she murmured: "*Mon petit loup!*" Birnier sat holding the letter. He fought with an impulse to abandon everything to go to her—if he could get out! How stale and monotonous the adventure and the scientific interest suddenly seemed! After all, what had he accomplished? What could he accomplish? Even yet he had learned but little of the secrets of the witch-doctor's craft. Perhaps there was little or nothing to learn? And zu Pfeiffer? He stared across at the portrait of Lucille. And as he gazed a wave of pity rose within him for this boy made mad by the witchery of those eyes and the music of that voice. A sentence in Lucille's letter appeared to stand out from the context: "*Mon Dieu, they are as thick as the blackberries!*"

And yet—and yet—Why the devil had she taken it into her head to come out to Uganda above all places? he asked himself. She was so damnably near to him. He smiled satirically as he recollected her phrase about those fools who made of love a nuisance, and yet now what was she doing? After all the suspicion in his mind that love is everything to a woman seemed proven true.

But how adorable she was! He fingered the letter as if it were part of her. Well, she was young; success and adulation from one capital to another had interested and amused her for a few years, but when Milady had suddenly discovered that the Career bored her she had thrown up everything and logically—to her mind—expected her mate to do likewise! With what insouciance had she treated the affair of zu Pfeiffer and the youngster whom he had struck. When Birnier had met her she had had a story of a young fool count in Paris who had shot himself, merely because she would not listen to his suit; and she had protested with one of those wonderful shrugs and a moue, saying that she could not marry all the men in the world! That apparently bloodthirsty indifference had of course tended to make more men "crazy wild," as she put it, about her. And that reputation had added to her numerous attractions even to Birnier.

He could escape if he wished—with zu Pfeiffer. He could take Mungongo with him. Yet would Mungongo dare the tabu at his bidding? Birnier doubted it. Would Mungongo even consent to let him, Birnier, who was now in his eyes the King-God, go and so imperil the foundations of the native world? Birnier was certain that he would not. They were all dominated by this confounded idol of wood, he reflected.

Bakahenzie, or even Mungongo, would cheerfully sacrifice him if either imagined that the damned Unmentionable One desired it, at the suppositious bidding of something which was nothing.

Through the sweet scent of her in the air like a compelling aura about him, came suddenly zu Pfeiffer's voice speaking in the accents of agony; yet all he said was:

"Herr Professor Birnier—I am compelled—to—to apologise for..."

The voice failed and the haughty blond head turned away, unable to complete to the uttermost the greatest sacrifice he had ever attempted.

"Please don't," said Birnier comprehendingly. "I understand."

And Birnier did comprehend; realised the small hell in zu Pfeiffer as a higher developed tabu did a childish tabu unto death. Zu Pfeiffer, white man, had been just as guilty of an attempt to commit murder at the suppositious inversion of a thumb of an idol as Bakahenzie; not an idol of wood but the projection of his subconscious desires. Zu Pfeiffer would sacrifice a million at the bidding of his Kaiser, whose divinity was the same myth, the projection of himself. Yet what had been Birnier's object in undertaking all these pains and penalties but to study mankind in the making, the black microcosm of a white macrocosm; to aid them to a better understanding of themselves and each other? Was not Bakahenzie an embryonic zu Pfeiffer? How could one aid a zu Pfeiffer if one did not know a Bakahenzie?

From the saturnalia in progress outside came another swirl of sound seeming to lap mockingly against the motionless figure of zu Pfeiffer silhouetted against a green sky; and above him towered the idol leaning sideways.

As if in drunken laughter of the follies of black and white humanity! mused Birnier. Yet what am I doing? At the crook of a dainty finger am I, too, to bow to an idol? Am I to pity zu Pfeiffer and these children?... Savages! Good God, what am I?

Choose from Thousands of 1stWorldLibrary Classics By

A. M. Barnard	Booth Tarkington	Edward Everett Hale
Ada Leverson	Boyd Cable	Edward J. O'Biren
Adolphus William Ward	Bram Stoker	Edward S. Ellis
Aesop	C. Collodi	Edwin L. Arnold
Agatha Christie	C. E. Orr	Eleanor Atkins
Alexander Aaronsohn	C. M. Ingleby	Eleanor Hallowell Abbott
Alexander Kielland	Carolyn Wells	Eliot Gregory
Alexandre Dumas	Catherine Parr Traill	Elizabeth Gaskell
Alfred Gatty	Charles A. Eastman	Elizabeth McCracken
Alfred Ollivant	Charles Amory Beach	Elizabeth Von Arnim
Alice Duer Miller	Charles Dickens	Ellem Key
Alice Turner Curtis	Charles Dudley Warner	Emerson Hough
Alice Dunbar	Charles Farrar Browne	Emilie F. Carlen
Allen Chapman	Charles Ives	Emily Bronte
Alleyne Ireland	Charles Kingsley	Emily Dickinson
Ambrose Bierce	Charles Klein	Enid Bagnold
Amelia E. Barr	Charles Hanson Towne	Enilor Macartney Lane
Amory H. Bradford	Charles Lathrop Pack	Erasmus W. Jones
Andrew Lang	Charles Romyn Dake	Ernie Howard Pie
Andrew McFarland Davis	Charles Whibley	Ethel May Dell
Andy Adams	Charles Willing Beale	Ethel Turner
Angela Brazil	Charlotte M. Braeme	Ethel Watts Mumford
Anna Alice Chapin	Charlotte M. Yonge	Eugene Sue
Anna Sewell	Charlotte Perkins Stetson	Eugenie Foa
Annie Besant	Clair W. Hayes	Eugene Wood
Annie Hamilton Donnell	Clarence Day Jr.	Eustace Hale Ball
Annie Payson Call	Clarence E. Mulford	Evelyn Everett-green
Annie Roe Carr	Clemence Housman	Everard Cotes
Annonaymous	Confucius	F. H. Cheley
Anton Chekhov	Coningsby Dawson	F. J. Cross
Archibald Lee Fletcher	Cornelis DeWitt Wilcox	F. Marion Crawford
Arnold Bennett	Cyril Burleigh	Fannie E. Newberry
Arthur C. Benson	D. H. Lawrence	Federick Austin Ogg
Arthur Conan Doyle	Daniel Defoe	Ferdinand Ossendowski
Arthur M. Winfield	David Garnett	Fergus Hume
Arthur Ransome	Dinah Craik	Florence A. Kilpatrick
Arthur Schnitzler	Don Carlos Janes	Fremont B. Deering
Arthur Train	Donald Keyhoe	Francis Bacon
Atticus	Dorothy Kilner	Francis Darwin
B.H. Baden-Powell	Dougan Clark	Frances Hodgson Burnett
B. M. Bower	Douglas Fairbanks	Frances Parkinson Keyes
B. C. Chatterjee	E. Nesbit	Frank Gee Patchin
Baroness Emmuska Orczy	E. P. Roe	Frank Harris
Baroness Orczy	E. Phillips Oppenheim	Frank Jewett Mather
Basil King	E. S. Brooks	Frank L. Packard
Bayard Taylor	Earl Barnes	Frank V. Webster
Ben Macomber	Edgar Rice Burroughs	Frederic Stewart Isham
Bertha Muzzy Bower	Edith Van Dyne	Frederick Trevor Hill
Bjornstjerne Bjornson	Edith Wharton	Frederick Winslow Taylor

Friedrich Kerst
Friedrich Nietzsche
Fyodor Dostoyevsky
G.A. Henty
G.K. Chesterton
Gabrielle E. Jackson
Garrett P. Serviss
Gaston Leroux
George A. Warren
George Ade
Geroge Bernard Shaw
George Cary Eggleston
George Durston
George Ebers
George Eliot
George Gissing
George MacDonald
George Meredith
George Orwell
George Sylvester Viereck
George Tucker
George W. Cable
George Wharton James
Gertrude Atherton
Gordon Casserly
Grace E. King
Grace Gallatin
Grace Greenwood
Grant Allen
Guillermo A. Sherwell
Gulielma Zollinger
Gustav Flaubert
H. A. Cody
H. B. Irving
H. C. Bailey
H. G. Wells
H. H. Munro
H. Irving Hancock
H. R. Naylor
H. Rider Haggard
H. W. C. Davis
Haldeman Julius
Hall Caine
Hamilton Wright Mabie
Hans Christian Andersen
Harold Avery
Harold McGrath
Harriet Beecher Stowe
Harry Castlemon
Harry Coghill
Harry Houidini

Hayden Carruth
Helent Hunt Jackson
Helen Nicolay
Hendrik Conscience
Hendy David Thoreau
Henri Barbusse
Henrik Ibsen
Henry Adams
Henry Ford
Henry Frost
Henry James
Henry Jones Ford
Henry Seton Merriman
Henry W Longfellow
Herbert A. Giles
Herbert Carter
Herbert N. Casson
Herman Hesse
Hildegard G. Frey
Homer
Honore De Balzac
Horace B. Day
Horace Walpole
Horatio Alger Jr.
Howard Pyle
Howard R. Garis
Hugh Lofting
Hugh Walpole
Humphry Ward
Ian Maclaren
Inez Haynes Gillmore
Irving Bacheller
Isabel Cecilia Williams
Isabel Hornibrook
Israel Abrahams
Ivan Turgenev
J. G.Austin
J. Henri Fabre
J. M. Barrie
J. M. Walsh
J. Macdonald Oxley
J. R. Miller
J. S. Fletcher
J. S. Knowles
J. Storer Clouston
J. W. Duffield
Jack London
Jacob Abbott
James Allen
James Andrews
James Baldwin

James Branch Cabell
James DeMille
James Joyce
James Lane Allen
James Lane Allen
James Oliver Curwood
James Oppenheim
James Otis
James R. Driscoll
Jane Abbott
Jane Austen
Jane L. Stewart
Janet Aldridge
Jens Peter Jacobsen
Jerome K. Jerome
Jessie Graham Flower
John Buchan
John Burroughs
John Cournos
John F. Kennedy
John Gay
John Glasworthy
John Habberton
John Joy Bell
John Kendrick Bangs
John Milton
John Philip Sousa
John Taintor Foote
Jonas Lauritz Idemil Lie
Jonathan Swift
Joseph A. Altsheler
Joseph Carey
Joseph Conrad
Joseph E. Badger Jr
Joseph Hergesheimer
Joseph Jacobs
Jules Vernes
Julian Hawthrone
Julie A Lippmann
Justin Huntly McCarthy
Kakuzo Okakura
Karle Wilson Baker
Kate Chopin
Kenneth Grahame
Kenneth McGaffey
Kate Langley Bosher
Kate Langley Bosher
Katherine Cecil Thurston
Katherine Stokes
L. A. Abbot
L. T. Meade

L. Frank Baum	Owen Johnson	Stephen Crane
Latta Griswold	P.G. Wodehouse	Stewart Edward White
Laura Dent Crane	Paul and Mabel Thorne	Stijn Streuvels
Laura Lee Hope	Paul G. Tomlinson	Swami Abhedananda
Laurence Housman	Paul Severing	Swami Parmananda
Lawrence Beasley	Percy Brebner	T. S. Ackland
Leo Tolstoy	Percy Keese Fitzhugh	T. S. Arthur
Leonid Andreyev	Peter B. Kyne	The Princess Der Ling
Lewis Carroll	Plato	Thomas A. Janvier
Lewis Sperry Chafer	Quincy Allen	Thomas A Kempis
Lilian Bell	R. Derby Holmes	Thomas Anderton
Lloyd Osbourne	R. L. Stevenson	Thomas Bailey Aldrich
Louis Hughes	R. S. Ball	Thomas Bulfinch
Louis Joseph Vance	Rabindranath Tagore	Thomas De Quincey
Louis Tracy	Rahul Alvares	Thomas Dixon
Louisa May Alcott	Ralph Bonehill	Thomas H. Huxley
Lucy Fitch Perkins	Ralph Henry Barbour	Thomas Hardy
Lucy Maud Montgomery	Ralph Victor	Thomas More
Luther Benson	Ralph Waldo Emmerson	Thornton W. Burgess
Lydia Miller Middleton	Rene Descartes	U. S. Grant
Lyndon Orr	Ray Cummings	Upton Sinclair
M. Corvus	Rex Beach	Valentine Williams
M. H. Adams	Rex E. Beach	Various Authors
Margaret E. Sangster	Richard Harding Davis	Vaughan Kester
Margret Howth	Richard Jefferies	Victor Appleton
Margaret Vandercook	Richard Le Gallienne	Victor G. Durham
Margaret W. Hungerford	Robert Barr	Victoria Cross
Margret Penrose	Robert Frost	Virginia Woolf
Maria Edgeworth	Robert Gordon Anderson	Wadsworth Camp
Maria Thompson Daviess	Robert L. Drake	Walter Camp
Mariano Azuela	Robert Lansing	Walter Scott
Marion Polk Angellotti	Robert Lynd	Washington Irving
Mark Overton	Robert Michael Ballantyne	Wilbur Lawton
Mark Twain	Robert W. Chambers	Wilkie Collins
Mary Austin	Rosa Nouchette Carey	Willa Cather
Mary Catherine Crowley	Rudyard Kipling	Willard F. Baker
Mary Cole	Saint Augustine	William Dean Howells
Mary Hastings Bradley	Samuel B. Allison	William le Queux
Mary Roberts Rinehart	Samuel Hopkins Adams	W. Makepeace Thackeray
Mary Rowlandson	Sarah Bernhardt	William W. Walter
M. Wollstonecraft Shelley	Sarah C. Hallowell	William Shakespeare
Maud Lindsay	Selma Lagerlof	Winston Churchill
Max Beerbohm	Sherwood Anderson	Yei Theodora Ozaki
Myra Kelly	Sigmund Freud	Yogi Ramacharaka
Nathaniel Hawthrone	Standish O'Grady	Young E. Allison
Nicolo Machiavelli	Stanley Weyman	Zane Grey
O. F. Walton	Stella Benson	
Oscar Wilde	Stella M. Francis	

www.ingramcontent.com/pod-product-compliance
Lightning Source LLC
Chambersburg PA
CBHW031109030726
47496CB00002BA/450